# WHERE GOD AND HUMAN MEET

# WHERE GOD AND HUMAN MEET

*The Paschal Mystery, Priesthood*
*and Sacrifice among the Igbos*

PASCHAL CHIDIEBERE MBAGWU

A Herder & Herder Book
The Crossroad Publishing Company
New York

The Crossroad Publishing Company
www.CrossroadPublishing.com
© 2017 by Paschal C. Mbagwu

**Imprimatur**
Francis Cardinal George, O.M.I., Ph.D.
Archbishop of Chicago

**Nihil Obstat**
Reverend Peter Damian Akpunonu, S.S.L., S.T.D.
Reverend Dr. Emery de Gaál

[Permission to publish is an official declaration of ecclesiastical authority that the material is free of doctrinal and moral error. No legal responsibility is assumed by the grant of this permission.]
Given at Chicago this 5th day of November 2013.

Book design by The HK Scriptorium

Library of Congress Cataloging-in-Publication Data
available from the Library of Congress.

ISBN 978-0-8245-2219-3

*To my parents,*
*Sylvester and Charity Mbagwu*
*For all their love, sacrifice, and prayer*

# Contents

## II
## THE PASCHAL MYSTERY,
## IGBO PRIESTHOOD, AND SACRIFICE

## III
## THE CHURCH IN IGBOLAND TODAY

# Preface

## Father Emery de Gaál, Ph.D.

Chairman and Professor of Dogmatic Theology
Mundelein Seminary, University of St. Mary of the Lake
Chicago, Illinois

We live in a world of gradual and accelerating globalization and integration. Historically viewed, this is a singular phenomenon brought about by the dynamics inherent in technology, the sciences, and economic development. Invariably this will produce a single, global consciousness, as Joseph Cardinal Ratzinger, the future Pope Benedict XVI, penned for Josef Cardinal Frings's memorable talk in Genoa on the eve of the Second Vatican Council in 1961. The world is "fated" to such a situation of integration, and it is most assuredly in of itself to be welcomed by us, as it holds the promise of overcoming the deleterious consequences of the vainglorious attempt to build the Tower of Babel. This process will bring about a heightened, universally shared appreciation of the *conditio humana*. It may not be a foregone conclusion, however, that such a globally integrated world will automatically be a desirable place to live. Every age and time requires again and again an ethical effort and an intellectual self-verification in order not to fall into uncouth barbarism. Ever again human beings need to take stock whether their present state is also a humane one.

This—that is, whether we can do justice to the grand vision of who the human person is—is indirectly challenged by the very vectors that bring about this unified world: technology, economic development, and the sciences. To the Israeli author and intellectual Amos Oz (1939–) it seems as if the human race is predestined to become free of historical identity, defining itself exclusively by way of performance and consumption. A radical reduction, horizontalization, and pragmatization of the human imagination seem the inescapable consequences.

At every Eucharist, the Church celebrates *anamnesis*, that is, the memory of the salvation of all of humankind, wrought once and for all times by Jesus Christ, the high priest on the cross. The Church actuates ever again history: the death and resurrection of Jesus Christ become present not only in the form of a retold narrative but "are," in the full sense of the verb, realized in the present and actualized in the past in the Eucharist. In a way more intensive than anything else human culture knows or could possibly imagine, Catholics are giving thanks for a past event, in which they may partake in the here-and-now of their respective existences. Past and present fuse in such a way that, together, both grant everyone a supratemporal identity, an inalienable dignity, and an everlasting future in Christ Jesus.

This is wholly unexpected for human beings, but the most thrilling form to live: with and for the Blessed Trinity through the historical, saving works of Jesus Christ, the Second Person of the Blessed Trinity, in the Eucharist.

All human cultures create social homogeneity and solidarity by way of a shared history. This is an incontrovertible anthropological fact. However, the future globalized society runs the danger of rendering such shared memory impossible. In the process, not only something constitutive for Christianity may be lost, but something that is indispensable for every human being and for any form of culture: identity and personhood.

Father Paschal Mbagwu ably succeeds in transposing this international challenge into the context of Nigeria, more specifically into the context of the rich Igbo culture. Using evidence spanning from the Judeo-Christian Bible to the Second Vatican Council and bringing it into dialogue with anthropological data from the Igbo tribe, he demonstrates beyond any doubt that the Christian understanding of priesthood is not an unreasonable imposition on the rich, indigenous Igbo way of life but, quite on the contrary, a logical fulfillment of the hope the Igbo people have harbored for long—that is, well before the arrival of missionaries: *gratia praesupponit (et perfecit) naturam* (grace presupposes [and perfects] nature), as St. Thomas Aquinas informs us.

The Catholic priest as *alter Christus* presiding at the sacrifice of the Eucharist is not an exotic figure in Igbo civilization but rather represents a deeper understanding of the institution of priesthood, the nature of sacrifice, and of hierarchy—all concepts not alien to, but central to, Igbo culture already well before the advent of Christianity. To the author's mind, it is the Easter joy that provides the most profound justification to reconcile the primordial and universal human yearning for reconciliation and Christian salvation. In fact, Father Mbagwu shows convincingly that the more recent Western European problematizations of combining institution and faith, as well as of uniting the priestly office and charism, are completely alien to the African genius.

I am delighted to warmly recommend Father Paschal Mbagwu's carefully argued study *Where God and Human Meet: The Paschal Mystery, Priesthood and Sacrifice among the Igbos.*

Feast of St. Gregory the Great,
September 3, 2015

# Preface

## *Most Reverend Edward J. Slattery,*

### Bishop of Tulsa, Oklahoma

After reading and reflecting on Fr. Mbagwu's doctoral dissertation, *Priesthood and Sacrifice in the Light of the Paschal Mystery,* I realized again the significance of that liturgical gesture at every Mass in which the priest or deacon mingles, at the preparation of the gifts, a few drops of water with the wine and prays quietly: "By the mystery of this water and wine, may we come to share in the divinity of Christ Who humbled Himself to share in our humanity." The water that represents our humanity is to be elevated to the divinity of Christ so that we become one in Him. At Mass and in Christ, you and I are to become an acceptable offering to the Father.

Fr. Mbagwu's love of the liturgy and of his personal identity as an Igbo is poured out on every page of his book, whose purpose is to keep Christ in the center of every liturgical rite celebrated by the Igbo people of southern Nigeria—probably the fastest growing Catholic part of the world. The Igbo people have found Christ during the past century and Christ has found them.

This scholarly, but quite readable, work gives an example of how a non-Christian culture becomes a Catholic culture without losing its identity as a people who have a long history. The reader will discover anew that all cultures tend toward Christ; instead of losing their identity, they find it—that the wine and water are meant to be mingled, that God's desire and design are that all of us be one in Christ.

Given on October 6, 2015,
Memorial of St. Bruno

# Acknowledgments

I wish to express my sincere gratitude to almighty God for the grace of patience that enabled me to finish this book. I thank God for the gift of good health, without which this book would not have reached the final stage. For all God's love, protection, and for many other blessings, I owe loads of gratitude to God.

May I acknowledge the support and help of my local ordinary, Archbishop Anthony J. V. Obinna, who, in his graciousness, chose me to study at the University of St. Mary of the Lake for my S.T.L. and S.T.D. I thank him for supporting me all through the rigorous process. I am grateful to His Eminence Francis Cardinal George (may he rest in peace), of the Chicago Archdiocese, who generously offered me the scholarship that enabled me to achieve this success. I thank the former Rector of Mundelein Seminary, Very Rev. Msgr. Denis Lyle, and the current Rector, Very Rev. Fr. Robert Barron, for giving me the required support and atmosphere for studies. I thank my dissertation director, Rev. Professor Peter-Damian Akpunonu, who painstakingly read through my manuscripts and directed me to a successful completion. I am also indebted to Rev. Dr. Douglas Martis, Director of the Liturgical Institute, for all his support. He gladly welcomed me and made me feel at home in the Liturgical Institute. I am grateful to Bishop Edward Slattery, the Bishop of Tulsa, who in his fatherly love assigned me to a parish in his diocese from where I was able to finish my writing. To all the priests of the diocese of Tulsa and to the parishioners of St. Patrick, Sand Springs, and Our Lady of the Lake, Mannford, Oklahoma, I say "thank you."

I am also grateful to Professor Fredrick Hansen, Rita and Maggie, Frank and Joyce Pacenza, Frank and Paquita Dudek, Julie Nichols, Frank Shuette, James and Linda Ward, John and Mary Knecht. To Roman and Virginia Albert, the Woodys and Rambos, I owe loads of gratitude. You really cheered me up in difficult moments. Your love, support, and encouragement really strengthened me.

To my brother priests, Msgr. Kevin C. Akagha, Frs. Mark Njoku, Eddie Njoku, Agapitus Ike, Very Rev. Father Jovita Okonkwo, Rev. Prof. Lawrence Iwuamadi, Fr. Kingsley George-Obilonu, Fr. Emmanuel Lugard Nduka, Fr. Louis Obirieze, Fr. Jude Ossy Okeke, Fr. Erasmus Okere, Fr. Christian Ekeh, Fr. Vita Anyanwu, and Fr Justin Okoro, I say a hearty thanks. I greatly appreciate all the support you offered me all through my studies.

To my parents, Sylvester and Charity Mbagwu, and all my siblings, Chim, Elechi, Ukachi, Chika, Kelechi, Ugochukwu, and Chima, I say thank you for your support and love.

Finally, to my family here in the United States, Sir Peter and Lady Dorothy Onyewu, Ogechi, Nonye, Chichi, Oguchi, and Uche, I remain indebted to you for all your sacrifices for me. I thank Henry and Chioma Ejimogu and Okwy for their support and encouragement. I cannot thank you enough, but I pray that God may bless you all.

# Introduction

This book is largely my doctoral dissertation. It is a research and inquiry into the importance and relevance of the priesthood and its relation to worship, with its implications for the Igbos. The study focuses on the biblical priesthood and sacrifice vis-à-vis the priesthood and sacrifice in the Igbo religion with the Paschal Mystery as its *terminus ad quem*. I hope that this study will foster a deeper understanding of sacrifice and priesthood in the Igbo society through the Church's eucharistic celebration and help the Igbos appreciate the mystery of the Eucharist as it developed with time. My contribution will be to apply the rich tradition of the Church to Igbo life, so that the Igbos can appreciate and participate with greater vigor and fervor in the great mystery of human salvation.

The book begins by tracing the origin of the priesthood from biblical tradition to the priesthood of Christ and ministerial priesthood in his Church. These will then be applied to the Igbos, with emphasis on the relationship between the priesthood and their daily life. I hope that it will help the Igbos appreciate the activities of God in their daily life. This is because priests of the Old Testament worked within a structure, and it is important and necessary to appreciate how their traditions developed within their own structures.

This study focuses on the revered traditions of the Igbos as they relate to the priesthood and to sacrifice in the Bible and tries to find ways to inculturate their sacred institutions, which are part of the culture of the people, in light of the Second Vatican Council, especially *Lumen Gentium* (the Dogmatic Constitution on the Church of Vatican II), *Sacrosanctum Concilium* (the Constitution on the Sacred Liturgy of Vatican II), and *Dominus Iesus* (the Declaration of the Congregation for the Doctrine of the Faith). These premier documents teach and encourage all peoples to study and explore "how the positive elements of other religions may fall within the divine plan of salvation."[1]

Among the Igbos of southeast Nigeria, there is the need to understand the nature of the Catholic priesthood as it relates to the Igbo priesthood. The Igbo priesthood and its sacrifices are sacred to the Igbos, and the priest is greatly revered in the community. The Igbos have gladly welcomed the Catholic faith,

---

1. Congregation for the Doctrine of the Faith, "Dominus Iesus": On the Unicity and Salvific Universality of Jesus Christ and the Church (Washington, DC: United States Conference of Catholic Bishops, 2000), 14. *Ad Gentes* 9; *Nostra Aetate* 2; *Lumen Gentium* 16.

but even after more than one hundred years of Catholicism, they are yet to fully imbibe the Christian faith and avoid certain forms of syncretism within the community.[2] Incidentally, Igbo communities have Christians who practice their faith but are nonetheless deeply rooted in traditional religious beliefs. The question then arises: what is it that makes the Igbo person so firmly attached to traditional beliefs and customs?[3] John S. Mbiti, writing about Africans in general, contends that in "that religious way of life, they know who they are, how to act in different situations, and how to solve their problems."[4] Following Mbiti's assumptions, one questions whether an Igbo can be fully a Christian without rejecting and surrendering his cultural identity. How is the Catholic Igbo to understand and appreciate the Church's sacrifice vis-à-vis the traditional sacrifices of the Igbo community? Of what value are the teachings of the Second Vatican Council for Igbo Catholics in moments wherein their problems seem not to be solved within the Church's tradition, whereas solutions seem available in the traditional religion?

Another major problem is the missionary method of evangelization. While Africans are very grateful for the gift of faith and the sacrifices of numerous men and women who labored under harsh conditions, nevertheless, the missionaries in many cases did not have a good command of the language or an appreciation of the people's culture, and were therefore very limited in what they could do, despite their good intentions. The work they did has often been called "shallow Christianity." It belonged to the next generation of Christians to continue from where the missionaries left off and to ensure that Christianity took deep root among the people and their culture.[5]

---

2. Peter Nlemadim DomNwachukwu, *Authentic African Christianity: An Inculturation Model for the Igbo* (New York: Peter Lang, 2000), 5. He affirms the above view thus: "Now we see a replacement of some of those shrines with prayer houses. The same persons are still the consultants, dressed not in shabby and awe-evoking costumes, but in white robes, normal native attire, or western-style dress. They do not divine with elements such as cowries, white chalk, pieces of stone, pieces of red cloth, and so on. Their main tool of divination and fortune-telling is the Bible."

3. John S. Mbiti, *Introduction to African Religion,* 2nd rev. ed. (London: Heinemann Educational, 1991), 14–33. Mbiti, though writing about Africans in general, may be of help here. He explains that, for Africans, religion affects every facet of their life—custom, tradition, music, drama, and so on. Hence, wherever Africans are found, they carry their religious affinities with them, for letting go may mean a renunciation of who they are.

4. Ibid., 14.

5. Deusdedit R. K. Nkurunziza, "Towards a New African Paradigm of Evangelization," *African Ecclesial Review* 50 (March–June 2008): 68. Nkurunziza supports this idea from his experience in Kenya: "Evangelization was further carried out with colonial mentality; there was no time to listen and learn. The evangelizer was the master who knew everything. It was urgent that the greatest possible number of persons be baptized, so as to afford them entry into heaven. . . . A pitiless struggle raged between

In the modern era, scholars like Hans Küng have argued against priestly ordination, holding that all believers are "priests," and "in principle all Christians are empowered to administer Baptism and Eucharist."[6] Raymond E. Brown, on the other hand, believes that leaving every element of priesthood to the wave of charismatics would amount to a dangerous situation.[7] These and similar problems raise the issue of the relevance and importance of the priestly sacrifice of Christ, whom the Scriptures call the high priest of the new and eternal covenant (Hebrews 8).

With the world moving toward relativism, there are questions whether the priesthood is still relevant in our world. This study will show through Sacred Scripture and the practice of the early Church that priests were not only servants of the people but, more adequately, ministers of God.

## Methodology

This study is primarily biblical and liturgical but, at the same time, analytical. I have chosen to base it on the Bible because it is the sourcebook of Christianity. The study has to be analytical to expose what was practiced in Israel and what is believed among the Igbos, as a way of making the case for the liturgy to be inculturated into the life of the Igbos. This approach will lead to the liturgical symbolism of the texts and the rituals therein. This method will clearly show that the gospel of Jesus is for all peoples in all places. Above all, the whole study is centered in Christ as a way of uniting everything in Christ who, as the new high priest, has restored all things to God through his Paschal Mystery. It is hoped that readers, and Igbos in particular, will come to a deeper appreciation of the salvific death of Christ and the benefits of being united with Christ.

I submit that belief in Christ, and especially in his Paschal Mystery, will wipe away the traditional dread of suffering held by the Igbo people and help shape their understanding of priesthood and sacrifice. The Catholic priest, by conforming his life entirely to Christ, becomes the strength of his people. It will help the average Igbo person to put away his fears and, with the priest as his guide, to enter into joyful freedom in Christ.

Some authors, for example, Johannes Baptist Metz and Leonardo Boff, have written works on political and liberation theology, proposing theories that

---

traditional healers and missionaries. Traditional practitioners were frequently labeled falsifiers of the truth and agents of the devil and their knowledge condemned as diabolical."

6. Hans Küng, *Why Priests? A Proposal for a New Church Ministry* (London: Collins, 1972), 80.

7. Raymond E. Brown, *Priest and Bishop: Biblical Reflection* (Paramus, NJ: Paulist Press, 1970), 7: "Too charismatic an understanding of the Christian ministry is just as dangerous as too professional an understanding of it."

should make every serious-minded Christian uncomfortable.[8] It is not only through solidarity with one another that people attain salvation. Salvation comes with and through the person of Jesus. With the theologies of Boff and Metz, the transforming qualities of Christ's sufferings are missed. It is through a true Christocentric shift that the genius of pre-Christian Igbo religiosity, seen in the Igbo culture, priesthood, and worship, can be redeemed.

### Division of the Book

This book is divided into three sections. The first is biblical: the understanding of priesthood from the biblical point of view. This section will also explore the priesthood of Jesus and the qualities of his priesthood, since he was not a priest by Jewish standards. I shall also study sacrifice from the Old and New Testaments' perspectives, the different types of sacrifice, and the Church's teaching on the sacrifice of Jesus Christ, the source and origin of the sacraments.

The second section centers on the Passover and the Church. It studies the Passover in relation to the eucharistic sacrifice. This section will also study the Igbos, specifically the Igbo understanding of priesthood and sacrifice from their traditional point of view. In this area, I shall study the Igbo worldview, their selection of priests, the different types of priests, and their areas of ministry.

The third and last section is about the Church in Igboland today. It has two chapters. Chapter 5 focuses on the Church in Igboland—its advent, the key missionaries, and their achievement in southeastern Nigeria. It also studies how the Igbos received the faith, what it meant to them and how they value it, and the practice of the faith today in Igboland. Further, it evaluates areas of concern and necessary catechesis and how inculturation may be implemented in Igboland. Chapter 6 is a synthesis of the work in the light of the Paschal Mystery and the issue of how to reposition the Church in Igboland. It draws on relevant teachings of the Second Vatican Council regarding peoples and cultures and the celebration of the liturgy, with emphasis on liturgical renewal and active participation, in which many have erroneously conceived and obscured the role and traditional understanding of the priest's uniqueness (*Lumen Gentium* 10). This book, however, is not intended to produce "a clericalized Church confronting a laicized world," but rather a people of God with an ordained minister—a priest, who is a liturgical leader and president, able to lead people from darkness to faith.[9] Finally, there are recommendations on the way forward, an evaluation, and a conclusion.

---

8. Johannes Metz and his student Leonardo Boff proposed an anthropocentric theological shift in which they held that the condition of one's being is the condition of one's being a Christian. That is to say, whatever or however I am is how God wants me to be.

9. Patrick J. Dunn, *A Re-examination of the Roman Catholic Theology of the Presbyterate* (New York: Saint Paul Publications, 1990), 25.

The priesthood of Christ and sacrifice have been studied all through the ages by scholars, but their emphasis has always been on either the priesthood alone or on sacrifice alone. Michael Keenan Jones in our age comes close to this work, though his focus is on the origin of Christ's high priesthood. He seems to favor the dogmatic reasoning, using Thomistic theology and the Fathers of the Church for his arguments. Joseph Okwor studied priesthood from an Igbo perspective, with emphasis on improving the formation of the future priests.[10] This book, on the other hand, has a case study of the Igbo priesthood and sacrifice vis-à-vis the biblical priesthood. It not only traces the origin of priesthood and sacrifice through the Bible and the Igbos' understanding and practice of priesthood in the traditional setting but also analyzes both understandings liturgically for the benefit of the Igbo Christians. To enhance that benefit one must recognize that God, who is invisible and utterly transcendent, has definitively revealed himself in Jesus of Nazareth. In Jesus, God speaks to human beings as friends, lives among them (Bar. 3:38), and invites them to communion and filiation in him. The mediation is manifested in a special way through the Church's liturgy so that those who are open to receiving the communication of God may have fellowship with him. As Walter Brueggemann states,

> The Creator and the creature should always have some contact, but God's transcendence and incommensurability does not allow that vis-à-vis human sins and finiteness. While the incommensurability of Yahweh would seem to require that they do not, Yahweh, in mutuality, moves out of incommensurability (kenosis) for the sake of contact, but it is contact that does not compromise Yahweh's sovereign incommensurability.[11]

The contact between God and human beings is experienced in the greatest measure in the liturgy of the Church. It is the bridge point where heaven and earth meet, where *katabasis* and *anabasis* take place.

This book studies these complex realities in the Igbo context, where God meets and interacts with the people. The study focuses on the liturgical locus of contact between God and humanity because, while the Old Testament

---

10. Scholars like Karl Barth, Karl Rahner, Edward Schillebeeckx (*Ministry: Leadership in the Community of Jesus Christ,* [New York: Crossroad, 1981]), Thomas Aquinas, Michael Keenan Jones, and Joseph Okwor, to mention a few, have done some work on the priesthood or sacrifice. See, e.g., Joseph Okwor, *The Priesthood from an Igbo Perspective: A Theological Study Aimed at Improving the Formation of Catholic Priests in Igboland* (Enugu, Nigeria: Fulladu Publishing Company, 1998); and Michael Keenan Jones, *Toward a Christology of Christ the High Priest,* Tesi gregoriana, Serie theologia 135 (Rome: Gregorian University Press, 2006).

11. Walter Brueggemann, *Theology of the Old Testament: Testimony, Dispute, Advocacy* (Minneapolis: Fortress, 1997), 568.

interprets the history of Israel in terms of the covenant, the New Testament was established in and through the person of Jesus, who by his Paschal Mystery created a new people for his God and Father. Christ's priesthood and sacrifice become the central hub around which this study revolves.

Through this book, I hope to give Christianity in Igboland an Igbo and African character, starting with the priesthood and sacrificial ritual in the Igbo tribe, which is the seedbed of Christianity in Nigeria, and finally suggesting areas in the Igbo culture and tradition that may be inculturated into the Church's worship. This will eventually give Christ and the Church a true home in Igboland.

# I

## PRIESTHOOD AND SACRIFICE

CHAPTER ONE

# PRIESTHOOD AND SACRIFICE
# IN THE OLD TESTAMENT

## 1.1 Priesthood in the Old Testament

Humanity, by reason of creation, has always sought ways to remain close to God or some Being that is believed to be behind the origin and the control of the universe. To achieve this, humans, despite their imperfections and weaknesses, devised means of bridging the gap with the Absolute and of communicating with this Being. The purported means of reaching God became necessary because people felt that God, who is pure spirit, could not be reached without the aid of spirits. Albert Vanhoye succinctly asserts, "Man perceives a terrifying difference of quality between the explosive force of the life of God and the fragility of his own existence, and recognizes his unworthiness to enter into relationship with the Thrice Holy."[1] The many forms humans devised include divination, soothsaying, adoration, and the offering of sacrifices. These activities were carried out individually, communally, or through an official representative of the community, and it is the duty and importance of this representative that this book is setting out to unravel. In this book, I call the one who leads the community in worship "priest."

Situating this study in the context of Israel, biblical tradition holds that the choice of Israel by God was a means of gathering all nations so that through Israel all may be united under God as his people. The singular initiative of

---

1. Albert Vanhoye, *The Old Testament Priests and the New Priest,* trans. Bernard J. Orchard (Petersham, MA: St. Bede's, 1986), 27. See also Josephus, *Jewish Antiquities,* trans. H. St. J. Thackeray, Loeb Classical Library (London: William Heinemann, 1926), 4.1.45-50. Josephus describes the sin of Adam and Eve and their withdrawal from God because of their iniquities as follows: "But, when God entered the garden, Adam, who ere then was wont to resort to His company, conscious of his crime withdrew; and God, met by action so strange, asked for what reason he who once took delight in His company now shunned and avoided it" (*Antiquities of the Jews* 1.1.4 §45).

God in manifesting Himself to Israel was the beginning of the relationship that would culminate in the covenant and cult. God preceded this great event with the call of Abraham (Genesis 12), the revelation of his personal name, "YHWH" (Yahweh; Exod. 3:13–15; 6:2–3), the exodus from Egypt (Exodus 12–13) and the Sinai covenant (Exodus 19–24). Israel could therefore honor and worship the God it has come to know through cult. Israel was to be a special possession, a kingdom of priests and a holy nation (Exod. 19:4-6). It was a call to be holy because Yahweh is holy (Lev. 19:2). The privilege granted to Israel involves a separation, a setting apart, a dedication, and a consecration. Israel was to be the means through which all nations were destined to attain salvation. J. H. Kurtz understands this call and invitation by God to Israel as a call to the entire nation to be a priestly nation.[2] Kurtz's position is still debatable, by the way. The election of Israel was the first step toward the choice of the tribe of Levi and the institution of the priesthood in the Old Testament.

### *1.1.1 Etymology of Kōhēn*

The usual word for priest in the Hebrew Scripture is *kōhēn*. There is no consensus among scholars as to the etymology of the word "*kōhēn*," a term used for both Israelite and non-Israelite priests. However, there are four hypotheses that this study will examine. These hypotheses can be summarized as follows:

a. *Kōhēn:* The word *kōhēn* is in the masculine nominative and comes from a Northwest Semitic root *kwn*, meaning "to be firm, lasting, established."[3] From the root *kwn*, the priest is the person who is "firm," "lasting," and "established" for and before God.

b. *Kanu:* Some derive the word *kōhēn* from the Akkadian *kanu*, which in the *shaphel* has a sense of "bowing," "adoring," and "doing homage."[4] In this sense, the *kōhēn* is the one who bows in adoration or adores the divinity. He is the man who pays homage to the divinity in worship.

Roland de Vaux follows the view that the word *kōhēn* is an expansion of *kanu*.[5] He differs from others, however, by saying that its verbal root of *kun* or

2. J. H. Kurtz, *Offerings, Sacrifices and Worship in the Old Testament*, trans. James Martin (German 1863; Peabody, MA: Hendrickson, 2000), 19. Kurtz argues that God chose the kingdom of Israel to be the "priests" of all nations but Israel renounced this right and delegated Moses instead. "On that occasion they said to Moses (Ex. Xx. 19), 'Speak thou to us, and we will hear; but let not God speak with us, lest we die' (cf Deut. V. 22sqq.). By these words they renounced the great privilege of the priesthood, that of drawing near to God, and holding personal and immediate intercourse with Him."

3. Aelred Cody, *A History of Old Testament Priesthood*, Analecta Biblica 35 (Rome: Pontifical Biblical Institute, 1969), 26.

4. Jeremy Black, Andrew George, and Nicholas Postgate, eds., *A Concise Dictionary of Akkadian*, Santag 5 (Wiesbaden: Harrassowitz, 2000), 146.

5. Roland de Vaux, *Ancient Israel: Its Life and Institutions*, trans. John McHugh

*kwn* means "to stand up."[6] I differ from the view of de Vaux on *kun* because *kun* could only mean "to be certain, be established, fixed, be set forth, be stable, set in order"[7] (Deut. 10:8). The *kōhēn* stands before the divinity ready to do his will, to minister.

    c. *Kahin:* Another possible cognate is the Arabic root *kahin,* which means "priest," but the *kahin* was in essence a "soothsayer" or "a wise man." A *kahin* may not be properly called a priest in the strict sense of the word because the priest's major function is to minister to the divinity. The soothsayer claims to foretell the future or reveal events by divination, while a priest performs other cultic ceremonies as well. Aelred Cody has the following suggestion:

> The existence of the Arabian word *Kahin* as a cognate to the Hebrew *Kohen,* however, has led to theories which sought to find the origin of the very institution and nature of the Hebrew priesthood in the type of soothsaying known to have been that of the Arabian *Kahin.*[8]

Cody, therefore, equates *kahin* with *kōhēn.* However, based on the information presented above, one can conclude that the *kōhēn* is basically a wise man or a soothsayer.

    d. Ugaritic *kun.*[9] The word *kōhēn* in Ugaritic and Phoenician comes from the root *kun,* which means "one who brings abundance, well-being, prosperity."[10] The *kōhēn* in this hypothesis is the man who brings plenty, abundance, well-being, and prosperity. The *kōhēn* is seen as a source of blessing, for he prays and blesses the people in the name of the divinity.

    One may be inclined to agree with Cody in this area: ". . . the earliest priests

---

(New York: McGraw-Hill, 1961), 346: "It is more common, though, to connect it with the root *kwn* meaning 'to stand upright'; the priest would then be the man who stands before God (cf. Dt 10:8) like a servant."

    6. Vanhoye, *Old Testament Priests,* 19-20.

    7. Robert Young, ed., *Young's Analytical Concordance to the Bible; Also, Index Lexicons to the Old and New Testament* (orig. 1900; Grand Rapids: Eerdmans, 1955), 21. Young explains *kun* as to "be certain," "be directed," "be established," "be fashioned," "be fitted," "be fixed," "be meet," "be perfect," "be prepared," "be ready." See also Black, *Concise Dictionary of Akkadian,* 146. The Akkadian dictionary states that *kanu* means "to be(come) permanent, firm, true." It could also mean "firmly established," "remain visible," "be stable." It could be of a person or of a statement.

    8. Cody, *History of Old Testament Priesthood,* 16.

    9. Cyrus H. Gordon, *Ugaritic Manual: Newly Revised Grammar, Texts in Transliteration, Cuneiform Selections, Paradigms, Glossary, Indices,* Analecta Orientalia 35 (Rome: Pontificium Institutum Biblicum, 1955), 277.

    10. Cody, *History of Old Testament Priesthood,* 28. Cody postulates that "we do not have the materials (in Old Aramaic . . .) we should like to have for verifying it. For the moment we have to be content with the word's meaning as it appears in usage already fixed, hoping for more clarification. . . ."

among the Israelites were essentially sanctuary attendants—not soothsayers, not diviners, not sacrificers, although oracular consultation was their principal activity and there was nothing to prohibit their offering a sacrifice like other men."[11] The above hypotheses offer useful information toward the understanding of the term "priest." However, the hypothesis I find most compelling is the derivative from the root *kun,* "to be firm, established for a purpose." In this case, it is for ministering to the divinity. There are other words used to describe the *kōhēn* such as the following:

a. *Kĕmārîm:* This word is from the root *kmr,* a noun used in Assyrian colonies but which always appears in the plural in Hebrew as *kĕmārîm.* It was used for pagan priests. De Vaux writes that some scholars have suggested that this noun, which is derived from the root *kmr,* was used about 2000 BCE.[12]

b. *Kĕhunnâ:* The noun *kĕhunnâ* denotes priests of a sanctuary and priesthood in general. It is used in the Old Testament to designate priests (Exod. 29:9; Num. 3:10; 1 Sam. 2:36). It shows the relationship the priest has with a sanctuary.

All these hypotheses show that the term *kōhēn* is a complex reality. There is no one definition that encompasses everything about the priest.

c. *Hiereus:* The word *hiereus* is the Greek equivalent of Hebrew *kōhēn.* It is found in the Greek texts of the Old Testament and New Testament and is used of priests. *Hiereus* is related to *hieros,* "sacred." The *hiereus* is a sacred man and also a man of the sacred.

From the etymology and the various hypotheses, the different nuances of the word for priest could point to a man chosen by God to minister to him. The priest mediates between God and the people. He is the man designated by God to relate to him in matters concerning religion and worship. He stands before God for the sake of ministering to God and for leading the people in worship. The *kōhēn,* therefore, is the man of the sanctuary who is chosen by the divinity to stand before him. The definition by Albert Vanhoye of the word *kōhēn* portrays this duty and sacred character of the office of the priest.

> The *Kohen* may be viewed as the man of the sanctuary, the one who has the right to touch the sacred objects and who is admitted into the presence of God, as the man charged with offering the sacrifices, or again as the one who utters oracles and who gives blessings and decides questions of ritual purity.[13]

---

11. Ibid., 29.

12. De Vaux, *Ancient Israel,* 345: "There is another noun, however, derived from the root kmr, which was used from about 2000 BC in Assyrian colonies of Cappadocia, then in ancient Aramaic, and later on in the dialect of Palmyra and in Syriac. The corresponding Hebrew word, always in the plural kemarim, occurs only three times in the Bible and always refers to priests of false gods (2 K 23:5; Os 10:5; So 1:4)."

13. Vanhoye, *Old Testament Priests,* 20.

This beautiful definition of the priesthood by Vanhoye may have had the Israelite priesthood in mind. The Israelites, like every other people, had the need for someone to mediate for them before God, and this function grew into an institution after so many years. It passed through the following stages:

### 1.1.2 Priesthood in the Tribal Period

The tribal period in Israel was when heads of families acted as priests. During this period, which spanned about five hundred years, blood was the bond that held members together. Vanhoye notes that an honor to a member of a family extends to all, while a sin against one extends to all as well.[14] Therefore, whatever a member of the family experienced in life was cause for thanksgiving or petition to God. It was the head of the family that presided over the prayers at the family ritual worship. This is the period that is situated mostly in the book of Genesis. Here, the head of the family was the priest. He directed, taught, prayed, and blessed his children. Abraham, Isaac, and the other patriarchs belonged to this period. After the exodus, the heads of families continued to immolate the paschal lamb in families and continued instructing the people until the centralization of cult under Josiah.

### 1.1.3 Priesthood as Institution

Before the call of Moses and Aaron, priesthood in ancient Israel was neither an institution nor a vocation, as there was no "call" from God to anyone to be his priest. The origin of the Israelite priesthood as an institution is the call of Aaron and his sons. Exodus 28 states it as follows: "From among the sons of Israel summon Aaron and his sons to be priests in my service: Aaron, Nadab and Abihu, Eleazar and Ithamar, sons of Aaron" (Exod. 28:1). This is the beginning of Israelite priesthood. When corruption set in among the priests in the later stages, God referred to the choice of the house of Aaron as a reminder to the priests of the privilege he afforded them. 1 Samuel 2:27–37, which is a later text, captures it in the following way:

> Thus the Lord said, "I revealed myself to the house of your father when they were in Egypt subject to the house of Pharaoh. I chose him out of all the tribes of Israel to be my priest, to go up to my altar, to burn incense, to wear an ephod before me; and I gave to the house of your father all my offerings by fire from the sons of Israel. . . . I promised that your house and the house of your father should go in and out before me forever."

---

14. Ibid., 10–11. See also John Bright, *A History of Israel*, 4th ed. (Louisville: Westminster John Knox, 2000), 162–63.

The above citation alludes to the choice of the house of Eli, who was a descendant of Ithamar, who is traced to the Aaronic lineage. Although Moses is also mentioned as a priest, scholars still debate whether that was so. The above reference seems to imply that Eli is a priest from the Mushite tradition—priests descended from Moses. Cody has some reservations on this issue, and Vanhoye has commented on it as well.[15] Moses was the leader and consultant in all matters that related to religion, wars, and the stability of the nation. Therefore, he is a priest since he belonged to the tribe of Levi, had priestly powers and prerogatives, and consecrated Aaron and his sons.

There are suggestions that Moses, being the intermediary between God and his people, performed the role of priest before the institution of the priesthood in Israel and at the consecration of Aaron and his sons. Moses, as leader of the people of God, was the great lawgiver. He solemnized the Sinaitic covenant and played the role of mediator between God and Israel. He played a role that was unique as the leader of God's people.

As for the division of the land, Yahweh spoke to Aaron and his sons as follows: "You shall have no inheritance in their land, no portion of it among them shall be yours. It is I who will be your portion and your inheritance among the sons of Israel" (Num. 18:20; cf. Ezek. 44:28; 45:1–6). The description in Lev. 8:1–8 of the consecration of Aaron and his sons to the priesthood is a way of adding grandeur and solemnity to the priesthood.

---

15. Cody, *History of Old Testament Priesthood,* 41. See also Jacob Milgrom, *Leviticus: A Book of Ritual and Ethics*, Continental Commentaries (Minneapolis: Fortress, 2004), 23. He argues on the role of Moses: "According to the Priestly source, here is where Moses enters the holy of holies (*adytum*) to stand before the ark. Other traditions in the Torah talk about Moses speaking to God 'face to face' (Exod 33:11) or 'mouth to mouth' (Num 12:8), but the Priestly source takes great pains to deny that Moses ever saw God's presence in the holy of holies. Moses' only distinction is that he sees visions of the kavod (the fire-cloud that envelopes God) in the tent and listens to the voice of God as he stands in front of the veil that conceals the ark. He needs to be alone to listen to God. In the Priestly source, visual theophany is public (Lev 9:23-34; Num 9:15-16), but listening to God is private." See also Jean Galot, *Theology of the Priesthood*, 2nd ed. (San Francisco: Ignatius Press, 2005), 21. Galot writes that Moses, "not a priest in the strict sense, performs in his capacity as leader of his people ritual functions such as the sacrificial ritual of the covenant (Exod 24: 3–8). See also Eugene H. Maly, *The Priest and Sacred Scripture* (Washington, DC: United States Conference of Catholic Bishops, 1972), 41. Maly wrote, "Any consideration of ministries in the Old Testament must acknowledge the unique role of Moses, who in God's providence and in the growing faith of Israel assumed an ever more comprehensive position touching all the categories of ministry without being adequately explained by any one. As unsurpassed mediator of revelation and instrument of unity, speaking in behalf of the transcendent God of Sinai, he was destined to reveal the concrete pattern of salvation offered by God who chose to save by inviting all men to join His people."

Yahweh spoke to Moses; he said: "Take Aaron, his sons with him, and the vestments, and the chrism, the bull for sacrifice for sin, the two rams and the basket of unleavened bread. Then call the whole community together at the entrance to the Tent of Meeting." Moses followed the orders of Yahweh; the community gathered at the entrance to the Tent of Meeting, and Moses said to them, "This is what Yahweh has ordered to be done." (Lev. 8:1–4)

It was Yahweh who chose Aaron and his sons, and Moses carried out the command of the Lord. Thus, priesthood is the Lord's choice. He calls and chooses whom he wishes. Leviticus 8:6–30 gives an explanation of the rite of consecration and investiture of Aaron and his sons.[16] The message of Lev. 8:6–30 is that the consecration and investiture marked Aaron and his sons for liturgical celebrations. They were ritually cleansed so that they could go in and out before Yahweh on behalf of the congregation of Israel. To go in and out implies a service and possibly a leadership position. Following this assumption, the postexilic documents exalted the position of the priesthood.

Samuel E. Balentine points out the significance of the anointing of Aaron and his sons (which is quite different from the anointing kings received) and the importance of the blood ritual. He also argues that priests have a great responsibility to fulfill before God and the people by virtue of being chosen for the task of mediation. He asserts:

> The anointing of priests served a different purpose. Among Israel's titular leaders, the priests were uniquely charged with the responsibility of ministering at *the intersection between the holy things of God and the common, profane world* in which God wishes the holy to be increasingly present and formative. Such a ministry required that they be specially prepared, for unlike kings, who exercise authority in the secular world, where success may be secured and failures corrected by legal statutes, the priests must safeguard God's most distinctive gift to the world—the capacity to be the earthly domain for the holy. On their shoulders, therefore rests the burden of implementing God's risky investment in the world.[17]

---

16. Samuel E. Balentine, *Leviticus,* Interpretation: A Bible Commentary for Teaching and Preaching (Louisville: John Knox, 2002), 73. Balentine wrote: "The ceremony proper begins with the ritual of *washing* (v.6) and *clothing* (vv.7–9). The washing ritually cleanses Aaron and his sons, preparing them, in a way similar to what has been described in animal sacrifices (1:9, 13; cf. 8:21), for contact with the holy. The clothing ritually vests them with garments that visually identify their holy status. Eight vestments in all comprise the attire."

17. Balentine, *Leviticus*, 76 (emphasis added). The words *intersection* and *profane* have much to do with the Igbo worldview and metaphysics. There is among the Igbos a

Although Balentine used a postexilic writing to buttress his point, one can draw from the analysis that Aaron was specially chosen for the privileged office of the priesthood.

In ancient Israel, only kings were anointed (1 Sam. 9:16; 10:1; 2 Sam. 2:4; 5:3; 1 Kgs. 19:15; 2 Kgs. 3:6). We can therefore assume, judging from the above instances, that all kings of Israel and Judah were anointed. Anointing of kings was a religious rite, as the Spirit of the Lord descended on the individual who was anointed (1 Sam. 24:7).

The texts about the anointing of priests are late passages from the Priestly source (Exodus 29; Lev. 8:12ff.). There is no preexilic or prophetic text that explicitly mentions the anointing of priests. Though priests were anointed in the postexilic era when they functioned as the political leaders of the people, anointing was not a rite of consecrating priests reserved for them from inception.

### 1.1.4 Millē' Yad (πληροῦν τὰς χείρας), *Filling the Hand*

The term *millē' yad* is the technical term in the Hebrew Scriptures for the consecration of priests. The ἱερος is one who is "filled with the divine power of the deity" and is "consecrated to the deity." The Septuagint translates *millē' yad* as πληροῦν τὰς χείρας), "filling the hand." The original meaning of *millē' yad* is very much debated. To "fill one's hand" was seen as a part of the rite by which one was consecrated priest. The candidate for the priesthood would receive the victim for sacrifice in his hand and then proceed to the altar for sacrifice.[18] It was a form of investiture of the priest. Leviticus 8:27–28 states that Moses put the parts of the victim to be burned on the altar into the hands of Aaron and his sons and made the gesture of presentation with them. He later took these offerings from their hands and burned them on the altar. It is not clear what that signified, but after a time it came to mean inaugurating an altar (Ezek. 43:26). The candidate was therefore consecrated and installed as priest to direct worship. However, the texts on "filling the hand" are late texts that were seeking to explain a phrase whose original meaning was forgotten. It might have been the reason for its early disuse.

As pointed out earlier in this chapter, the first sons in the families in Israel exercised the priestly duties before the institution of the priesthood. God chose the tribe of Levi for ministry at the sanctuary, with Aaron and his sons

---

crossroad or an intersection that is believed to be the meeting point of the spirits. Offerings are provided to the spirits in such places so as to occupy them and distract the bad ones from interfering in the affairs of people in the world.

18. De Vaux, *Ancient Israel*, 346–47. De Vaux explains "filling the hand" as an expression whose meaning was understood as referring to the investiture of the priest. De Vaux also wrote that it is assumed by some authors to mean the salary of the priest (Judg. 17:10; 18:4). See also Cody, *History of Old Testament Priesthood*, 153–54.

as the first priests (Num. 3:1–4, 5–10; Deut. 10:8–9). The succession to the Old Testament priesthood was by genealogical descent. The priest had to be from the family of Aaron and of the tribe of Levi. It was a family affair as it was passed from father to son. When Aaron approached his end, Yahweh ordered Moses to strip him of the high priest's vestments and put them on his son Eleazar, who would succeed his father. This instruction was carried out by Moses (Num. 20:22–29). The consecration of Aaron and his sons implies that at the earliest period in the formation of the *Qehal Yahweh* (assembly of Yahweh) and the institution of the priesthood, there was a distinction between the office of rulers and priestly function.

The high priest was the symbol of the Israelite priesthood, as he was empowered and authorized to carry out liturgical functions on behalf of the people. He was called "the priest who is preeminent over his brothers, on whose head the anointing oil has been poured" (Lev. 21:10), "the chief of the Levite leaders" (Num. 3:32), "the priest" (Num. 3:6), "the head priest" (2 Kgs. 25:18), "the anointed priest" (Lev. 4:3). His priestly vestments, with the turban on his head bearing the inscription "holy to Yahweh" (Exod. 28:4–39; Lev. 8:7–9), summed up his mediatory role and the high dignity he enjoyed. Besides the normal dress worn by other Israelite males, the high priest had the following liturgical vestments:

a. The Ephod. The meaning of *'ēpōd* in the Old Testament is uncertain. It could mean the instrument of divination (1 Sam. 2:28). It was also called the *'ēpōd bad*,[19] a linen loincloth worn by the ministers of the sanctuary. The Bible indicates that David wore it when he danced before the ark of the Lord (2 Sam. 6:14). There is also the *'ēpōd* of the high priest, which is a breastplate that hung over his chest. In the case of the high priest, it was made of fine-twined linen of gold, purple, violet, red, and crimson colors. It had two onyx stones on each shoulder, on which were engraved the names of the tribes of Israel—six on each stone. "In this way Aaron will bear their names on his shoulders in the presence of Yahweh, so as to commemorate them" (Exod. 28:12). The priest "carries" the whole congregation of Israel into the presence of Yahweh. It was an indispensable object for obtaining oracles. It raises the question of whether it was a garment for the priests or an object for obtaining oracles (1 Sam. 14:3ff.; 23:6–9).

b. Pectoral of Judgment (Breastplate). This pectoral plate was worn over the chest of the high priest with twelve precious stones engraved with the names of the twelve tribes of Israel. The *Urim* and *Thummim* were also attached to the pectoral plate as a reminder that the high priest bore the divine oracle to the sons of Israel (Exod. 28:30). By means of the *Urim* and *Thummim* the high priest could consult with Yahweh (1 Sam. 23:2–6).

---

19. De Vaux, *Ancient Israel,* 349.

c. The Robe: This garment was called "the robe of the ephod" to show its liturgical character when worn by the priest. It had a round opening for the neck and was woven from linen and extended from the neck and shoulders to the ankle. The lower hem was decorated with pomegranates and purple and golden colored bells alternately. It was the official vestment of the high priest when he presided.

Exodus 28:40–43 gives the list of the other vestments worn by the high priest and all the sons of Aaron (the priest). The first of these was the tunic. It was of unbleached linen or wool and was worn over the linen loincloths. Next was the "girdle and headdress to give dignity and magnificence" (Exod. 28:40).

The sacred vestments were for cultic purposes. Only the priests who wore them had access to the sacred areas of the temple, which were not open to the lay congregation of Israel. On the social aspect, they indicated dignity, beauty, and glory. This is rendered in a sublime way in Sir. 45:7–22. The priestly vestment was a form of protection against the demons who may want to kill one seeking audience with God.

d. The Turban and the Plate of Pure Gold. The turban was the "crown" that the high priest wore on his head. In the postexilic period when the high priest was the leader of the people, the crown was called "the plate of pure gold." The turban, bearing the inscription "Holy to the Lord," signified that the high priest was dedicated to the Lord and set apart for service. This was probably a tall, cone-shaped headdress and was for the high priest alone. It was seen as a royal sign (Ezek. 21:26; Zech. 3:5).

Looking at the high priest in his vestments, one would conclude that he was someone with authority as a leader, a prince in the temple of Yahweh, bearing symbolically the twelve tribes of Israel on himself into the presence of Yahweh. In the splendor of their vestments, priests represented God to the people, while the high priest in particular represented the whole nation of Israel before God (Exod. 28:29–30).[20] To underline the importance and significance of the high priest, his death marked the end of an era and a year of favor. Those who were exiled from the land for manslaughter were welcomed back home from their city of refuge (Num. 35:25).

On some occasions, the Bible shows certain kings who played the role of priest-kings. In 2 Samuel 6, David wore a linen ephod and blessed Israel. The linen, described earlier, was one of the vestments worn by the priests during religious rituals. In 1 Kings 8, Solomon dedicated the temple of Israel and blessed the congregation of Israel.

The above instances show that kings performed roles that were reserved for priests in the later stages of Israelite history.

---

20. Philip Jensen, "*khn*," in *The New International Dictionary of Old Testament Theology and Exegesis,* ed. Willem A. VanGemeren, 5 vols. (Grand Rapids: Zondervan Press, 1997) 2:600–605.

The office of the priesthood could not be appropriated by anyone, as those who tried to usurp it were punished with death (Num. 16:3–35; 17:5). Vanhoye captures what befell Korah and his sons in the following words: "When Korah stirs up a movement of protest against the privileges of the priests and declares: 'All the congregation are holy, every one of them,' his claim is rejected in the most forceful manner, by a crushing divine intervention."[21] Therefore, priesthood was not for anyone who aspired to it; only those called by God could minister to him.

### 1.1.5 Functions of Priests (Num. 18:1-8; Deut. 33:8-10)

The priest in ancient Israel performed many functions for the people, especially in the liturgical celebrations.[22] He is first and foremost a man of God, called to minister to God. He is also "a man of the sanctuary."[23] The numerous services the priest renders are as follows.

------

21. Vanhoye, *Old Testament Priests*, 248. Vanhoye also argues that the Book of Deuteronomy shows that the Israelites were near to the mountain but could not bear the thunderous voice of Yahweh. Thus, they told Moses to play the intermediary role.

22. Abraham E. Millgram, *Jewish Worship* (Philadelphia: Jewish Publication Society, 1971), 114: ". . . precedence is given to one who is of priestly descent and after him to one who is of Levitical descent." Millgram says further that "the practice has therefore been to follow the set hierarchy and to call to the reading of the Torah first the Kohen and then a Levite, if they are in attendance." What Millgram is citing here refers to the liturgy of the Jews in the synagogue. His book *Jewish Worship* is about the liturgy as found in the modern era; however, it follows the tradition put in place by the Torah, which gives precedence to the priests and the Levites in a liturgical function.

23. Vanhoye, *Old Testament Priests*, 30–31. Vanhoye further explains that the priest has a twofold movement: the ascending movement and the descending movement. The ascending movement is that which takes him to God by means of sacrifice. Through this he mends the severed relationship between God and his people. The descending movement is the consequence of the ascending movement whereby the priest conveys God or the oracles/blessings/message to the people. See Brueggemann, *Theology of the Old Testament*, 664. He notes that "cult mediates Yahweh's presence, and priests are required for the cult." He also gives another dimension of the role of priests which points out their supervisory role in worship. My impression is that the priests themselves do not mediate, but they supervise and attest the visual, material, physical acts of worship that do the mediation. See also de Vaux, *Ancient Israel*, 348. De Vaux shares this opinion and asserts that the "transference into the order of things sacred conferred a real dignity on the priest. When Mikah engaged the Levite he said 'Be a father and a priest to me' (Jg 17:10), even though the Levite was only a young man (cf. vv. 7 and 10). The significance of this remark is that the priest had inherited those religious prerogatives which, in the patriarchal period, had belonged to the head of the family."

1.1.5.1 The Service of God and Care of the Sanctuary.

The priest has as the first function, the service of God. According to Walther Zimmerli, it is accepted that priests are the ones who are at the service of God.[24] Thus, the priest was rightly called in the earliest periods "the man of the sanctuary" because his primary responsibility is "to minister to me" (Exod. 28:1; Num. 18:7). As man of the sanctuary, the priest attends to the cleanliness and decorum of the place, ensuring that nothing unworthy of the divinity takes place. He locks and unlocks the temple, and provides for sacrifices and other cultic needs.

1.1.5.2 Receiving Divine Oracles

It is the function of the priest to seek out and interpret the will of God. The *Urim* and *Thummim*[25] were used for consultation only in the days of Samuel, David, and Solomon.[26] The origin, etymology, and use of these oracular objects are shrouded in mystery, which may account for their early disuse.[27] Priests continued to proclaim oracles even as the latter prophets were called upon to assume this function.

1.1.5.3 Teaching the Torah

In the history of God's chosen people, it was the priests who taught the people the law of God. The law was given by the Lord, while the priests taught the people. The teaching of the ethical laws was associated with the Levites, who were in charge of the people's day-to-day activities (Hos. 4:6; Deut. 31:9, 26; Zeph. 3:4). However, the priests were to teach the Torah, along with the statutes. 2 Kings 17:27 notes that the northern priests were sent back to Israel after the deportation in the late eighth century BC to teach the people the statutes of

---

24. Walther Zimmerli, *The Old Testament and the World*, trans. John J. Scullion (London: SPCK, 1976), 85–86. Here Zimmerli writes about the priest as follows: "The priest stands in the privileged place of one who has ready access to the holy and . . . can be near to God. His access to and nearness to God is a priestly service for others."

25. The *Ephod* and *Urim* and *Thummim* were used to determine a yes or no answer from God or to determine innocence or guilt. These instruments were means of relaying God's immediate response to the one seeking the will of Yahweh.

26. Cody, *History of Old Testament Priesthood,* 115–16: "Even though the statement of Ezra 2:63 = Neh 7:65 that in the Second Temple there was no one to use the urim and thummim makes us wonder if memory of them as objects to be manipulated was based on a practice which had really ceased completely so long before, there seems little room for doubt that in the monarchical period urim and thummim as objects actually used in oracular consultation became obsolete."

27. De Vaux (*Ancient Israel,* 353) writes that, according to Esdr. 2:63 (Neh. 7:65), "there was no priest to handle the *Urim* and *Thummim*; this is confirmed by the Jewish tradition which often repeats that there was neither *Urim* nor *Thummim* in the Second Temple."

the God of the land. Negligence of this duty ushered in religious decadence, as the prophet Hosea noted: "But let no man denounce, no man rebuke; it is you, priest, that I denounce. Day and night you stumble along . . . and you are the ruin of your people. My people perish for want of knowledge" (4:4–6).

During the exile and subsequent return, the teaching function of priests was extended to the Levites. Then followed a new body of teachers in the doctors of the law, the scribes, the Pharisees, and the Sadducees. Malachi the prophet captures this idea very well: "The priest's lips ought to safeguard knowledge. His lips are where the law should be sought since he is the messenger of Yahweh Sabaoth" (2:7). The priest is the channel through which God makes known and manifests his glory.

1.1.5.4 Separation of the Sacred from the Profane (Deut. 33:8–10)[28]

It was the role of the priests to remind the people of the necessity of keeping some distance from the sacred. In the desert it was mainly the priests and Levites (*ḥakkōhănîm wĕhallĕwîyîm*) who carried the ark in the desert until it was placed in the temple in Jerusalem. The priests were the ones who instructed the people on special topics and answered questions related to legal purity and cult (Hag. 2:11–13). They also performed this duty when the ark was finally enthroned into the temple constructed by Solomon (1 Kgs. 8:6).[29]

1.1.5.5 Therapeutic Functions Based on the Clean and
the Unclean Ritual Pronouncements

One of the duties assigned to the Aaronic priesthood was that of seeing, examining, and monitoring the bodies of the sick and giving support to the sick. This function includes the examination of skin diseases, diagnosis, quarantine,

---

28. Vanhoye (*Old Testament Priests*, 29) writes on the separation even of the priests from the most sacred place reserved for only one priest on only one day of the year: "The priest's encounter with God requires even further rites of separation. One does not encounter God just anywhere, or at any time, or in any manner, but only in a holy place at a specific moment and in the performance of particular sacred gestures. The holy place is the sanctuary, a place separated from profane space and reserved for worship. Only priests have access to it, and even they cannot go everywhere in the holy place: the holiest area is forbidden to them; it is open only to a single person, the high priest, and to him on one day only, the Day of Atonement (Lev 16)." See also Michael Kunzler, *The Church's Liturgy*, trans. Placed Murray et al. (New York: Continuum, 2001), 28. Here Kunzler supports the idea of a sacred space: "The salvation of the fallen world and of man in it [Here we recall that humans from the time of Adam have always had a concept of sin or offense to the Supreme Deity and needed to appease Him] can only consist in restoring the life-giving but disturbed communication with the triune God. Its completion will be the complete re-sacralization of the profane."

29. 2 Chronicles 5:7 gives a description of the priests carrying the ark into "the back chamber of the house" for only one time—at the enthronement of the ark.

observation, and, if necessary, sacrificial rites when a person was pronounced clean (Lev. 14:1–20).

### 1.1.5.6 Offering of Sacrifice

Priests offered sacrifices to God. Until recently, this has been considered their most important function, but that is misleading. It is strange because, from the earliest period, it was not a prerogative of the priest to offer sacrifices. The situation arose as functions were allotted in the organized liturgy of the temple. The offering of bloody sacrifice involves the manipulation of the blood of the victim upon the altar of the deity. It was at the point of the blood ritual that the sacrifice is believed to be offered through the hands of a priest. Aaron and his sons were chosen by God in the Old Testament to offer sacrifices for themselves and the people—thus, the manipulation of blood (Leviticus 9).[30] However, this study notes the following:

1.1.5.6.1. The patriarchs were their own priests and individual heads of families offered sacrifices. For example, the Passover was offered by family heads.

1.1.5.6.2. When it came to the issue of killing the victim, it was not the priest who slaughtered the animal, but the individual who brought the animal (Exod. 24:3–8). This was stipulated by law.

1.1.5.6.3. When it was time for the most sacred part of the ritual, it was then that the priest became involved. This includes manipulation of the blood of the victim and the placing of the victim on the altar, which is the symbol of God (1 Sam. 2:28).

### *1.1.6 Development of Priesthood*

From the biblical perspective, the history of the priesthood of ancient Israel is long but lacking in detail. What is available is the history of the chosen people of Israel. The authors of the various books of the Bible were intent on handing on the story of the covenant between God and Israel. Rodney K. Duke argues that the biblical writers were more interested in the divine origin of the priesthood and the holiness of the office.[31] From the time of Adam to Moses, there was no official priesthood in Israel. Exodus 19: 20–24 suggests that a kind of

---

30. Cody, *History of Old Testament Priesthood*, 41–42; see also Vanhoye, *Old Testament Priests*, 24–25.

31. Rodney K. Duke, "Priests, Priesthood," in *Dictionary of the Old Testament: Pentateuch*, ed. T. Desmond Alexander and David W. Baker (Downers Grove, IL: InterVarsity, 2003), 646–55.

priestly system of worship existed among the Israelites who had just exited from Egypt before the giving of the law. It was at the giving of the law to Moses that priesthood became an official institution with the consecration of Aaron and his sons. Aaron and his sons, Nadab, Abihu, Eleazar, and Ithamar, were the first official priests in Israel, with Aaron functioning as the high priest (Exod. 28:1). One can get the impression that the priestly office was given to the tribe of Levi from which the Aaronides emerged. Cody has argued, along with some texts of "P," that the Aaronides claimed the exclusive responsibility of bearing the Israelite priesthood themselves, while neglecting the Levites.[32] His position on this issue is questionable because the Scriptures make it clear that God chose Aaron and his sons as the first official priests of Israel (Lev. 8:1–13). Aaron and his sons were chosen for the office of priesthood, but I differ from the view that they claimed it exclusively—they were called. Priesthood is always a call and a choice on the part of God.

The first mention of priests for Israel in the Bible is in Exod. 28:1–4 and the consecration in Exodus 29. From then on, priesthood became a dynastic succession of the Aaronic family and was passed from generation to generation. The office was passed on to Eleazar after his brothers were consumed by fire for offering unholy fire to the Lord (Lev. 10:1–3). They tried as much as they could to protect the office of the priesthood and to choose men from the lineage of Aaron. This protectiveness of the priestly lineage shows the necessity and importance of a priestly figure in relation to worship, though some may argue that the Canaanite priests influenced the Israelites to some extent.[33] It is true that the Israelites faced the constant temptation to be like the other nations, whereas God had called them to be unlike the other nations. That was a struggle they had to deal with, and they had prophets calling them back each moment they strayed. Cody wrote about what was practiced in the ancient Near East before Israel settled in the area.

> The religious institutions of Sumer, Babylonia, Assyria, and Egypt are known . . . through documents which already reflect highly organized urban civilizations whose complex priesthoods and cultic groups, with distinct classes of cultic personnel assigned to distinct types and differentiated cultic functions, are far removed from the society of the semi-sedentary Israelites before the days of the monarchy.[34]

---

32. Cody, *History of Old Testament Priesthood,* 41: "Those texts of P which justify the claims of the group calling themselves 'Aaronides' to the rights of exclusiveness in priestly functions at the expense of all other groups, including 'the Levites' (in its late sense as a name of subordinate function), insist that only Aaron and his descendants can be legitimate priests (Exod. 28:1, 43; Num. 3:10)."

33. Cody, *History of Old Testament Priesthood,* 60.

34. Ibid., 7.

Israel was late when it comes to organized liturgy. It did not have an organized liturgy before the monarchy.

1.1.6.1 Priesthood in the Time of the Judges
In the Book of Judges, there is a constant refrain at the beginning or end of each major story. "In those days there was no king in Israel; every man did what was right in his own eyes" (Judg. 17:6; 18:1; 19:1; 21:25). This statement by implication refers to the lapses and chaos experienced in Israel because of the lack of a political/kingly figure. Judges 17–18 describes the erection of a sanctuary by Micah, the Ephraimite who made one of his sons a priest. To emphasize the importance of priests, Micah saw a passing Levite and hires him as a priest in place of his son. Cody has the following to say on this issue:

> This episode reveals some very interesting things. Micah's son, an Ephraimite, can be priest-attendant of the sanctuary, but a Levite is so much to be preferred that Micah is eager to hire a Levite in place of his own son. The significance of this is that it was already accepted that Levites were the right people to have as sanctuary attendants.[35]

In Judg. 18:5ff., some Danites passing by made some consultations with the Levite, as they wanted to know the will of God for them. The above instances allude to the importance and necessity of the priestly class. They also highlight the esteemed position the priestly class enjoyed in the communities.

1.1.6.2 Priesthood during the Monarchy
The Israelites demanded a new form of government that resulted in the appointment of Saul as the first king of Israel (1 Samuel 8–10). He was the visible representation of Yahweh and carried out liturgical sacrifices; thus, he was often referred to as "Yahweh's anointed." In 2 Sam. 13:8–15, Saul offered sacrifice to God and was condemned by the prophet Samuel for the act of disobedience to the word of God. Popular opinion is that Saul was condemned because he performed a function reserved for the priests, that is, the offering of sacrifice. One must not lose sight of the fact that the kings functioned as priests too. This position could not have been the reason for the condemnation in light of what later kings did (2 Sam. 6:18). My next paragraph describes David and other kings offering sacrifices to God, and it proves the assertion that kings offered sacrifices. During such periods in Israel, kings performed rituals without undermining the role of priests.[36] The threshing floor of Araunah the Jebusite (2 Sam. 24:17), on which David offered sacrifice to God, later became the site of Solomon's temple. 2 Samuel 8:18 refers to the sons of David as priests—*kōhănîm*.

---

35. Ibid., 54.
36. Lawrence Boadt, *Reading the Old Testament: An Introduction* (New York: Paulist Press, 1984), 278.

They also had the responsibility of ruling the people of Israel with David, their father (1 Chr. 18:17), and, in that capacity, could also minister at the shrine.

When Solomon became king, he offered sacrifices to God at Gibeon before he built the temple (1 Kgs. 3:4). Solomon was sleeping in the high place at Gibeon when Yahweh appeared to him (1 Kgs. 3:5–14). King Solomon not only offered sacrifices to God; he also dedicated the temple (1 Kings 8), and the smoke of Yahweh's presence filled the temple such that priests were not able to go in to offer sacrifices in the temple (1 Kgs. 8:10–11). Smoke in the biblical tradition was an element either of theophany or of the anger of Yahweh. It symbolizes the presence of God in the temple (*'āšān, 'āšē*, Exod. 19:18; 20:18; Isa. 6:4; Ps. 104:32).[37] The word used in the case of 1 Kgs 8:10 is in the same sense as Isaiah used it in 6:4. It describes a theophany just like the Sinai experience. Therefore, if God came down to the sacrifice of Solomon, it follows that God approved of the offering at Solomon's hands. Lester L. Grabbe, explains the action of Solomon as follows:

> Solomon himself was able to stand and pray before the altar of God (1 Kings 8:10; 22, 54). . . . Solomon consecrated the entire center of the Temple court for burning the sacrificial parts (v 64). This action was taken by the *king* rather than priests; Solomon acted as a priest among priests.[38]

Consecration of a place meant for worship could be done only by one who has been chosen and authorized by God to stand before him. In the case of Solomon, God confirmed his support for the king's actions in the above instance by saying, "I have heard the prayer and plea you have made before me; I have consecrated this temple, which you have built, by putting my Name there forever. My eyes and my heart will always be there" (1 Kgs. 9:3). The kings, positively or negatively, had some roles to play in the cultic ceremonies. They often served as priests in ceremonial worship. The king could do this because, as head of the nation, he was a high priest par excellence (*Summus Pontifex*). He could depose a high priest too (1 Kgs. 2:26–27).

During his reign, Jeroboam I made two golden calves and placed them in the shrines at Bethel and Dan. He appointed priests from ordinary families who

---

37. The word *'āšēn* comes from the root verb *'šn*, meaning, "wrapped in smoke, *ashan*—be angry." When *'šn* is used in this verbal form or in adjectival form *'āšēn*, it describes a theophany. When it appears in its noun form, *'āšān*, it is being used figuratively to describe Yahweh's anger (2 Sam. 22:9; Isa. 65:5). See Jeffrey J. Niehaus, "'*šn*," in VanGemeren, *New International Dictionary of Old Testament Theology and Exegesis*, 3:556–57.

38. Lester L. Grabbe, *Priests, Prophets, Diviners, Sages: A Socio-historical Study of Religious Specialists in Ancient Israel* (Valley Forge, PA: Trinity Press International, 1995), 23.

were not from the tribe of Levi to these shrines. He led the northern tribes to apostasy and schism. Jeroboam could organize worship because he was king and had the authority to delegate priests to the shrines. He instituted feasts and mounted the altar to offer sacrifices and incense (1 Kgs. 12:26–33). He was able to do these things because it was the prerogative of kings to preside at liturgical worship if they wanted. His action unfortunately led the ten tribes away from the true worship of Yahweh.

During Israelite history, individuals could offer sacrifices at the shrines in various parts of the nation. When it came to the official national sacrifices, only the appointed priests from the Aaronic lineage could perform such functions. During the period of judges, the judges performed this function as well in their capacities as representatives of the people before Yahweh (Judg. 6:19–32; 1 Sam. 7:9; 1 Kgs. 15:9–24; 2 Chronicles 14–16). Josiah was a king with the "fear of God" who repaired the temple. As leader and guide, he sent his scribes to help maintain justice and oversee the activities in the temple. This could have been done only by one who was vested with authority to restore dignity and decorum in the house of worship. The case of Uzziah is a peculiar case. He attempted to offer incense on the altar, for which he was struck with "leprosy," from which he suffered until death.[39] The historicity of this event is doubtful, especially since it was recorded only in Chronicles, a didactic writing. The above shows that it was not the exclusive responsibility of priests to offer sacrifices; and neither is sacrifice the most important function of priests. Kings, as I have shown, also offered acceptable sacrifices (Leviticus 1–7). Though kings offered sacrifices and prayers as the history of Israel was being shaped, there are suggestions that one may be wrong to think that kings had the ultimate role and official responsibility of offering sacrifices or of serving as high priests in Israel. De Vaux supports the view that young men in Israel, priests and kings, all immolated animals in sacrifice.[40] Though various classes of people offered sacrifice, there is a distinction in the roles of kings and the priests.

A king, of course, had nothing to do with oracular work or the giving of Torah, and his *raison d'être* was not service at the sanctuary but

---

39. The Book of Chronicles is not a historical book, and the passage is absent from the Book of Kings. This Priestly, postexilic document was at a loss how Uzziah, a very good king, suffered "leprosy" in his last days. The Chronicler attempted to explain the tragedy and so recorded that only the Aaronides were to offer incense on the altar (2 Chr. 26:18).

40. De Vaux, *Ancient Israel*, 355–56. De Vaux has an interesting passage on the offering of sacrifice in Israel: "Saul, David and Solomon all offered sacrifice, and . . . this does not mean that kings of Israel were priests; but neither does it mean that priests did not offer sacrifice at the time. Achaz himself offered the first sacrifice on the new altar he had built, but the priest Uriyyah was entrusted with the care of it afterwards (2 Kgs 12–16)."

the sovereign rule of a kingdom. There, precisely, lies the important distinction to be made.[41]

The reign of Hezekiah sparked a cleansing and pulling down of shrines in Israel, so that the cult was centralized in Jerusalem. It was a struggle for independence as well. In 2 Kgs. 19:9–34, Hezekiah takes a more direct role of praying in the temple for the preservation of Israel, laying Sennacherib's letter before the Lord—a function that could be assumed only by one in charge of a people as their religious leader. Hezekiah abolished and knocked down the bronze serpent made by Moses in the desert because the people had deviated from the true religion of Israel and worshiped the bronze serpent (2 Kgs. 18:4). The activities of Hezekiah paved the way for the reform of Josiah, who celebrated the Passover in a manner that had never been seen since the monarchy began. He restored the correct priestly organization and took the active role of a leader who had the responsibility of making sure that the cult and the priesthood are functioning as the law required. These activities of the kings of Israel show that they had roles to perform in the liturgical life of their people. Cody clarifies the role of kings in the liturgical celebrations as follows:

> [Kings] of Israel were representatives of the people as a whole, responsible for the welfare of the people as a whole even in relations between people and God. As such they were responsible for the organization and administration of the state of worship.[42]

Sacrifice was performed by various kings as leaders in politics, religion, and the social life of the people. The kings ensured the faith-unity of the people through military prowess and social justice. However that may have been, Brown offers an insight into the distinction of roles:

> The prophet, the judge, and the king were the recipients of a charism, for they were called and specially gifted by God. But the levitical priest

---

41. Cody, *History of Old Testament Priesthood,* 101.
42. Ibid., 100. See also Maly, *Priest and Sacred Scripture,* 42: "One of the figures responsible for continuing the Mosaic ministry of establishing and maintaining the unity of each succeeding generation of God's covenantal people was the king. This role crystallized only after several centuries which saw a variety of governmental forms in Israel: patriarchs, judges and nazirite leaders of the holy wars, and finally kings. Basic to each of these was an awareness of a direct charismatic calling, by which the individual was acknowledged as elected by God, filled with the Spirit of wisdom and strength and leadership, and chosen for a particular mission." Maly further states, "In a more specifically religious framework, the King of Israel was expected to show constant concern and care for worship, fulfilling the traditional role of the paterfamilias in sacrifice as well as that of the traditional role of the priest-king in prior Canaanite culture."

was born into the priesthood; he could serve as a priest because by
birth he was a member of a priestly tribe and family.[43]

Here lies the major distinction of functions and roles. Priesthood was hereditary, and the priests came from the tribe of Levi. Others who had duties to perform in the temple may have been helpers or servants, like the Gibeonites, who
supplied water to the temple (Josh. 9:27). Vanhoye gives a systematic account
of the priesthood from the institution of the monarchy through the exile and
the return from exile. He shows how the priesthood wielded power in the civil
affairs of the nation.[44] As time went on, there was a growing expectation of the
coming of the Messiah, who would hold the titles of priest, king, and prophet.
He would be a priest who would offer sacrifices pleasing to the Lord and would
gather the scattered children of God.[45]

### 1.1.6.3 Priesthood in the Maccabean Period

The Maccabean period witnessed another crisis in the history of Israel. The
members of the priestly family of Mattathias, whose roots were traced to the
family line of Asamonaios (Ἀσαμωναῖος), are the main characters. There were
many changes in the history of the Israelite priesthood in the Seleucid period.
The Zadokite priestly family maintained the office of high priest through
Joshua, son of Jehozadak, for three hundred years, until Menelaus, with a different connection, became high priest in 172 BC (2 Macc. 4:23). 1 Maccabees
7:5 and 2 Macc. 14:3 mention Alcimus, a man with an uncertain family background who became high priest by appointment (162 BC). He is called a priest
from the lineage of Aaron, though there is no proof. The years between 162 and
152 have been called by scholars a "sacerdotal black hole."[46] This is because
there were irregularities in the appointment and exercise of high priesthood
and no one person was seen and acknowledged as high priest until Jonathan
became high priest in 152 BC. Devout Jews, not satisfied with their religious
situation, began a revolution to liberate themselves from the shackles of Hellenism.

The revolution began within the priesthood when Mattathias, out of zeal
for God, killed a man who, because of Seleucid Hellenism, came to organize

---

43. Brown, *Priest and Bishop*, 7.
44. Vanhoye, *Old Testament Priests*, 39–42.
45. Ibid., 43. Vanhoye cites Isa. 2:1–5; Mic. 2:1–9; 3:3–4; 1 Sam. 2:35, and the Qum-
ran writings to show that there was a growing concern for the coming of the royal
Messiah who would institute true worship of Yahweh in Israel. Even in the Hasmonean
period, it was the priestly family that kept the priesthood and the traditions in place
until the time of Herod in 37 BC.
46. Alison Schofield and James C. Vanderkam, "Were the Hasmoneans Zadokites?" *Journal of Biblical Literature* 124 (2005): 73–87, esp. 73.

public sacrifice to pagan gods. Mattathias organized his sons and began a revolution to maintain the Jewish religion and traditions. His third son, Judas, the commander of the army, pioneered the cleansing of the temple in 164 BC. Jonathan, a son of Mattathias, became the first Maccabean high priest, and members of his family held the office until 37 BC.

There is an argument among scholars that the Hasmoneans were not Zadokites,[47] and that they merely assumed the office of the priesthood (1 Macc. 2:1–2). 1 Chronicles 24:7 gives the genealogy of Mattathias, with Jehoiarib as an important name in the genealogy. Jehoiarib was the first of the twenty-four ancestral high priests who served in the temple. H. G. M. Williamson argues that the name was a later addition to the Pentateuch by the Priestly writers.[48] In all, the family of Mattathias was from a priestly lineage, and, as such, the Israelite priesthood continued with them until Herod wiped out the Hasmoneans in 7 BC. The Hasmoneans had a considerable influence on the Jewish religion and political life up to the time of Herod. Vanhoye succintly puts it as follows:

> The priestly dynasty of the Hasmoneans kept itself in power through various vicissitudes until the time of Herod, whose reign began in 37 BC. The political power of the high priest was then reduced to a secondary level, but it did not disappear. Even when the Roman Empire made Judea into one of its procurational provinces, the high priest continued to be the highest authority of the Jewish nation. He pre-

---

47. Victor Tcherikover, *Hellenistic Civilization and the Jews* (New York: Atheneum, 1970), 492–93.

48. H. G. M. Williamson, "The Origins of the Twenty-Four Priestly Courses: A Study of 1 Chronicles xxiii–xxvii," in *Studies in the Historical Books of the Old Testament*, ed. J. A. Emerton, Supplements to *Vetus Testamentum* 30 (Leiden: Brill, 1979), 76. Williamson writes that "commentators maintain that one can in fact determine the family affiliation of the individual priestly houses in 1 Chronicles 24 from v.6: 'the heads of the ancestral houses of the priests and of the Levites; one ancestral house being chosen for Eleazar and one chosen for Ithamar. . . . From the last part of the verse they conclude that the principle was one of alteration, with the first group chosen from Eleazar, the second from Ithamar, and so on until the eight Ithamarite divisions were selected. The last eight of the twenty-four, then, all being from Eleazar's line, would have cast lots to determine their order. In support of their reading they cite the fact that in 1 Chronicles 25 the Levitical singers are also selected in this way. This appears to be a reasonable influence, although others have suggested that the pattern was two for Eleazar and then one for Ithamar. If we follow the latter approach, it would have the advantage of making both J(eh)oiarib and Jedaiah Eleazarites and therefore Zadokites. . . . On either reading, it is very likely that Jehoiarib is envisioned as belonging to the family of Eleazar via Zadok."

sided over the Sanhedrin, whose competence as a regional power the Romans acknowledged.[49]

In conclusion, priesthood was bought and sold for a period during the Maccabean era. It became involved with politics in such a manner that it was not easy to decipher whether the Hasmoneans were fighting a religious war or a political one, because religion was identified with politics. Corruption and struggle for power were the hallmarks of the period. Such was the Israelite priesthood and the authority of the high priest until the Christian era. It was also at this time that there was a growing expectation of the Messiah who would sit on David's throne forever. Having witnessed so many priests and kings, and still having experienced wars and slavery, all were expecting the new era of peace promised by God through his prophets. It was against such a background and longing that Jesus began his public ministry.

### 1.1.6.4 Summary

The above section has dealt with the etymology, origin and development of the priesthood. This chapter surveyed the beginning of Israelite priesthood, when individuals and family heads were priests. Even kings were not left out in the sacrificial rituals.[50] At each given moment in the history of Israel, there was someone, whether a family head or the head of the nation, who would stand before God in service, on behalf of others. When Aaron and his sons were chosen, it became the responsibility of Aaron and sons to minister to God. This is important to this study because the Igbo community, which this book studies, has the same progression in their traditional religion until the advent of Christianity. A priest, as he executes his duties, offers sacrifice either in thanksgiving or in reparation or for other purposes. Hence, the importance of sacrifice to this study.

## 1.2 Sacrifice in the Old Testament

This section studies sacrifice in the Old Testament to show the relationship between biblical priesthood and sacrifice. It is evident from world religions that humans believe they are drawn closer into the mystery of God through the ritual of sacrifice, and the people of Israel are no exception. Repentance may help one to refrain from evil but may not be enough to restore one to full com-

---

49. Vanhoye, *Old Testament Priests*, 42.

50. Cody (*History of Old Testament Priesthood*, 107) clarifies this idea more by stating that "Israelite ideas of both monarchy and priesthood, and of their relation to one another, went through a process of development from the early days of the monarchy, when kings performed acts which had about them a character that was indisputably priestly in an ancient Semitic sense, and the later days of monarchy, when the growth of priestly power led more and more to reservation of properly sacral functions to professional priests."

munion. The Bible bears witness to that. In some situations, the offender comes to make reparation with gifts (Lev. 3:1-5). Thus, both the ancient religions and the religion of Israel show that humans have approached God with offerings and gifts.

Worship, therefore, is often accompanied by gifts and sacrifices. There is always someone who receives or presents the gifts to God in a place appointed by God. It was done according to prescribed rites and rituals. The composition of the altar in ancient Israel shows this exclusiveness. The bronze screen, which covered the lower outer base of the altar, though serving as ornamentation, prevented profane hands from touching the altar. However, "[c]ult means social worship through ritual performance."[51] It involves the community, the assembly—it is essentially public. As Millgram noted, "[I]n bringing an offering to the shrine of worship primitive man was also expressing his submission to the gods who control the forces of nature which make for plenty or scarcity, for life or death."[52] As humans express submission to the deity, they also hope to swing the divine favor to their advantage through the ritual of sacrifice.

### 1.2.1 Etymology of Sacrifice

The word *sacrifice* comes from two Latin words *sacrum* and *facere,* meaning "to make sacred." The idea of making sacred indicates that what is offered in sacrifice is being moved from the sphere of the "profane" to that of the sacred; that is, from the general and everyday use of people to a separate and distinct use of/for God. Being in the realm of the sacred, what is offered belongs to God. Sacrifice is commonly used in religion to denote that which is "given" or offered to the deity. From the moment it is offered or sacrificed, it belongs exclusively to God. Moreover, God issued a warning in Exod. 23:15; 34:20 thus: "No one shall appear before me empty-handed," meaning that God requires people to present gifts to him. In the light of the above, whatever is presented to God is a sacrifice of some sort, just as prayer alone is a sacrifice of praise. The ultimate purpose of sacrifice is to provide a means of approaching the deity, and to maintain that presence by preserving the purity and holiness that are required by the individual or the assembly.

### 1.2.2 Origin and Different Types of Sacrifice

Sacrifice is as old as the history of humanity. Human beings have always felt drawn to the divine and felt a need to communicate with the spiritual realm. To communicate with the spiritual is also a means of controlling forces both known and unknown to humans. These forces could bring suffering, evil, and death. To win divine favor, human beings devised some means of rapproche-

---

51. John L. McKenzie, *A Theology of the Old Testament* (Garden City, NY: Image Books, 1974), 39.

52. Millgram, *Jewish Worship,* 43.

ment or thanksgiving, including sacrifice. It is also plausible to affirm that humans had some sense of sin, an infringement that distorted the right order of creation,[53] and needed to do "something"[54] to restore the severed relationship between them and God. To rectify the severed relationship and pacify God, humans used sacrifice to procure divine favor.[55]

In the Book of Genesis, though a meta-history, Cain and Abel were the first to offer sacrifices to God (Gen. 4:4). Noah offered a sacrifice to God on the altar he built after the deluge (Gen. 8:20). Abraham offered sacrifices and would have offered his son Isaac in perceived obedience to God if he had not been stopped (Gen. 22:13). The patriarchs offered sacrifices, too (Gen. 31:54; Exod. 24:5). In the above instances, the persons involved performed rituals as means of seeking favor from God or of thanking God for his blessings. Family heads offered sacrifices and led their families in prayers. Gideon offered sacrifice (Judg. 6:19) along with Manoah (Judg. 13:16–23) and Elkanah (1 Sam. 1:3–4, 21). This evidence shows that humans have an innate attraction to the supernatural and a desire to communicate with the divine, specifically through sacrifice and prayer. Individuals were their own priests in the earliest period of the chosen people up to the Passover in Egypt.

As Israel was being shaped into a nation, Jethro offered sacrifice to God on behalf of Israel (Exod. 18:12). This phrase "on behalf of Israel" singles out

---

53. S. Mark Heim, *Saved from Sacrifice: A Theology of the Cross* (Grand Rapids, MI: William B. Eerdmans Publishing Company, 2006), 22: "Sin catastrophically unbalances the human–God relation so that it can never be evened again. Not from our side. A gap exists." It is this gap that has been created by sin that humans seek to mend with their ritual of sacrifice.

54. Man had to do something to restore that relationship, but he had no idea how. All the past generations knew that there was something wrong with the created order. They had the sense of sin and so were trying to appease God. It became clear to man only with the incarnation, passion, and resurrection of Jesus. Hence, a broken world has been renewed and man is once again made whole. Cf. Heim, *Saved from Sacrifice*, 21: "We might summarize the doctrine this way. We are guilty of sin, against God and our neighbors. The continuing sinful acts themselves, the self loathing or malicious desires that prompt them, the twisted social patterns that become the environment for human development, the guilt we bear for such ungrateful response to God's good gifts—all of these together separate us from God, poison our relations with each other, and are far beyond any human power to mend."

55. Milgrom, *Leviticus: A Book of Ritual and Ethics*, 17: "[T]he system of sacrifice provided a metaphor, a method, for the Israelites to reach God, responding to the deep psychological, emotional, and religious needs of the people. Indeed, this is the meaning of the Hebrew word for 'sacrifice'; it comes from a verb meaning 'to bring near.' Thus a sacrifice is that kind of an offering that enables us to approach God." Inasmuch as Milgrom has his own ideas of sacrifice, which I do not wish to dispute at the moment, the important message from Milgrom becomes that sacrifice gives the sacrificer/offerer a belief that he is able to have access to God—he can approach God through that means.

someone as the person who stands between the people offering sacrifice and God. It is interesting that those chosen to stand before God, to minister to God, performed this role of offering "on behalf of others." Standing before God on behalf of others is a privilege specifically given to some humans by God. This, however, does not in any way negate the possibility of one approaching God with his own sacrifice on a personal basis or for the needs of his family. That is very valid, but the line of argument here is that, when it comes to the community sacrifice, a national sacrifice, or a group of worshipers in an assembly, there is a guide and leader duly chosen by God (Lev. 16:1ff.).

In Israel, these communal sacrifices were carried out only in locations where there were divine manifestations. Israel set up altars at any place of theophany to serve as a memorial. These altars marked out those spaces as sacred, a practice found in later shrines of Israel. The priests, through these rituals, make Yahweh present to the people. When later in Israel's history the temple was built, the high point of the people's celebrations was to offer sacrifices in the temple, especially on their most solemn feasts: Unleavened Bread, Passover, Tabernacles, and Pentecost. The Book of Leviticus describes one of the effects of the ritual of sacrifice. According to Alfred Mark,

> Leviticus 1–16 culminates in chapter 16 with the description of the Day of Atonement. This ritual is of special importance, as it gives Israel, at the turning point of every year, the possibility of removing all the sins and impurities which had polluted Israel in the past year, so that YHWH can again be fully present among his people.[56]

It follows that sacrifices of atonement and reparation have cleansing power. Appropriate rituals are required to achieve the desired results.[57] Priestly writers teach that humans are sinful and unclean and, as such, should not venture into

---

56. Alfred Marx, "The Theology of Sacrifice according to Leviticus 1–7," in *The Book of Leviticus; Composition and Reception*, ed. Rolf Rendtorff and Robert A. Kugler, Supplements to Vetus Testamentum 93 (Leiden: Brill, 2003), 103–20. Marx takes chaps. 1–16 as a division of the Book of Leviticus. The use of the word pollution refers to abomination or evil or sin, which injures the relationship with God and causes evil consequences for the community. It is called pollution because it affects every member of the community and literally or figuratively "pollutes" and defiles the land. See also Millgram, *Jewish Worship*, 44. Millgram supports the idea of the priest helping the worshiper to offer sacrifices: "It was customary for the officiating priest to bless the offering and consecrate it. This brought the supplicant into actual contact with the deity."

57. Jacob Milgrom, *Leviticus: A Book of Ritual and Ethics*, 18. According to Milgrom, man felt God's presence in the sacred space: "Then they could reach God by their sacrifice. The officiating priest would choose the appropriate sacrifice that corresponded to the emotional needs of the offerers. And when the latter saw the aromatic smoke rising from the altar, they felt that their prayers/requests were also ascending."

sacred space. The idea is prevalent in worship because the holiness of God is conceived as creating a distance between God and man, and sinful man cannot bridge that gap. In the view of the Priestly writers, humans can drive God away from his sanctuary by their iniquities. This is also found in prophetic writings, especially in Jeremiah.[58] Commenting on the Book of Leviticus, Milgrom notes:

> Valid worship requires a recognition of inadequacy on the part of the worshippers, or a prior spontaneous sense of gratitude for previous and gracious divine initiatives. This proper mentality then may result in a valid sacrificial gift to the deity. Otherwise put: Proper and prescribed visible forms of worship should arise from the recognition of one's crea-turehood and be accompanied by the determination to lead a holy life.[59]

The above idea of "valid worship" seems to bring out the qualities of true worship, which first stems from creaturehood and is then followed by the element of worship, namely, thanksgiving and acknowledgment of God as the source and controller of the world. Acknowledging God goes deeper than the recitation of words. It also involves the whole person, for which sacrifice is an excellent form of expression. In sacrifice, humans share what they have purportedly received from the deity with the deity, as an act of showing their loyalty to the deity. Modern ideas, though, show a different view of sacrifice.[60] A survey of sacrifice in ancient Israel is important to this study and may help one appreciate how a localized and inculturated liturgy would help a people worship and live out fully the mysteries they believe.

The Bible mentions types of sacrifices:

1. *Qorban* is the word used in Leviticus, Numbers, and Ezekiel for all kinds of offerings. It comes from the Hebrew word *qārab* (Lev. 16:1), the verbal root *qrb*. It was used commonly in northwest Semitic and Akkadian in a sense that is similar to the use in the Hebrew language. The word *qrb* has a sense of "being

---

58. Ibid., 9. Milgrom wrote in support of this idea thus: "The priestly theologians make use of the same imagery, except that the demons are replaced by humans. Humans can drive God out of the sanctuary by polluting it with their moral and ritual sins. All that the priests can do is periodically purge the sanctuary of its impurities and influence the people to atone for their wrong."

59. Ibid., 31.

60. Lloyd R. Bailey, *Leviticus – Numbers,* Smyth & Helwys Commentary (Macon, GA: Smyth & Helwys, 2005), 47. Bailey wrote that moderns have a different interpretation of sacrifice, which I find interesting. He wrote, "(1) Deities are, in some measure, thought to be dependent upon human beings to provide for their needs. (2) Sacrifice originated in the idea of a shared meal between deity and worshipper. (3) Sacrifice originated in the idea that human potency could somehow merge with that which the sacred animal contained. (4) Sacrifice originated in the need for a controlled outlet for human aggression. (5) Sacrifice originated in the desire to provide a gift to the deity in connection with a request for help."

near" or in "close proximity" to an object. It is an offering that brings people closer to God (Exod. 32:19).

*Qorban,* therefore, is the general term for offerings of all kinds. The desire for closer relationship with God is of paramount importance to humans, as it is believed to open the way to blessings from God.

2. *Zebaḥ:* This word is from the verbal root *zbḥ,* meaning "slaughter," "kill," "slaughter for sacrifice," or "offer." In Akkadian, *zibu* is used for food offering and is related to the verb *zebu,* the Hebrew *zevaḥ,* Aramaic *debaḥ* and Ugaritic *dbḥ,* which all refer to animals slaughtered in sacrifice. The old Aramaic Zenjirli dialect uses the extended form of the verb *zbḥ* to mean "do sacrifice" and "sacrifice."[61] *Zebaḥ* is usually used in the Bible for bloody sacrifices, in which the victim is always immolated. It occurs prominently in Leviticus 3. It further stresses a variety of community sacrificial actions (Judges 16; 23; 2 Kgs. 10:18–27; 1 Sam. 20:6–20). The root *zbḥ* first occurs in the Bible as a means of ratifying the covenant between Jacob and Laban (Gen. 31:54). "He offered" (*zbḥ*) "a sacrifice" (*zebaḥ*). It was used again in Gen. 46:1, when Israel "offered (*zbḥ*) sacrifices (*zebaḥ*) to the God of his father Isaac." In 1 Kgs. 3:4–5, the verb *zbḥ* is used, though the action was for a burnt offering. Richard E. Averback argues that this root continued to be used for all bloody sacrifices to the Lord (Exod. 3:18; 5:3, 8, 17) and for the Passover sacrifice, *zebaḥ pesaḥ* (Exod. 12:27).[62] The basic meaning of the verb *zbḥ,* however, is "to slaughter." Through *zebaḥ* one communes with the Lord. Its normal use refers mainly to sacrifices that are slaughtered, whether private, communal, legal, illegal, or idolatrous. *Zebaḥ* is often associated with *šālôm,* which conveys the idea of well-being, goodness, and peace—hence the term *zebaḥ šĕlāmîm,* "peace sacrifice."

3. *Minḥāh:* The word *minḥāh* is found in the Bible in two contexts: cultic and secular. In the cultic context it can serve as (a) a general term for sacrifice, or (b) a specialized term for grain offerings. In the secular context it is used as (a) a word for gifts or presents for people (Gen. 32:20–21), and (b) a word for tribute to a superior in political circles (Judg. 3:15, 17).[63] De Vaux uses *minḥāh* to depict gift offerings that accompany the main sacrifices,[64] but his view does not seem plausible because he seems to follow only one of the cultic usages of the term—a specialized term for grain offerings, which was a meaning it acquired at a later period. *Minḥāh* appears in the Bible first in Gen. 4:3–5, in the sacrifices of Cain and Abel. It was used for both the animal offering of Abel and the grain offerings of Cain. No matter how one decides to view the use of *minḥāh,* the Bible portrays it as a sacrifice either of meat or bread offer-

---

61. Richard E. Averback, "*zbḥ,*" in VanGemeren, *New International Dictionary of Old Testament Theology and Exegesis,* 1:1066–73.

62. Ibid., 1068.

63. Richard E. Averback, "*minḥah,*" in VanGemeren, *New International Dictionary of Old Testament Theology and Exegesis,* 2:978–90.

64. De Vaux, *Ancient Israel,* 416.

ings (Judg. 6:18), animals or incense (Num. 16:15), or vegetable offerings (Lev. 2:1–16; 23:9–14; Num. 15:17–21; Deut. 26:1–11). Animal sacrifice is invariably accompanied by *minḥāh*: grain, cereal, oil, and so on. Following the distinctions and the hypotheses, sacrifice in the OT may be grouped into the following:

### 1.2.2.1 Holocaust

There are two Hebrew words for the category of offering: *'ōlāh,* which means "that which goes up," and *kālîl,* meaning "entire," "whole." Averback suggests that the term *'ōlāh* in the original form was *kālîl,* which would account for the use of the two interchangeably. The Hebrew *kālîl* means "entire," "whole," "complete," thus a total sacrifice.[65] It is translated in the LXX as *holokaustos,* from *holos* and *kaustos,* meaning,"fully burnt" and in the Vulgate as *holocaustum.* The entire victim is placed on the altar, on which everything is burnt. The sacrifice is given back to God by destroying it on the altar. It assumes a spiritual form as it rises in smoke (*'ōlāh*) from the altar toward God.[66] In this sense, it could be that the name also derives from the act by which the smoke rises.

The ritual of holocaust is performed with a male lamb without blemish (Leviticus 1; 22:17–25). The person offering the sacrifice lays hands on the victim as a sign of ownership. He is the one who receives the graces accruing from the sacrifice. The man who brings the victim cuts the throat of the animal, and then it is skinned, cut into four parts and placed on the altar by the priest. The whole parts are burned on the altar, including the hooves, intestines, and head. The work of the priest begins when it comes to the point of placing the victim on the altar and the handling of the blood. The priest as the one chosen by God to minister to him, to go in and out before him, pours the blood around the altar. Since "blood is life" and "the life of the flesh is in the blood" (Lev. 17:14; Deut. 12:23), it was proper to give it back to God, the Author of Life.

If the victim is a bird, the offering of the poor (Lev. 5:7; 12:8), the priest does all the functions involved in the ritual because everything is done on the altar and he is the one authorized to touch or place things on the altar.

### 1.2.2.2 Communion Sacrifice

The communion sacrifice is that in which the participants share in a meal of the victim as part of the ritual. In the classical term it is the *zebaḥ šĕlāmîm* or *zebaḥ.* According to de Vaux, "the rituals in Israel present it rather as a sacrifice of thanksgiving to God which brings about union with him."[67] Communion sacrifice is divided into three parts:

1. *tôdāh.* Sacrifice of praise (Lev. 7:12–15). The ritual for this sacrifice is the same as the other communion sacrifices. However, Lev. 7:12 notes that "there

---

65. Richard E. Averback, "*kalil,*" in VanGemeren, *New International Dictionary of Old Testament Theology and Exegesis,* 2:657–58; and *'ōlāh,* 3:405–15. See also de Vaux, *Ancient Israel,* 415.

66. De Vaux, *Ancient Israel,* 452.

67. Ibid., 417.

must be added to it an offering of unleavened cakes mixed with oil, unleavened wafers spread with oil, and wheaten flour in the form of cakes mixed with oil." In this sacrifice, the flesh of the victim must be entirely eaten on the same day of the sacrifice.

2. *nĕdābāh:* This is a voluntary sacrifice, a freewill offering or a free inclination. It comes from the root *ndb* meaning "to incite, offer freely, give a free something." It describes the inner motivation of someone who is moved to give, act, or speak (Lev. 7:16–17, 18–23). It is a sacrifice offered not out of any promise or law but merely out of devotion to God. The offering was a major part of Israel's sacrificial system (Lev. 7:16), and it is seen as a part of the sacrifice of well-being. The whole idea of *nĕdābāh* is an offering out of one's own volition.

3. *nēder.* Votive sacrifice (Leviticus 7). It comes from the Hebrew root *ndr,* meaning "make a vow." It is a sacrifice offered to God by a person who has bound himself by a vow. According to de Vaux, there is no precise differentiation between the three communion sacrifices. Upon examination, however, one realizes that there are important differences. Though they all go by the name "communion sacrifice," the distinction lies in the intention of the one offering the sacrifice. Vows in Israel were made to Yahweh, and when the petitioner received favors he usually came back to God to offer a votive sacrifice for God's provision and/or realization of ambition (Gen. 28:20–22; 2 Sam. 15:7–12; Prov. 31:2). If one believed that God had blessed him with success in his military exploits or riches, for example, then it is easy to say that such a person offered a sacrifice of praise. When one made a vow as he prayed for a favor, on the other hand, then it became a votive sacrifice. An example is Hannah, Samuel's mother (1 Sam. 1:1–28).

4. *thysia.* The word for sacrifice in Greek is *thysia.* It is used to translate the Hebrew *minḥāh* and *zebaḥ* (Lev. 17:5; 19:5). These Hebrew words are similar in meaning to the Greek *thysia* as they also end in a communion meal.

### 1.2.2.3 Expiatory Sacrifices

Expiatory sacrifice arose to reestablish the covenant relationship when it was broken by sin. The Israelites offered two kinds of expiatory sacrifices: the sacrifice for sin (*ḥaṭṭā't*) and the sacrifice of reparation (*'āšām*). For de Vaux, it is difficult to determine the exact significance of each sacrifice or to say why they are distinguished from each other.[68] There are some notable differences in the two kinds of expiatory sacrifice. Under expiatory sacrifice, the Israelites have the following:

1. *Sacrifice for Sin (ḥaṭṭā't).* This word stands both for sin and sin offering. It can stand either for sin, the sacrifice for sin, or the victim. There are variations in the victim according to the status of the sinner and the gravity of the sin. The ritual is described in Lev. 4:1–5, 13; 6:17–23. Following the narrative in the Book of Leviticus, this rite is distinguished from all other sacrifices by the use of blood. De Vaux explains that the goal of sacrifice is not the destruction

---

68. Ibid., 418.

of the offering, for "we must maintain that God, who is Lord of life and of all being, cannot be honored by the destruction either of being or of life."[69] The major purpose of the blood ritual was to purify and "reconsecrate" a person or thing from the effects of the iniquities of the people (Lev. 8:15; 16:19). The blood from the sin offering was never applied to the bodies of people but only on the altar and some other sacred objects. The Israelites believed that through the sacrifice for sin, peace with God was achieved.

2. *Asham* (*'āšām*). The word *'āšām* is a semicognate of the Hebrew root *'šm,* which is traced to Arabic *'tm,* which means "sin, transgression, and guilt." Ugaritic texts referred to *asam* as a disease which the healing god had power to heal through some sacred fine imposed by the priests also called *asam.*[70] The Hebrew *'āšām,* however, is a nominative word meaning "guilt offering." De Vaux calls it "an offense, the method by which the offense is corrected and the rite of reparation."[71] The offense is a violation of the Lord's property or another person's property. In either of the two, the violator brought an offering to the Lord in reparation for the rights he violated. Leviticus 5:6 states, "the offerer shall bring his offering as a penalty (*'āšām*) for the sin he has committed . . . and the priest shall make atonement for him for his sin." The word *'āšām* empha-sizes guilt—the sin committed is willful and grave and has therefore disturbed the sinner's relationship with God and neighbor. Hence, reparation involves some form of penalty. The rite was the same as in the sacrifice for sin, but the distinction is that the blood was never taken into the holy place. It was a sacri-fice for private individuals; thus, the blood was on some occasions smeared on the bodies of humans to cleanse them (Leviticus 14). The only victim it refers to is a ram. On some occasions, the sacrifice was accompanied by payment (Lev. 5:14–16, 21–26; Num. 5:5–8). Restitution was a major part in this type of sacrifice but was not an integral form of sacrificial rites. Therefore, the result for the violator was that his sins would "be forgiven him" (Lev. 5:16, 18; 6:7).

1.2.2.4 Sacrifice of Reparation: Day of Atonement (Yom Kippur)
The words *Yom Kippur* are a combination of two Hebrew words *yôm* and *kpr.* The noun *yôm* means "day." *Kpr* is the verbal root for *kippur* and means "cover," "smear," "paint." Following the root verb *kpr,* the "Day of Atonement" was technically a day when all the sins of the congregation of Israel were "cov-ered" by the Lord. Just as the name implies, *Yom Kippur* was a day dedicated to making atonement for the sins of the high priest, the congregation of Israel, and the slaves living in Israel. The purpose was to "decontaminate" the people from all sin and from the effects of impurities and iniquities, and reconsecrate them to God. It was a day of prayer and penance. It was a later celebration in Israel

---

69. Ibid., 452.
70. Richard E. Averback, "*'ašam,*" in VanGemeren, *New International Dictionary of Old Testament Theology and Exegesis*, 1:557–66.
71. De Vaux, *Ancient Israel*, 420.

and, most probably, postexilic. It was one of the most solemn days in the Israelite calendar, and no work was done on that day. The ritual for the day is given in Leviticus 16. There are indications that this ritual text has undergone several editions with a number of doublets (Lev. 16:6 and 16:11; 16:9b and 16:15; 16:4 and 16:32). Leviticus 16 is, therefore, a later text. Two conclusions ensue.

1. The high priest offers a bull for his sins and the sins of his family and sprinkles the blood behind the *kapporet* (mercy seat) and incenses it. It is the only occasion on which the high priest enters the Holy of Holies.

2. The high priest draws lots on two goats and offers one marked "for Yahweh" as a sacrifice for sin. He lays hands on the second goat for *Azazel* and confesses the sins of the people onto the goat, which is eventually sent into the wilderness bearing the sins of the people.[72] The high priest goes back to the altar to sprinkle with the blood of the bull the horns of the altar with his finger seven times. Leviticus 16:19 states that "this is how he will render it clean and sacred, purified and separated from the uncleannesses of the sons of Israel." The high priest then blesses the people with the Holy Name as the ceremony comes to a close.

The Hebrew word for holiness, *qdš*, bears the connotation of separateness and distinctiveness.[73] Separateness and distinctiveness are the key words in this type of sacrifice because they are used with reference to God and to things pertaining to the divine. This means that the gift (sacrifice) is separated from public usage and is entirely dedicated to God. It has been removed from the sphere of the "profane" and transferred to the sphere of God, making it holy. This whole idea is portrayed in the Old Testament and especially in connection with the issue of rituals and cult. What comes from the people is perceived as "profane" and must be transferred to the holy sphere, that is, to the realm of God, which is separate and distinct. To achieve the holiness required to maintain the sacred space, Israel created and maintained certain structures of time (festivals and Sabbath), space (temple and the courtyards), and personal statutes (ritual purities/impurities and sexual ethics). The Book of Leviticus gives the idea that what humans do can have a sacred dimension and quality if it is transferred to the divine sphere. All are invited to move from the sphere of the profane to the sacred in order to encounter God.

### 1.3 Summary

The above chapter studied the priesthood and the need of humans to bridge the gap between themselves and God. Humans, however, cannot find God,

---

72. Rabbinic tradition holds that the goat was taken to Beth Hadudun, the modern Khirbeth Khareidan, which is overlooking the Kidron Valley. The Kidron Valley is of interest to John the Evangelist, for he wrote that Jesus was arrested in the Kidron Valley. Perhaps Jesus is seen as the goat Azazel.

73. Cf. Jackie A. Naunde, *qdš*, in VanGemeren, *New International Dictionary of Old Testament Theology and Exegesis*, 2:877–87.

and so God comes down to reveal himself. God's presence is mediated through priests chosen by him. All the regalia of the priest serve to show that he is one chosen and separated from others for the ministry of service. Ancient Israel practiced priesthood and sacrifice from its earliest years in various forms. First, Israel believed that God could be approached through sacrifices. Second, Israel offered sacrifices to win the favor of God. Finally, humans believed they were empowered through the sacrifice. The material presented above, therefore, calls to mind the question of God's contingency and immutability.[74] One may ask: Is sacrifice necessary in the world today, and what role does it play in the life of peoples? Different cultures and traditions have different views on the necessity of sacrifice depending on how attached and rich their cultural heritage may be. I have taken some time to explore extensively sacrifice in ancient Israel. All the details are important, as they point to the various roles that the patriarchs, judges, kings, and priests performed in sacrifice. Cody, however, supports the proposition that, in liturgical celebrations, only priests could place things on the altar in sacrifice to God.

> [I]n Dt. 33:10 is the mention of sacrifice in a context showing it to be a property—or claimed to be a property—of priestly circles. The days when Israel looked upon sacrifice by heads of families, clans, and tribes, and by kings as heads of entire people, as a perfectly normal thing, without reservation, were drawing to a close. Israelites who were not priests would continue to have a certain active part to play in sacrifices they might wish to make, for the individual Israelite in the requisite state of ritual purity would continue to immolate the victim he was offering (Lev. 1:15; 3:2, 8, 13; 4:24, 29, 33), but everything which made it necessary to come in contact with the sacrificial altar would be reserved to a priest. This . . . is the reason for the reservation to the priest of the blood-rites (Exod. 30:10; Lev. 17:11, 14).[75]

In all sacrifices, humans, through those duly chosen, brought offerings to the shrine in hopes of swinging the divine wheel of fortune in their favor.[76]

---

74. De Vaux, *Ancient Israel*, 451. "Man deprives himself (of something that he needs) in order to give them away: by doing so he loses the gift, but he also gains something, for the acceptance of the gift involves God in an obligation."

75. Cody, *History of Old Testament Priesthood*, 119.

76. Millgram (*Jewish Worship*, 43–44) supports the idea of offering to restore a distorted relationship: "In bringing an offering to the shrine of worship primitive man was also expressing his submission to the gods who control the forces of nature which make for plenty or scarcity, for life or death. When primitive man suffered from a sense of guilt, a feeling of having offended the deity, he longed for reconciliation."

CHAPTER TWO

# PRIESTHOOD IN
# THE NEW TESTAMENT

This section studies the priesthood of Jesus in the Gospels and other New Testament writings. Obviously Jesus never called himself a priest, but his followers after some years began to refer to him as one. This study, however, seeks to establish the authenticity of Christ's priesthood and thereby prove the higher status of Jesus' priesthood compared to tribal or national priesthood. There arises a problem when one considers that Jesus is not of a priestly family or genealogy. While the New Testament ministry is predominantly charismatic in nature,[1] this study focuses on the priesthood of Jesus, who has united the visible and the invisible in his person and is called the chief minister of God's grace and "high priest of our confession" (Heb. 3:1).

## 2.1 The Priesthood of Jesus

To understand the priesthood of Jesus, one has to juxtapose it with the Old Testament, which will highlight the major differences and show any similarities that might be present.[2] The ministry of Jesus was prophetic, not ritualistic (Matt. 16:14; Luke 13:33; Mark 6:15; John 4:44). "The ministry of Jesus was an eschatological manifestation . . . which clearly set it apart from that of the Old Testament."[3] Setting it apart from the old shows a sharp difference between the Old Testament and New Testament priesthoods. The mission of Jesus is described in terms of the kingdom. There is absolutely one basic theological

---

1. Maly, *Priest and Sacred Scripture,* 28: "In the last analysis, there is only one ministry and one service, that which the Father lavishes on all creation through His Son in the wisdom and charity of the Spirit. All material and spiritual gifts seem to coalesce into one expression of divine love for men. Since, in this economy of salvation, however, limited creatures must be agents and instruments of that love, creation acts as one cosmic prism diffusing God's charity into so many varied hues. Those colors are scattered throughout . . . , each reflected in some group or individual, and each serving to make visible some aspect of the Father's concern for men."
2. Brown, *Priest and Bishop,* 5.
3. Maly, *Priest and Sacred Scripture*, 3.

principle that guides any meaningful investigation into the priesthood of Jesus, namely, his incarnation, which is the perfect and eschatological channel through which God communicates with humans.

### 2.1.1 Priesthood in the Synoptics

In the Synoptic Gospels, priesthood was understood in terms of carnal descent from Aaron. Hence, Jesus was not a priest. In the Gospel according to Matthew, Jesus presented his mission in terms of the kingdom, which was one of the first words that came from his mouth at the beginning of his public ministry (Matt. 4:17; 12:28; 16:19). He was preoccupied with the proclamation of the kingdom. For Jesus, the true disciple was the one who did the will of his Father (Matt. 7:21). Jesus is presented by Matthew as the "chosen servant of God who would proclaim the true faith to all nations," fulfilling the prophecy of Isaiah (Matt. 12:15–21; Isa. 42:1–4). Hence, he healed many who were sick, cared for women and children, and had concern for the poor. Matthew also presents Jesus as the royal son of David (Matt. 21:9) who would be king according to the prophecies (Pss. 132:11; 89:29; Matt. 2:1–2; 26:64; 27:29, 37). He cast out demons through the "Spirit of God" (Matt. 12:28), showing that God backed his actions. At the Sermon on the Mount, he proved to be the new lawgiver, teaching with authority (Matthew 5–7).

In the Gospel according to Mark, Jesus is presented as having the approval of his Father: "You are my Son, the beloved; my favor rests on you" (Mark 1:11). Jesus is therefore empowered to preach the kingdom (Mark 1:15; 9:1). He casts out demons and would not allow them to speak because they knew who he was: "the holy One of God" (Mark 1:24). Jesus prohibits demons from speaking about him "because they knew him" (Mark 1:34). This is the first instance of the so-called Messianic Secret, which refers to the fact that Jesus hides his identity as Son of God until it is made known on the cross. In the cure of the paralytic, the bystanders raise objections, asking how Jesus can speak the way he does when he says, "My child, your sins are forgiven" (Mark 2:5). Jesus responds by saying, "to prove to you that the Son of Man has authority on earth to forgive sins," he says to the paralytic, "Rise, pick up your mat and walk" (Mark 2:10). God is the source of Jesus' power and ministry (Mark 2:1–12). He manifested divine authority in his miracles and preaching. Peter's confession in chapter 8 was devoid of the notion of suffering, and so Jesus greeted it with the command to silence. Raymond Brown suggests that "Peter rejects this portrait of the suffering Son of Man; and so Jesus categorizes his lack of understanding as worthy of Satan."[4]

---

4. Raymond E. Brown, *An Introduction to the New Testament,* Anchor Bible Reference Library (New York: Doubleday, 1996), 138–39.

At the Transfiguration, God confirms his approval of Jesus as the promised Messiah when the hidden glory of Jesus was made manifest and a voice was heard: "This is my Son, the Beloved. Listen to him" (Mark 9:8). Thereafter, Jesus makes the third prophecy about his passion and death. What is at stake here is the concept of the Messiah among the Israelites at the time of Jesus. Their tradition had an idea of a Messiah-king, a descendant of David. He was expected to be a warrior and, to some, a son of God. The event of the Transfiguration becomes the avenue by which Jesus reveals his glory and strengthens the faith of his apostles before his passion.

The Gospel according to Luke is portrayed as a priestly and sacrificial Gospel because of the temple images that open the Gospel and conclude it (Luke 24:53). Luke presents Zechariah, a priest who, upon leaving the "sanctuary of the Lord" (Luke 1:22), was unable to speak the *habbĕrākāh* (Hebrew, "the blessing"). At the end of the Gospel, Jesus blesses the apostles (Luke 24:51).[5] However, this does not necessarily mean he was a priest because a rabbi or head of a household could pray and bless his disciples. In sum, before the Jews and during Jesus' earthly life, he was not seen as a priest and did not presume to be one. All three Synoptic Gospels have one thing in common on this issue: Jesus is not a priest by Jewish standards.

### 2.1.2 Priesthood in Johannine Literature

In the Gospel of John, there is no single mention of Jesus as a priest. When priests are mentioned, the reference is to the Jewish priests and the high priest (John 7:32, 45; 11:45, 49; 18; 19). John situates Jesus within the Passover context in the temple of Jerusalem, which was turned into a marketplace, and the evangelist presents Jesus' body as the new temple (John 2:19). This does not in any way indicate that Jesus was a priest, but rather that he was the Messiah, who was expected to purify the temple (Mal. 2:1–5). The Book of Revelation, which is attributed to John the Evangelist, sees Christians in the generic sense as "priests" (Rev. 1:5–6). The followers of Jesus are called "priests" in a figurative way. They are called to become "a kingdom of priests" (Rev. 5:9–10).

### 2.1.3 Priesthood in Pauline Literature

Paul understands the death of Jesus as a sacrifice. He does not use the term "priest" in relation to Jesus. He refers to himself as one appointed by God "as a priest of Jesus Christ, and I am to carry out my sacred duty (Greek ἱερουργέω) by bringing the Good News from God to the pagans, and so make them accept-

---

5. Judging from the pairs regularly found in Luke's Gospel, this action of Jesus is adjudged to be a priestly action. Luke installs Jesus as the new priest who does what Zechariah could not do because of his lack of speech.

able as an offering, made holy by the Holy Spirit" (Rom. 15:15–16). He uses the word ἱερουργέω, which the Jerusalem Bible translates as "priestly duties." However, ἱερουργέω means "sacred ministering," and in the Pauline context, the preaching of the word is interpreted in terms of a sacred ministry and likened to the work of sacred functionaries.

Paul describes his functions in terms of offering and service (Rom. 12:1) and uses the Greek word *leitourgos,* which means performing sacred duties in a worshiping assembly, or working publicly. In other New Testament passages where *leitourgos* is used, it always refers to the idea of performing sacred duties (Acts 13:2; Rom. 15:27; Heb. 10:11). 1 Corinthians 9:13 gives another insight into ministry in the New Testament, "that they minister about holy things." The word used for minister in this instance is *ergazomai,* which means "commit," "do," "labor," "minister about" or "work."[6] For Paul, therefore, he and the other apostles are "committed" to the work entrusted to them; they "labor" *(ergazomai)* over such duties.

Paul refers to himself as a minister delivering God's message to the gentiles (Col. 1:26–29). Paul goes on to speak of himself and the other apostles as "stewards of the mysteries of God" (Rom. 4:1), which means that he saw himself and the other apostles as "ambassadors of Christ, and God makes his appeal through us" (2 Cor. 5:20). As ambassadors, they are representatives of Christ, who is the sole mediator. However, these statements never in any way imply that Paul addressed Jesus as priest. Ministers, successors, and ambassadors are not priests.[7] Paul understood his authority to be from God himself (1 Cor. 1:1; 2 Cor. 1:1), an authority to function and serve vicariously. He calls it a command received from the Lord (1 Thess. 4:2; 2 Thess. 3:6), and he was bound to follow the command in obedience.

Timothy, who was appointed by Paul, was charged with authority to teach and to minister (διακονεῖν, "to serve") to the people of God (1 Tim. 4:1-5). Paul uses the word διάκονος in other areas in the Scripture as a servant, deacon, or laborer (Rom. 13:4; 15:8; Gal. 2:17; Eph. 3:7; 6:21; Col. 1:7). Such were the first delegates of the apostles, and they were to succeed in the apostolic ministry of preaching, teaching, and governance. Paul reiterates the ancient *kērygma* in his letter to the Corinthians, which points to the continuation of the ministry of Jesus in his followers. "I delivered to you as of first importance what I also received, that Christ died for our sins in accordance with the scriptures" (1 Cor. 15:3-5). The line of argument of Paul is to prove his missionary and apostolic mandate from the Church and the authority to function as a presbyter. There-

---

6. Robert Young, ed., *Young's Analytical Concordance to the Bible; Also, Index Lexicons to the Old and New Testament* (orig. 1900; Grand Rapids: Eerdmans, 1955), s.v. "Index Lexicon to the Old Testament and the New Testament."

7. A priest as described earlier is one called "to minister to God." A minister is a servant. A successor could be any person who takes over an office after the office is vacant, while an ambassador is a representative of another, a city or country.

fore, "the local ordained ministry they set in place was an application of their own apostolic ministry."[8] Apostolic ministry consists in preaching the Word, which is the *kērygma,* and the breaking of Bread by the head of the assembly, the *presbyter.* The apostles were commissioned to work and speak in the name of Jesus who sent them. The sending is not a mere bearing and delivering of the message but a sending that bore and conveyed the presence of the one who sent them. Brown argues in support of this view by saying that "in the Jewish notion of apostolate the one sent . . . represents the one who sends, bearing not only the sender's authority, but even his presence to others."[9]

From the New Testament account, it is very probable that the apostles appointed successors to their office and established various ministries in their missionary journeys because they believed they were mandated by Jesus to do so.[10] The words of Jesus were understood as their authority to teach. "Anyone who listens to you listens to me; anyone who rejects you rejects me, and those who reject me reject the one who sent me" (Luke 10:16).

From the postapostolic era there were three major threats to apostolic succession and the order of established ministry. The Marcionists, the Gnostics, and the Montanists[11] posed threats to the authority and tradition handed on by Jesus, that is, the authority of the ministry or to teach what was received from the apostles.[12] What was at stake is not whether Jesus handed on a priesthood; that was only presumed and widely accepted as the Fathers of the Church attest.

---

8. Aidan Nichols, *Holy Order: Apostolic Priesthood from the New Testament to the Second Vatican Council* (Dublin: Veritas, 1990), 3.

9. Raymond E. Brown, *Priest and Bishop: Biblical Reflections* (Paramus, NJ: Paulist, 1970), 28.

10. Nichols, *Holy Order,* 33. He supports this view when he says, "What we should say is, rather, that the apostles, in instituting local ordained ministries for the good order of the communities they had founded, necessarily conceived such ministry as involving good order in cultic presidency, teaching and pastoral discipline."

11. Cyril Richardson, ed. and trans., *Early Christian Fathers* (Philadelphia: Westminster, 1953), 26. Montanus is quoted by Richardson as saying, "I am come neither as an angel, nor as an ambassador, but as God the Father." That was a challenge and a threat to the authority and Godhead of Jesus. If Montanus is God, then Jesus cannot be God and the Church has no authority to proclaim as such—if we follow Montanus's line of thought.

12. Jaroslav Pelikan, *The Christian Tradition: A History of the Development of Doctrine,* vol. 1, *The Emergence of the Catholic Tradition (100–600)* (Chicago: University of Chicago Press, 1971), 109. In tracing the apostolicity of the Church and the controversy posed by Marcion, the Gnostics, and the Montanists, Pelikan notes, "Each of these systems of doctrine asserted that authentic continuity lay with it, and that the catholic claim to continuity was illegitimate. The question was: What are the criteria of doctrinal continuity? And if the answer was 'the consanguinity of doctrine with that of the apostles,' or the claim that 'Christ comes with a message from God, and the apostles with a message from Christ,' this simply moved the question over one notch,

The major issue was to know with certainty the group to which he handed the authority to direct Church affairs and preside at liturgical ceremonies. In a bid to resolve this controversy with the Gnostics, Irenaeus called the Church "the priest of God."[13]

### 2.1.4 Priesthood in the Letter to the Hebrews

The Letter to the Hebrews is the only New Testament writing that explicitly calls Jesus a priest, the high priest. The Letter to the Hebrews gives the most striking interpretation and analogy on the priesthood of Christ vis-à-vis the Jewish priesthood. The author calls him "the high priest of all the blessings that were to come" (Heb. 9:11–14). Being a document addressed probably to Jewish Christians, the letter seeks to remind them that they have a high priest in Jesus who enjoys a higher status than the angels (1:5–14), Moses (5:1–10), and Aaron (7:11–28). The letter contrasts Jesus with the high priests of old, who were impeded in their ministry by sins and death. This high priest, on the other hand, is beyond death and lives eternally interceding for his people (chap. 7). The author of the document juxtaposes Old Testament and New Testament passages with his argument to prove that Jesus is the new high priest. He is believed to have taken up an idea existing already in the Church and system-atized it.[14] That is the reason behind the many references to the Old Testament found in the Letter to the Hebrews. Occasionally, the Old Testament priests were punished by God or died because of their disobedience and sins (1 Sam. 3:14; Heb. 7:23-25). Jesus, on the other hand, through his perfect obedience to God was made perfect and so "became the source of salvation to all who obey him" (Heb. 5:9).

Jesus is called "the great high priest" (ὁ ἀρχιερεὺς ὁ μέγας) for the whole human race. Being acclaimed as the great high priest, he is the perfect mediator

---

to the issue of apostolic continuity." Further on, Pelikan refers to Iranaeus "citing a presbyter who had been a pupil of the apostles" (p. 111).

13. Richardson, *Early Christian Fathers*, 351. According to Richardson, Irenaeus of Lyon emphasized the new life in Christ, the problem of authority, and the right of the Church to offer sacrifices to God as "priest": "This new life is a life of faith, which certainly for Irenaeus means the acceptance of sound belief, but in the sense of joyful turning to God. . . . In the circle of the new life God's world, created good, returns once more to its right relation to him. In contrast to all Gnostic or falsely spiritual deprecia-tion of the material universe, Irenaeus stresses the significance of the offerings of bread and wine which the Church, as the priest of creation, offers to God."

14. It is a common belief that Hebrews is not an isolated work in the New Testa-ment; rather the author takes up existing themes current in the apostolic Church and elaborates on them. These are themes that concur with its central argument that the death of Jesus is the one true sacrifice that can take away sin. The priesthood of Jesus is one of those common New Testament themes. For the author, Jesus is the one and only true high priest of whom the Levitical priests of the Old Testament were prophetic types.

of the new covenant (Heb. 4:14; 12:24). The Letter to the Hebrews teaches as follows:

> At various times in the past and in various different ways, God spoke to our ancestors through the prophets; but in our own time, the last days, he has spoken to us through his Son. . . . He is the radiant light of God's glory and the perfect copy of his nature, sustaining the universe by his powerful command. (Heb. 1:1–3)[15]

Jesus is able to sustain all things because he is at God's right hand in heaven. From his vantage position and by his twofold nature, he is able to understand perfectly the plight of humans, and he helps. This implies that Christ is the only priest. The above statement has an ecclesiological importance attached to it.[16] The ecclesiological importance is the gathering that accrues from the sacrifice and leadership of Jesus. Jesus gathers the new children of God and leads them to God in the new way of worship. The word *archēgos* from *archē* ("beginning/source") and *agein* ("to lead") could mean "originator, founder of a city, leader." *Archēgos* could therefore be interpreted as "originator," "initiator," "founder," "pioneer leader," "leader-captain." In all the senses and usages of the word, the idea could be summed up as the beginning of the new order. Thus, the epistle portrays Jesus as the founder, pioneer, leader, and perfecter of the new people of God.

### 2.2 Characteristics of Jesus as Priest in the Letter to the Hebrews

#### 2.2.1 Identity with Humans

The Letter to the Hebrews teaches that Jesus must be "like his brothers to be a priest." By his Incarnation, he becomes one with human beings (Heb. 2:14–18). To be a priest he has to be authentically human because "[e]very high priest has been taken out of mankind and is appointed to act for men in relations

---

15. See Thomas F. Torrance, *Royal Priesthood: A Theology of Ordained Ministry*, 2nd ed. (Edinburgh: T&T Clark, 2003), 7. Torrance agrees regarding this definite revelation in Jesus who has united the Word and cult in his being: "[A]t last the Word of God, who cast His shadow over the cult of Israel and came to the prophets, was made flesh and tabernacled among men, full of grace and truth (John 1.14f). The Shekinah glory of God dwells in a man. He is Himself both the Lamb of God and the Temple of God (John 1.29–36; 4.21f)."

16. Benedict M. Ashley, O.P., "The Priesthood of Christ, the Baptized, and the Ordained," in *The Theology of Priesthood*, ed. Donald J. Goergen and Ann Garrido (Collegeville, MN: Liturgical Press, 2000), 153. "As Moses was the mediator of the imperfect former covenant sealed in the blood of animal sacrifices, so Christ is the mediator of the perfect new and final covenant sealed in his own sacrificial blood, shed as a proof of the divine love for humanity."

with God" (Heb. 5:1). The Old Testament had instructed that a priest has to be taken from among men (Lev. 8:2; Num. 8:6; Sir. 45:16). Jesus was not different from other men, and so the Letter to the Hebrews develops the theme "in which the Son has 'taken hold of' the children of Abraham rather than angels (Heb. 2:16): they have the same origin (Heb. 2:11), they have blood and flesh and must face the terrors of death (Heb. 2:14–15)."[17] This means that Jesus' suffering and death completed his identification with humanity. It is in his divine nature that Jesus is able to be *Immanuel* —God with us—and it is in his human nature that God stooped down to humans' level in communication. Michael Kunzler argues in support of this point as follows:

> In Christ God goes to meet man with a human face not as if he had only placed a mask over the burning light of the Godhead, but because in a manner never realized hitherto, Christ's genuine human existence is the created and already divinized "space between" in which God through the Incarnate Son enters into relationship with men.[18]

Albert Vanhoye adds that a priest is a mediator and must fully belong to both sides he is mediating. "He is intimately united to God in heavenly glory and yet remains close to us. In him, therefore, life-giving communication between God and mankind is assured: he is effectively high priest"[19] (Heb. 5:9).

### 2.2.2 Trustworthy High Priest

The quality of Jesus' being trustworthy takes on more meaning when it is examined in the context of Num. 12:7, which states: "My servant Moses is the man of trust in all my house." The reference shows the authority of Moses among the children of Israel and his role among God's people. The important word here is *pistos,* which is translated as "worthy of trust." It should be understood as trust, in the light of the function Moses performed. As Moses had the exalted position in leading the children of Israel, Jesus is most worthy and most glorious because he is the reflection of God's glory (Heb. 1:3).

In the Old Testament, God calls Moses and the prophets his servants. In the biblical period, a servant was someone who had no autonomy. He was completely dependent on the master. The master could do whatever he wanted with the servant. The servant was entirely at the master's service. Vanhoye notes that, in the case of Moses, "servant has nothing demeaning about it. On the contrary, it is an honorable title, for it expresses a personal relationship with

---

17. Luke Timothy Johnson, *Hebrews: A Commentary,* New Testament Library (Louisville: Westminster John Knox, 2006), 93.

18. Michael Kunzler, *The Church's Liturgy,* trans. Placed Murray et al. (New York: Continuum, 2001), 41.

19. Albert Vanhoye, *The Old Testament Priests and the New Priest*, trans. Bernard J. Orchard. Petersham, MA: St. Bede's, 1986), 83.

God."[20] In the case of Jesus, he is called "Son." By being "Son" and not "servant" Christ takes a special place and has a far deeper relationship with God than Moses (Heb. 3:5–6).[21] Jesus is the master above the house because "he has been found to deserve a greater glory than Moses," who was master in the house (Heb. 3:3). The author therefore calls Jesus the "trustworthy high priest" (Heb. 3:1–6). As a way of conclusion,

> [The author] is inviting Christians to contemplate the glorious Christ, enthroned with God and therefore fully "worthy of trust." Only this rendering completely fits all the requirements of the text and only the same serves to accurately define one of the fundamental aspects of the priesthood, which would disappear completely without it.[22]

### 2.2.3 The Compassionate High Priest (Heb. 2:17; 4:15–16) (ἐλεήμων)

The Greek word ἐλεήμων means "merciful," though some translations use "sympathetic" or "compassionate." It is a word that is emphatic in and of itself. It refers to Jesus' relationship to humans and describes his motivation as high priest. The author uses a double negation to strengthen the force of his argument. "For it is not as if we had a high priest who was incapable of feeling our weaknesses with us" (Heb. 4:15). Alan C. Mitchell states that the verb *sympathesai* in the LXX "expresses a quality of God manifested in the fact that the Law was given to humans as an act of God's sympathy."[23] Jesus shows this quality of God and thereby distinguished himself from the Old Testament priests. In the Letter to the Hebrews, the author reminds readers that Jesus, the new priest, is different. He is compassionate, in contrast to Old Testament priests, who never showed mercy (Exod. 32:25–29; Numbers 25). He is able to show mercy because he had been through weakness and suffering and yet did not sin, in contrast to Old Testament high priests, whose weaknesses led them to sin. Mercy and trustworthiness are aspects of Jesus' priesthood that separate him from other priests. The author concludes this section by exhorting all to be confident in approaching the throne of grace (Heb. 4:16), implying that grace and mercy flow from Jesus.

---

20. Ibid., 103. Vanhoye further says that the Bible uses the word *therapōn*, which is "servant," instead of *doulos*, meaning "slave." Hence, *therapōn* is a nobler term because it denotes one who is admitted freely into the presence of the king.

21. Alan C. Mitchell, *Hebrews*, Sacra Pagina (Collegeville, MN: Liturgical Press, 2007), 83: "The reason for Moses' appointment over the house of Israel is spelled out, so that he might testify to things that would be spoken later. . . . It is the example of Moses' trustworthiness that testifies, as it looks forward to a greater trustworthiness on the part of the Son. So for the author of Hebrews, Moses is a witness to Christ, and because he is an authoritative spokesman for God his testimony is trustworthy."

22. Vanhoye, *Old Testament Priests*, 95–96.

23. Mitchell, *Hebrews*, 106.

### 2.2.4 Jesus, Greater than Melchizedek

Chapter 7 of the Letter to the Hebrews argues that Jesus enjoys a higher status than Melchizedek and the Levitical priesthood. The author argues that, if Abraham gave "a tenth of all he had to Melchizedek," it follows that Melchizedek was greater than Abraham, since the inferior pays tithes to the superior. "It could be said that Levi, who himself receives tithes, actually paid them in the person of Abraham, because he was still in the loins of his ancestor when *Melchizedek came to meet him"* (Heb. 7:9–10). The Aaronic priests were subject to sin and death. The Son, Jesus, was made a priest with an oath. He is also "holy, innocent, uncontaminated, beyond the influence of sinners, and raised above the heavens" (Heb. 7:26). Jesus' priesthood remains eternal because he conquered both sin and death. Consequently, he lives forever as priest (Heb. 7:24–25).

### 2.2.5 Jesus, Priest of a Higher Sanctuary

Jesus has a more legitimate sanctuary where he ministers as a priest. The author comes to what he calls the principal point of all that is being said. The κεφάλαιον is translated as "the principal point," "main point." On this subject, J. Harold Greenlee makes the following observation:

> Since he is not summarizing what he has been saying, but passes to a new point, it is usually taken to mean that he is now reaching the main point in the argument and this crowning affirmation is . . . that Christ is performing his priestly ministry in heaven.[24]

The *kephalaion*, the main point, is that we have a priest of this kind. This is the key point of all that is being said, that we have a priest in God's heavenly sanctuary. Jesus is a priest higher in status than Moses, Aaron, and the angels. All the qualities mentioned earlier converge in this point because Jesus "has his place at the right of the throne of divine majesty in the heavens" (Heb. 8:1). The aorist tense of καθίζω could mean "to sit down," "to be seated," "to sit," "to have his place." The word refers to one who has accomplished a task. What it implies is that Christ has completed his work on earth and now has his duly deserved place of honor with God.

### 2.2.6 Superior to Angels (Heb. 1:4)

The author uses the word *kreittōn*, which means "better" or "superior" (Heb. 1:4; 6:9; 7:7, 19, 22; 8:6; 9:23; 10:34; 11:16, 35, 40; 12:24). The author makes use of this comparison to show that Jesus is not only superior to the prophets and messengers of the past but also superior to angels (Gal. 3:19). It is believed by

---

24. J. Harold Greenlee, *An Exegetical Summary of Hebrews* (Dallas: Summer Institute of Linguistics, 1998), 275.

the author and Israelites that the law was mediated through angels. He therefore makes a bold claim by saying that the Word in this context is spoken in Jesus. Another of such texts is Heb. 1:5: "To which of the angels did God say: 'You are my son, today I have begotten you?'" Jesus is superior to the angels because of the name he was given which is more excellent than the names of the angels. The fact that he is called "Son" sets him apart from the angels and implies that his name is above every other name. For the completion of Jesus' work on earth, the author uses a strong biblical image of "sitting at God's right hand" to prove Jesus' exaltation over the angels after his humiliating death on the cross.

### 2.2.7 *Jesus, Priest of the New Covenant*

The foundation of the priesthood of Jesus is his Incarnation. The Incarnation is the union of both the divine and human natures in the one person, the Logos. By the union of the two natures in the Logos, Jesus stands in perfect relation with the Father to mediate between God and humans because he belongs equally to both. His priestly offering consists in his human existence on earth, which culminated in his death and resurrection (Heb. 5:7–9; 9:12). Christ, by nature is the "Word which became flesh."[25] As such, he is the only person to mediate effectively between humans and the Father. In Jesus Christ, there is a merging of the Word and humanity.[26] Jesus establishes a new covenant through his Paschal Mystery. At the Last Supper, he gave a new meaning to the Passover when he called the wine "the new covenant in my blood" (Luke 22:20). He therefore inaugurated a new covenant through his blood. This explains why Jesus is rightly and ideally called the new high priest.[27] Christ becomes the

---

25. Torrance (*Royal Priesthood*, 14) supports and argues in defense of this view as follows: "In Jesus Christ, as Apostle and High Priest, both aspects of priesthood are fulfilled, but they are fulfilled in His Sonship and the ground of His Sonship. He is not priest in the sense that He symbolizes, or bears witness to something else, what God does. No, He is the Son of God, God Himself come down as Priest to share our humanity. On the ground of His Sonship and His incarnational qualification he ascends into the Holies. Here we pass beyond the conception of Aaronic priesthood to priesthood of another order. He is Priest in final reality, fulfilling the Mosaic priesthood because His Word is identical with Kingly act; fulfilling the Aaronic priesthood because His offering is identical with His Person. This is Royal Priesthood, in the coincidence of Grace and Omnipotence, in the identity of Person and Work. As such it is as unique as God Himself."

26. Heinrich Denzinger, *Enchiridion symbolorum definitionum et declarationum de rebus fidei et morum, Latin-English,* 43rd ed., ed. Peter Hünermann (San Francisco: Ignatium Press, 2012), 125–26, 150, 250–68; the Councils of Nicaea, Chalcedon, Constantinople 1, and Ephesus respectively.

27. Torrance, *Royal Priesthood*, 2. Torrance goes further to say that "priestly action rests upon God's self-revelation in His Word" (p. 3). Confer also Joseph Ratzinger, *Behold the Pierced One,* trans. Graham Harrison (San Francisco: Ignatius Press, 1986), 28–29. Here Ratzinger notes that it was absolutely necessary for God to mend the

new shepherd and leader of the people of the new covenant, which he ratified with his blood. He is the true shepherd "who lays down his life for his sheep" (John 10:11). Mark writes that Jesus sees the people "as sheep without a shepherd." The fathers of the Second Vatican Council proclaimed that "the deepest truth about God and the salvation of man shines forth in Christ, who is at the same time the mediator and the fullness of all revelation" (*Dei Verbum* 2). He becomes the last Adam, who gathers the chosen people of God and leads them to the kingdom of heaven.

In Deut. 18:18 there is the promise of the new and faithful prophet, and John 1:21 confirms the expectation of the promised prophet of Israel. Thus, salvation and redemption coalesce in concrete human history. The Twelve were called to be with Jesus (Mark 6:7) and to witness to him to the new Israel. The forming of the new people of God is to be a channel through which the promises of the old covenant would be fulfilled and the grace of redemption and restoration of the universe actualized. The choice of the Twelve is very significant because it represents symbolically the twelve tribes of Israel and therefore the new Israel.[28] Under the leadership of the new priest, human beings can therefore approach God with a new order of worship in and through Jesus.

### 2.2.8 Summary

From the above section it is evident that there is no mention of Jesus as priest in the Synoptics. Priesthood was applied to Christ after the death and resurrec-

---

severed relationship between him and humans. Ratzinger writes, "No one can build a bridge to the infinite by his own strength. No one's voice is loud enough to summon the infinite. No intelligence can adequately and securely conceive who God is, whether he hears us and how we should act toward him. . . . Negatively, this shows that man is not in a position to produce a relationship with him." See also Luke 22:20; 1 Tim. 2:5; 1 Cor. 11:25. See also Ignatius of Antioch, *Letter to the Ephesians* 7.2. However, Ignatius approaches this issue from a pneuma–sarx (spirit–flesh) point of view, which this book is not following. The point can be grasped that Jesus is the mediator, the link between God and man.

28. Pope Benedict XVI, *Jesus, the Apostles and the Early Church*, General Audiences, 15 March 2006 – 14 February 2007 (San Francisco: Ignatius Press, 2007), 9. Benedict notes thus: "The number twelve, which evidently refers to the twelve tribes of Israel, already reveals the meaning of the prophetic–symbolic action implicit in the new initiative to re-establish the holy people. As the system of the twelve had long faded out, the hope of Israel awaited their restoration as a sign of the eschatological time (as referred to at the end of the Book of Ezekiel: 37:15–19; 39:23–29; 40–48). In choosing the Twelve, introducing them into a communion of life with himself and involving them in his mission of proclaiming the kingdom in words and works (cf. Mk 6:7–13; Mt 10:5–8; Lk 9:1–6; 6:13), Jesus wants to say that the definitive time has arrived in which to constitute the new people of God, the people of the twelve tribes, which now becomes a universal people, his Church."

tion, which Christians began to view as salvific and redemptive (1 Cor. 5:7).[29] The persecution of Jesus and his followers was another factor that challenged the early Church to reflect on the importance and significance of the death of Jesus. Hence his death and resurrection were seen by the early Christians as a sacrifice called the "Paschal Mystery," replacing the old Passover sacrifice. Since Jesus' passion and death were viewed as a sacrifice, there was need to reflect on the character of the priest who offered the sacrifice. The followers of Jesus believed him to be the fulfillment of the Old Testament promise.[30]

Jesus' priesthood is unique because it is ontological. He is of "one substance with the Father"[31] and, as man, he had to offer worship to God. The uniqueness of Jesus' priesthood is by virtue of his Incarnation, about which the Letter to the Hebrews testifies thus: "When he came into the world, he said, 'Sacrifices and offerings you did not desire, but a body you prepared for me; holocausts and sin offerings you took no delight in.' Then I said, 'As is written of me in the scroll, Behold, I come to do your will, O God'" (Heb. 10:5–7). That promise has been fulfilled in Jesus through his obedience and sacrifice.

### 2.3 Sacrifice in the New Testament

#### 2.3.1 Sacrifice in the Synoptics

Sacrifice occurs in the New Testament primarily as bloody sacrifices. The New Testament mainly uses the Greek word θυσία to refer to sacrifice, particularly when making references to Old Testament sacrifices. The Synoptics do not refer to Jesus offering sacrifice but tell us that Jesus went to Jerusalem to worship and to observe the Passover. The Gospel of Luke opens with Zechariah in the temple performing his priestly duties (Luke 1:5–22). Jesus himself also makes references to sacrifice in Matt. 5:23. Jesus instructs believers to be reconciled to one another before offering their sacrifice (Matt. 9:13; 12:7; Mark 12:13; Luke 2:24; 13:1), thereby emphasizing the relational dynamics in the new kingdom he came to inaugurate rather than mere ritualistic sacrifices. Though at the presentation of Jesus, Mary and Joseph offered the sacrifice of two pigeons in the

---

29. Vanhoye (*Old Testament Priests*, 42–43) raises many questions on this issue, as it is the striking point/innovation that Christianity brought into the world; namely that the one who was crucified for "insurrection" is seen as a high priest. However, Vanhoye questions why the Christians of the first century CE drifted from the faith of their fathers and the priesthood, "this institution [that] had been founded on the word of God and guaranteed by an impressive collection of biblical texts."

30. Frank C. Quinn, O.P., "Ministry, Ordination Rites, and Language," in Goergen and Garrido, *Theology of Priesthood,* 55. Quinn argues that "Jesus was not *a sacerdos*, a (cultic or ritual) priest. He belonged to no sacred *sacerdotium*. Yet, following Hebrews, we speak of him as priest and even High Priest. Such use of sacerdotal metaphor allows us to understand Christ's role as mediator in a most profound way."

31. Denzinger, *Enchiridion symbolorum*, 125–26 (Council of Nicaea).

temple, the Bible does not tell us of any instance when Jesus offered sacrifice as the Old Testament priests did. Rather, in the New Testament Jesus made comments either for or against sacrifice.

The Gospel of Matthew presents Jesus as the Son of David, the Son of Abraham (Matt. 1:1). Matthew sees him as the king promised to David who would reign on his throne forever. He is very quick to make references to Old Testament prophecies that point to Jesus' life as the new leader, prophet, and king of God's chosen people and the gentiles as well.

In Mark, Jesus recognizes Jewish sacrifice when he orders the cured leper to go and offer sacrifice as prescribed by the law (Mark 1:44). He also praises the poor widow's offering (Mark 12:41–44). There is a criticism of the wrong application of *qorbān* (Mark 7:11). In Mark 10:45, Jesus gives the most striking remark on sacrifice, which implicitly inserts him into the messianic prophecy of Isaiah (Isa. 53:10–12). By saying that "the Son of Man came not to be served but to serve and to give his life as a ransom for many" (Mark 10:45), Jesus presents himself as the Suffering Servant of Isaiah. "Giving his life as a ransom for many" is sacrificial language that points to ransom from evil, which any first-century Jew would have understood. This sacrificial motif comes up again in the narrative of the institution of the Eucharist, and all the Synoptic Gospels accept and affirm the eucharistic supper and the death of Jesus as sacrifice (Matt. 26:17–29; Mark 14:12–27; Luke 22:7–20).

### 2.3.2 Sacrifice in the Pauline Letters

Paul, as one of the apostles, had at the center of his message the death and resurrection of Jesus. He speaks of believers as being justified by the death and resurrection of Jesus. "Jesus who was put to death for our sins and raised to life to justify us" (Rom. 4:25). It is a justification by the gift of God's grace through the sacrifice of Jesus' life (Rom. 3:24-25). Sacrificial language is freely used by Paul in the same sense as the Old Testament rituals (2 Cor. 5:21): "Christ, who had not known sin, God made 'sin' (*ḥaṭṭā't*), in order that we might become, in him, God's justice." He gives a striking theological interpretation that portrays Jesus as a Passover lamb by saying: "Christ our Passover has been sacrificed" (1 Cor. 5:7). He is implying that Jesus has become the sacrificial victim. Analogically, just as the Passover sacrifice was a sign of God's abiding help to Israel and their deliverance from Egypt, Jesus is the sign of God's deliverance of his people. For Paul, what the blood of the Passover lamb accomplished for the Israelites, the blood of Jesus has performed for believers. What mattered most for Paul was the Jesus who died and rose from the dead and would one day return in glory. Hence, the death of Jesus is a sacrifice that gains salvation for his followers, because Jesus "emptied himself of the divine glory" (Phil. 2:2–12). Paul focuses on believers to offer spiritual sacrifice to God (Rom. 12:1).

In the Pauline theology of sacrifice, Jesus' sacrifice has become a new way, and all must leave the old way for the new (Rom. 5:6-8). To buttress his point,

Paul uses the word "leaven," which was a symbol of putrefaction for the Jews. He goes on to say that evil must be eliminated from the lives of believers because of the Paschal Mystery. Therefore, through the death and resurrection of Jesus, believers are set free.

### 2.3.3 Sacrifice in the Johannine Writings

The Gospel of John is of prime importance to this study because it is a Gospel that is liturgically based as it brings into focus the belief, worship, and life of the Church in its early stages. It is a Gospel that is of high theology, and high Christology in particular. One of the striking images one finds in the Fourth Gospel is the motif of the lamb and its significance for John. To be able to understand how John uses the lamb imagery in the Gospel, it is necessary first to focus on his use of "life," "light," and "love."

The arguments and hypotheses of John about Jesus being the Son of God are based on his understanding of Jesus as the "Life of the World"—the "Light of the World" who has given the greatest "love to the world." John character-izes this love as being sacrificial. "A man can have no greater love than to lay down his life for his friends" (John 15:13). It is against this backdrop that the prologue proclaims Jesus as "the Word who has taken flesh and dwelt among us . . . and we have seen his glory, the glory of the only Son of God" (John 1:14). John presents Jesus as "the Lamb of God" (John 1:35). To call Jesus "the Lamb of God" at that time would be understood by any first-century Jew in terms of sacrifice or "Servant of God." This is because it would remind them of their temple sacrifices with their elaborate rituals of offering lambs, bulls, and oxen. The major sacrifice of the Jews, however, which with time commemorated the deliverance from Egypt, was the Passover, and it was celebrated with the Pass-over lamb. John, calling Jesus "the Lamb of God," was situating his listeners in the context of the Passover. At that early moment in the ministry of Jesus, John was already presenting Jesus as the new Passover lamb for sacrifice. It is not surprising to read, in John, that Jesus was crucified at the time the Passover lambs were being slaughtered on the preparation day (John 19:14, 31, 42). John has a subtle way of using words that have a deeper meaning. One of such words is "temple," which was later understood, after the resurrection of Jesus, as his body and later developed into the concept of the Church as the Body of Christ in the Pauline letters (see 1 Cor. 3:16; 2 Cor. 6:16; Eph. 2:21).

For John, Jesus is "the just one who takes our sins away and, indeed, the sins of the whole world" (1 John 2:2; 4:9–10). The above statement draws a com-parison with the lamb of sacrifice in the Old Testament, and it was precisely in the Passover meal/sacrifice that lambs or goats were used (Exod. 12:5). Just as no bone of the Passover lamb was broken, so no bone of Jesus, the new Passover lamb, was broken (John 19:31–37; Exod. 12:46; Num. 9:12; Ps. 34:20). With these striking similarities John wants his readers to grasp the importance and significance of Jesus' sacrifice. By his death and resurrection, John calls Jesus the lamb that is "worthy to take the scroll and open its seals" (Rev. 4:11; 5:6–10, 13; 13:8). "The lion of the tribe of Judah, the root of David" (Rev. 5:4–5), is the only one worthy to open the scroll and break its seals. Jesus, for John, holds the key to the kingdom (Rev. 1:8, 18). He has the authority vested in him by God because he submitted to the will of God.

The Book of Revelation ends with the Lamb enthroned as the life and salvation of the world (chap. 22). In the Book of Revelation, the Lamb that was slain is equated with God as sharing the same glory, honor, power, and kingdom (Rev. 5:1, 6–7).

To conclude, I state that the priesthood is an institution from God. The Old Testament priesthood developed from family heads to the leaders of the people. It became an institution from the call of Aaron and was passed on by genealogy. The Old Testament priests did not show mercy to sinners when they applied with full force the law, which often resulted in death to the sinner (see Exod. 32:25–29; Num. 25:4–8). The New Testament, on the other hand, has a priesthood that is not tied to a particular family, race, tribe, or even to a particular sanctuary. The New Testament high priest is a "sympathetic high priest," because he had been through suffering himself.

Both the Old Testament and New Testament priests were men chosen by God as mediators. They received the word of God, taught in his name, guided the congregation in worship, and offered sacrifices. The Old Testament prepared the ground for the New Testament when the apostles after Christ took up the leadership of the people of God. It is within the new community of believers, the Church, that the Paschal Mystery is celebrated.

### 2.4 Summary

This chapter surveyed the development of priesthood in the New Testament. It looked at the progression of priesthood and how Jesus was termed "priest" by his disciples after his passion, death, and resurrection. It looked at the activities of Jesus in the temple, his teachings and his Passover with his apostles, and interpreted the actions of Jesus as priestly actions. The early followers of Jesus understood his actions as priestly and believed him to be the Son of God. It is in the Pauline Letters and the Gospel of John that the sacrificial motif is brought up. The disciples of Jesus began to shape their belief in Jesus' death as sacrifice, a new Passover. This belief guided their conviction in the one sacrifice of Jesus as the summation, perfection, and fulfillment of the Old Testament promise of a new sacrifice and worship (Mal. 1:11; Ps. 113:3). The belief was the guiding light that contributed to the fast spreading of the gospel of Jesus to the "gentile" nations, among which are the Igbos.

# II

## THE PASCHAL MYSTERY, IGBO PRIESTHOOD, AND SACRIFICE

# CHAPTER THREE

# THE PASSOVER AND THE CHURCH

Having written about the priesthood and sacrifice in Israel, I now turn to the Paschal Mystery, which is the redemptive life, passion, death, and resurrection of Jesus, his Ascension into heaven and sitting at the right hand of the Father. Etymologically, "paschal" is from the Hebrew *pesaḥ* and the Greek *pascha,* which can be translated as "Passover."[1] The word *pesaḥ* is found in one of the oldest sources of Scripture (J, the Yahwist). Passover was originally a shepherd's feast celebrated to protect shepherd and flock as they moved from winter to spring pastures, while the unleavened bread (*maṣṣôt*) was the farmer's feast, which in spring celebrated the firstfruits of the earth after winter (Lev. 23:4–13). The Feast of Unleavened Bread was celebrated at the local sanctuaries in earliest times. Tamara Prosic argues that most theories on the Passover "are built on the assumption that the ancient Israelites were ethnic foreigners [and] nomads."[2] As nomads, they were always on the move for better pasture. Passover, therefore, was the religious meal of those who were ready to move, as all who participated in the meal wore traveling attire.

There are historical texts that mention the celebration of certain Passovers in the history of the Israelites.[3] These Passover celebrations commemorated

---

1. The etymology of the word *pesaḥ* is much debated. Some try to derive it from the Akkadian *pasahu,* "to appease," or Arabic *fasaha,* "be or become wide." *Pasahu* was used in Akkadian to refer to the rite of sacrifice which appeased the deity. William A. Van Gemeren, *New International Dictionary of Old Testament Exegesis,* s.v. "Pesah," by Hendrick K. Bosman. *Pasahu* was used in Akkadian to refer to the rite of sacrifice which appeased the deity. Theories on the Passover go back to the assumption that Israel was a nomadic tribe and, like all nomads, had similar cultures and traditions until their separation by God's covenantal laws. The most appealing theory is that the Passover was a feast celebrated by shepherds.

2. Tamara Prosic, *The Development and Symbolism of the Passover until 70 CE,* Journal for the Study of the Old Testament Supplement Series 414 (London: T&T Clark International, 2004), 5.

3. There is the first Passover on the night of the exodus from Egypt (Exodus 12), the first Passover in Canaan (Josh. 5:10–12), the Passover under Hezekiah (2 Chronicles

the stages in the development of the feast and how different generations celebrated the feast, and the responsibilities of the priests in the Passover sacrifice.

## 3.1 The Passover Feast in Israel

Passover is one of the principal feasts in Israel. The Passover became an official feast in Israel from the night of the exodus (Exod. 12:1–20; Lev. 23:5–12; Num. 28:16–25; Exod. 12:1–20, 40–51).[4]

With the first celebration of the Passover recorded for Israel, it then became an annual celebration according to the command of the Lord. "This day is to be a day of remembrance for you, and you must celebrate it as a feast in Yahweh's honor. For all generations you are to declare it a day of festival, forever" (Exod. 12:14).

### 3.1.1 Passover: A Shepherd's Feast

The primitive Passover was celebrated as a shepherd's feast even before the Israelites celebrated it on the night of their departure from Egypt. As a shepherd's feast, Passover had its origin in the nomadic life of the shepherds who were always on the move in search of greener pastures for their flocks.[5]

In the earliest stages of the Passover among the Israelites, they celebrated

---

30), the Passover celebrated by Josiah (2 Kgs. 23:21–23; 2 Chr. 35:1–18), and the Passover celebrated after the return from exile (Ezra 19–22).

4. What is peculiar about this feast is that the heads of families presided over their households and no portion of the meat of sacrifice was reserved. The Lord commanded that the sacrifice be celebrated in the homes. It was celebrated with an unblemished one-year-old lamb, slaughtered in the evening, and the lamb's blood was put on the lintels and doorposts. The lamb was roasted and eaten that very night with unleavened bread and bitter herbs (Exod. 12:1–13). The Lord promised to "pass over" the houses of Israel to strike down the firstborn of the Egyptians. "The blood shall be a sign for you, upon the houses where you are; and when I see the blood, I will pass over you" (Exod. 12:13). The smearing of blood on the doorposts and lintels with hyssop was an apotropaic ritual. Leaven, which was a sign of corruption, was removed from the house. This is because it could ferment and lead to putrefaction. Passover at this time did not completely lose its primitive ritual elements, as it was a period to muster the young men in the army in the Bedouin tribes. In Israel, therefore, protection of their firstborn would be a reminder of the "strength of hand with which Yahweh brought us out of Egypt, from the house of bondage" (Exod. 13:14).

5. In the celebration of Passover, the shepherds offered a lamb or goat in sacrifice as a protection for their flocks from unwanted spirits and dangers. The lambs were killed and the blood was smeared on their flock. It is likely that the sacrifice was offered when they were ready to move to a new location and they believed that it would protect them as they ventured into new and unfamiliar territory. Since they were nomads, they roasted the lamb with bitter herbs, with sandals on their feet and their shepherd's staff in hand ready for the journey. The lamb was eaten with unleavened bread because it

the feast separate from the Feast of Unleavened Bread.[6] In this form, they, like the other ancient Arab nations, occupied themselves with the assessment of the previous year and on how to gain the blessings of the new year. Segal also points out that the rituals were led by the chief of the particular Bedouin community and was directed to a particular deity they believed controlled the forces of nature. Myths of creation were recited, followed by eating and dancing, and a procession to the desert.[7]

When the Israelites came into Canaan, they continued to celebrate this feast in obedience to the Lord. Judah B. Segal argues that there was a "broad scheme" which viewed the Passover as a single item following the directions in Exodus 20–23 and 33–34. There is also the line of thought that follows Num. 9:1–14, which deals with the particulars of the feast and specifically with the *pesaḥ*, while Deut. 16:1–8, 16–17 has detailed regulations and looks like a contradiction to the rest.[8] Passover continued to be a night ritual, and heads of families were the principal sacrificers. As Israel mingled with other nations, the Lord commanded that no foreigner shall eat the Passover lamb (Exod. 12:43–49). It was only upon being incorporated into the covenanted people through circumcision that a foreigner would be allowed to participate in the Passover meal. This exclusiveness shows that the Passover was a sacrificial meal shared only with those who had the same faith and hope.

The celebration of the feast was extended sometime after the settlement in the land. The first celebration after the Sinaitic covenant marked the beginning of Israel as a nation.[9] At the time of Josiah, the Passover was celebrated on the 14th day of the Jewish month of Nisan. It was celebrated in a manner that the people of that time had never seen or experienced before, but all in strict obedience to the law. The Deuteronomic writers made Passover a pilgrimage feast, which is a consequence of the centralization of cult. Roland de Vaux argues that the two feasts (Passover and Unleavened Bread) were eventually combined

---

was easy and quick to bake. The celebration was also an occasion to number the flock in preparation for the journey.

6. Hendrik L. Bosman, "*pesaḥ*," in *New International Dictionary of Old Testament Theology and Exegesis,* ed. Willem A. VanGemeren (Grand Rapids: Zondervan, 1997), 3:642–44.

7. Judah B. Segal, *The Hebrew Passover, from the Earliest Times to A.D. 70* (New York: Oxford University Press, 1963), 155. For Segal, Passover was a time of reunion with the deity and of courting the favor of the deity. It was therefore necessary to observe ritual purity demanded by the deity for the blessings of the new year to flow. This feast, for Segal, was celebrated among the Arabs at approximately the time of the Passover in the Israelite calendar.

8. Ibid., 188–92.

9. Roland de Vaux, *Ancient Israel: Its Life and Institutions,* trans. John McHugh (New York: McGraw-Hill, 1961), 492–93.

(Ezra 45:21), following the "Priestly" code.[10] The feasts pointed to the deliverance from Egypt.

> The commemorative elements of the feasts were the sacrificial blood, which pointed to God's protection against the tenth plague of the first-born, the unleavened bread, which signified the haste of Israel in preparing for Exodus, and the bitter herbs, which referred to the Egyptian bondage.[11]

### 3.1.2 Passover: A Pilgrimage Feast

With the centralization of cult, Israel made the feasts of Passover and Unleavened Bread pilgrimage feasts. People would come to Jerusalem for the festival. The two feasts became occasions to remember "what the Lord had done" (Exod. 12:42) when he freed their fathers from Egyptian bondage. In the celebrations of Passover during the times of Josiah, Hezekiah, and Ezra, the emphasis was more on the sanctification of the people, though a postexilic praxis records that the Levites were the ones who killed the lambs (2 Chr. 29:34; Ezra 6:20). The essential aspect of the celebration was the family offering a lamb and consuming it in the temple area. Each family brought its lamb to the temple, and, as the head of the family sliced the throat of the lamb, the priests lined up in the temple and collected the blood, which they poured at the base of the altar. There was a strict rule on where to slaughter the paschal lamb (Deut. 16:5-6). The sacrificer then returned to his home to eat the lamb roasted according to the specifications of the law. When the temple was destroyed, the ritual killing of the lamb in the temple area became difficult, and so the paschal lamb had to be eliminated from the Seder (ritual). Every other aspect of the ritual had to be situated in the home.[12] This continued even after the Babylonian exile in the Second Temple period, and it was during one of the Passover feasts that Jesus instituted the Eucharist before his passion and death.

### 3.2 Passover in the New Testament

Paul was the earliest New Testament writer to use the word "Passover" in connection with Jesus, when he said, "Christ our Passover has been sacrificed" (1 Cor. 5:7). His statement confirmed what was believed and practiced by the followers of Jesus after his death. Paul and the early Christians believed and called Jesus' passion, death, and resurrection a "pasch." There is a parallel here between the belief in ancient Israel and the Christian belief. It is a parallel that

---

10. Ibid., 486.

11. Bosman, "*pesah*," 3:642–44. See also de Vaux, *Ancient Israel*, 486–88.

12. Abraham E. Millgram, *Jewish Worship* (Philadelphia: Jewish Publication Society, 1971), 301–2.

gives meaning and relation to the two covenants, the old and the new. Jon D. Levenson makes a remarkable contribution to the parallels.[13] The paschal connection is one that joins the ritual meal to the sacrifice and the death of Jesus on the cross. It makes the cross central to Jesus' ministry. The centrality of the cross to Jesus' mission was mentioned during Jesus' ministry (Luke 9:22; Matt. 16:21), and he laid emphasis on it at the Last Supper with his disciples (Matt. 26:20–29; Luke 22:14–22; Mark 14:17–25). The Last Supper and the crucifixion are two events that constitute the new covenant.

In the New Testament writings, allusions and statements about Jesus sacrificing himself (John 10:11-18; Phil. 2:6-11) abound. Robert J. Daly points to what he calls the three key moments in the understanding of sacrifice in the New Testament. He describes it in three stages involving the Father, Son, and Holy Spirit.[14] Though Daly has made an important contribution, he rather transfers all sacrifices to the spiritual realm. He fails to center sacrifice on Jesus but focuses his attention on what Christians can do. That Christians are able to perform any sacrificial function at all is due to the merits of Jesus' sacrifice.

In the New Testament, the Passover did not lose its emphasis on liberation and the activity of God in Israel. It was within this ritual, after each institution, according to Luke and Paul, that Jesus gave the command to "do it in memory

---

13. Jon D. Levenson, *The Death and Resurrection of the Beloved Son: The Transformation of Child Sacrifice in Judaism and Christianity* (New Haven, CT: Yale University Press, 1993), 174–75. Through the ancient Israelite Passover, there was a communion with God. In the Christian perspective, communion with God is effected through Jesus. In rabbinic Judaism, it was believed that the Israelite community exists only because of the obedience of Abraham, who wanted to offer his son Isaac in sacrifice. Christianity is therefore a religion founded on the cross of Jesus. It is a religion founded on the Father's willingness to actually offer his Son. "The paschal connection will prove central to the parallel Christian belief that the Eucharist is a reenactment of Jesus' final meal before his sacrificial death. Both the Jewish and Christian systems of sacrifice come to be seen as founded upon a father's willingness to surrender his beloved son and the son's unstinting acceptance of the sacrificial role he has been assigned in the great drama of redemption. Though this is more obviously the case in Christianity, it holds for Judaism more than is generally recognized. The Christian doctrine is incomprehensible apart from the history of Jewish biblical interpretations."

14. Robert J. Daly, *Sacrifice Unveiled: The True Meaning of Christian Sacrifice* (New York: T&T Clark, 2009), 9: "The first 'moment' is the self-offering of the Father in the gift, the sending, of his Son. The second 'moment' is the unique 'response' of his Son, in his humanity and in the Spirit, to the Father and for us. The third 'moment'— and only then does Christian sacrifice begin to become real in our world—consists in the self-offering of believers in union with Christ by which they share in his covenant relationship with the Father . . . (Romans 12:1). In other words, Christian Sacrifice is a profoundly personal, eschatological, and trinitarian event, an event in which we Christians, in the power of the same Spirit that was in Jesus, and in *our* concrete humanity, begin to do in this world what we will be able to do completely only in the next."

of him" (Luke 22:19; 1 Cor. 11:23–25). A major point to consider is that Jesus used bread, as any father or host in an Israelite community would do at a meal. He blessed and broke it and handed it to the apostles.

> Now as they were eating, Jesus took some bread, and when he had said the blessing he broke it and gave it to the disciples. "Take it and eat," he said. "This is my body." Then he took a cup, and when he had returned thanks he gave it to them. "Drink all of you from this," he said, "for this is my blood, the blood of the covenant, which is to be poured out for many for the forgiveness of sins." (Matt. 26:26–28)

Luke, however, insists that the cup was given after supper: "And likewise the chalice after supper, saying, 'This chalice which is poured out for you is the new covenant in my blood'" (Luke 22:20). I submit, however, that the Eucharist was instituted sequentially. The "Body of Christ" was given at the very beginning after the blessing. After the prayer, Jesus added, "Take and eat, this is my body" (Matt. 26:26). The "blood of Christ" was given after supper. Some time elapsed between them.

Some issues arise from what Jesus did, and it is probable that the apostles were amazed at the statements of Jesus at the Passover meal. He went beyond what was required and called the bread his body and the wine his blood. Any first-century Israelite would recall that the Passover lamb was eaten and the blood poured out.

At the Passover with his apostles, Jesus projected himself as the liberator. He added a new dimension to the traditional feast by indicating that the bread was his body. Jesus called the cup "the blood of the covenant" (Matt. 26:28), which might have reminded his apostles of the Old Testament covenant, which was sealed similarly by Moses with the "blood of the covenant" (Exod. 24:8). The blood of the Passover lamb was for the preservation and safety of the Israelites. Jesus in this "new Passover" meal calls the wine his blood, "the blood of the covenant," which will be "poured out" for many. This statement is reminiscent of the Old Testament covenant between God and Israel when Moses "poured out" the blood of the covenant (Exod. 24:8; 29:12; Lev. 4:7). Jesus was therefore saying through his symbolic acts that he was the Savior and that the "new covenant" was ratified in his blood. By that act, he gave a new dimension to the Passover meal.

### 3.2.1 Mark

In Mark, the preparation for the Passover supplies a ritual context (Mark 14:12–16) for the prediction of Jesus' betrayal. The ritual context suggests that Jesus freely offers his life in sacrifice. Raymond Brown suggests that the prediction of Jesus' betrayal and subsequent handing over to the chief priests and elders counter the idea of Jesus' self-giving in the Eucharist.[15] It seems that Jesus was taken against his will until one reads the prediction in the light of Jesus' Passover meal with the disciples. Mark emphasizes that it was the first day of the Feast of Unleavened Bread, "when the Passover lambs were sacrificed" (Mark 14:15). Mark immediately launches the reader into the Passover feast. The words of the institution and actions occur in the course of the meal "as they were eating" (Mark 14:22). Jesus "blessed and broke" the bread, which he called his body (Mark 14:22–25). There is no break between the actions of handing the disciples the bread and the cup. It was after they had drunk from the cup that Jesus said to his disciples, "This is my blood of the covenant, which is poured out for many." For Mark, the Last Supper provided an opportunity for another prediction of Jesus' death. There is a self-giving of Jesus which the bread and wine symbolize.

### 3.2.2 Matthew

In the Gospel of Matthew, the disciples come to Jesus to inquire about the preparation for the Passover. Matthew portrays Jesus as the head of the household as "he sat at table with the twelve" (Matt. 26:20). It was required that the head of the household recline with the family for the Passover meal (Exod. 12:1–21). Matthew also writes that, within the Passover meal, Jesus blessed the bread, broke it, and gave it to the disciples and said, "Take, eat; this is my body" (Matt. 26:26). Matthew emphasizes that the cup that will be poured out is "for the remission of sins," thereby pointing to the atoning power of the blood (Matt 26:28). For Matthew, there is a change from the old.

To show the change in world order and the new worship, Matthew employs eschatological imagery in his description of the death of Jesus.

> If the birth of Jesus was marked by a sign in the heavens (a star's rising), his death is marked by signs on the earth (a quake) and under the earth (tombs). His death brings judgment on the temple but also the resurrection of the saints of Israel. Human relationships to God have been changed, and the cosmos has been transformed.[16]

### 3.2.3 Luke

In Luke, the phrase "giving thanks" is very prominent. The evangelist captures the line of tradition followed by Jesus, as an Israelite head of the family would "give thanks" for the gifts of grain and grapes. In Luke, Jesus gives thanks and then hands the chalice to his disciples. Luke does not say anything about the

---

15. Raymond E. Brown, *An Introduction to the New Testament,* Anchor Bible Reference Library (New York: Doubleday, 1997), 145.

16. Ibid., 202.

remission of sins through the blood of Jesus. In Luke, the body is "given for you," and the cup is of the new covenant in his blood which is "poured out for you." Luke mentions a cup (the *kiddush* cup) that preceded the bread before another cup of wine, the cup of *haggadah*. In Luke 22:19, Luke uses the verb ἐκχυννόμενον, which is a present participle used when an action is taking place while one is speaking, or to take place in the immediate future. Thus, Luke is portraying that what Jesus is doing at that very moment is effecting a change in the bread and wine. He is projected as a family head offering the Passover sacrifice. He is acting as the priest offering the sacrifice.

For Luke, the Last Supper was a Passover meal that was celebrated by Jesus and his disciples (Luke 22:15). When it was concluded, a new Passover was instituted (Luke 22:19).[17] At the Last Supper, a new story was added to the Passover as captured in the Synoptics. The new story is one that will be told for ages to come.[18] It is the story of Jesus' Paschal Mystery, which is the new covenant and a new order. Instead of retelling the story of the exodus, Jesus was instructing the apostles that his Paschal Mystery would be a new story that would be told for all ages as a memorial of the new covenant in his blood. Hence, a new *anamnēsis* motif is added to the Passover.

### 3.2.4 John

John describes Jesus as the fulfillment of the Passover through his passion and death (John 19). He inserts the trial at dawn and the crucifixion of Jesus about the sixth hour, which is the hour the priests began to slaughter the Passover lambs (John 19:14, 32–36; Exod. 12:46; Lev. 23:5–8). It was also the fulfillment of the preaching of John the Baptist, who called Jesus "the servant of God" (John 1:29). A sponge soaked with vinegar was raised on a hyssop branch to Jesus' mouth as he hung on the cross. This was the type of branch that was used to sprinkle the blood of the Passover lamb (John 19:29; Exod. 12:21–23). It indicates a fulfillment of the covenant in Jesus and a new order of worship.

At the death of Jesus on the cross, John wrote that not one of his bones was broken. This reminds the reader that no bones of the paschal lamb were broken (Exod. 12:46). The garment of Jesus, which was not torn because it was seam-

---

17. Ibid., 256. Brown has a different view on the issue of the two cups in Luke. He calls the first cup the cup of the Passover meal, while the second cup preceded by the bread he calls Luke's description of the Eucharist.

18. C. P. M. Jones, "The New Testament," revised by C. J. A. Hickling, in *The Study of Liturgy,* ed. Cheslyn Jones et al., rev. ed. (New York: Oxford University Press, 1992), 196: "On the night before the crucifixion he lays bare his own inner purpose in approaching and accepting death; he makes it into a sacrificial offering, to provide the blood for a new alliance between God and the twelvefold Israel (cf. Exod. 24.4) and for 'many' (= all, cf. Isa. 53.12) by the twofold sign; by accepting bread and cup the disciples accept his intention and their own share in it."

less (John 19:23), reminds one of the high priest's vestment, which was woven in one piece (Exod. 28:32). For John, Jesus was establishing the new covenant, and he is the priest mediating the covenant. His passion, therefore, becomes a memorial taking place within the Israelite Passover feast in a manner that likens it to the Passover of the Old Testament (Exod. 12:14).

### 3.2.5 *Paul and the Passover*

The Paschal Mystery has a central place in the writings of Paul. He stressed the importance of the cross of Jesus for the salvation of the world. According to Paul, "Christ our Passover has been sacrificed" (1 Cor. 5:7). The Old Testament typology is understood in the Christian sense of a new covenant in Christ. There is a new deliverance in Jesus just as there was the deliverance from Egypt. For Paul, the death of Christ granted liberation to the world. In Jesus, there is a newness that cannot be produced by humans themselves. With a new liberation, the "leaven" of sin and iniquity should no longer be found in the new people of God. Paul defined the death of Jesus as a covenant-making sacrifice and a sacrifice for his followers. Therefore, "Jesus died for our sins, in accordance with the scriptures" (1 Cor. 15:3). The cross becomes the key to God's salvation of human beings. For Paul, then, "to live is Christ and to die is gain" (Phil. 1:21).

In Rom. 3:21–26, Paul states that the cross is God dealing with human sinfulness. It is the remedy for human sins. Hence, the leaven of unrighteousness must be cast away. In his First Letter to the Corinthians, Paul often took sacrifice for granted in the sense that he saw it as a part of the religious portrait, and he expected the Corinthian church to follow in the same line. The Eucharist, for Paul, is a communion sacrifice (1 Cor. 10:14–22). One who participates in it shares in the life, death, and resurrection of Jesus.

Paul makes an argument for participants in the cup and the bread presuming the belief of his audience. "The blessing cup which we bless, is it not a participation in the blood of Christ? The bread that we bless, is it not a participation in the body of Christ?" (1 Corinthians 10 and 11). Paul calls it "a cup of blessing" (1 Cor. 11:25), showing a specific act of praise, a praise coming from the people of God through the new priest. Any celebration of the Lord's Supper is a participation in the body and blood of Jesus and therefore the new Passover. For Paul, Christ's death was a self-giving, a self-emptying for humans (2 Cor. 5:14–15; Rom. 5:6–11; Gal. 2:20). The sacrifice of Christ, which Paul terms a "paschal sacrifice" stems from the idea of Christ being a sin offering for the sanctification of his people. "For our sake he made him to be sin who knew no sin, so that in him we might become the righteousness of God" (Gal. 3:13). God sent his own sinless Son in the likeness of sinful flesh and for sin (2 Cor. 5:21). He condemned sin in the flesh (Rom. 3:24–25). Paul used the technical term ἐν ὁμοιώματι σαρκὸς ἁμαρτίας ("in the likeness of sinful flesh"; Rom. 8:3) for a sin offering as it was used by the LXX (Lev. 4:3).

Paul therefore identifies the passion, death, and resurrection of Jesus with the sin offering of the Old Testament.

In Phil. 2:5–11, Paul uses an ancient christological hymn in the most exquisite statement about Jesus' position in the economy of salvation. It is also in line with his statement to the Corinthians that, though Jesus was rich, he became poor for the sake of humans (2 Cor. 8:9). Paul shows two important aspects of Jesus: the reality of his divinity and the reality of his humanity. He teaches that Jesus was in μορφῇ Θεοῦ (the form of God), and yet Jesus did not see his divine nature as something to be grasped—ἁρπαγμόν—("clutch" or "hold on to").[19] He instead emptied himself—ἀλλὰ ἑαυτὸν ἐκένωσεν—and took on the human *morphē*. He also died on the cross. For Paul, then, the self-renunciation of Jesus was the basis for his glorification. Jesus did not want to exalt himself but gave up everything, including his life, for the sake of the world. This act of sacrificial love brought him a greater glory, the glory of a new name that is above every other name—the name "Lord."[20]

In the Letter to the Galatians, Paul makes a case for the superiority of the gospel of Jesus. For Paul, there are three stages in the history of salvation.

1. A period without the law: from Abraham to Moses.
2. The period of the law: from Moses to Jesus Christ.
3. An era of grace: from Christ until the end of time.

To sum up Paul's theology of sacrifice, the death of Christ is a redemptive sacrifice. Paul saw the death of Jesus in terms of the two Israelite sacrifices of Passover and sacrifice of reparation (*'āšām*), which are associated with redemption and forgiveness, respectively. Jesus is the new Passover and sin offering for the redemption of the world, since his death is a single paschal celebration for all ages, and those who are baptized into him gain the blessings of the promise (Gal. 3:14). This idea continued into the early Church as they celebrated the Passover. The notion that "Jesus became accursed for sinners" (Gal. 3:14) and a ransom for human sins draws the fourth Servant Song of Isaiah into focus (Isa. 52:13–53:15).

---

19. William Barclay, *The Letters to the Philippians, Colossians, and Thessalonians*, 3rd rev. and updated ed., New Daily Study Bible (Louisville: Westminster John Knox, 2001), 43. Barclay writes that the statement can mean two things: "It can mean that Jesus did not need to snatch at equality with God, because he had it as a right. (2) It can mean that he did not clutch at equality with God, as if to hug it jealously to himself, but laid it down willingly for the sake of men and women."

20. In the Bible, a new name was a sign of a change in a person's life. Cf. Gen. 17:5; 32:28; Rev. 21:17.

### 3.3 The Passover in the Early Church

In obedience to the words of her Lord, who said, "Do this in memory of me," the early Church celebrated this memorial of the Paschal Mystery in a most sublime manner in the liturgy of the Eucharist. Hence, what the Church believes, she manifests in her liturgy and way of life. One can draw the logical conclusion that, at the Last Supper, Jesus offered himself up to his Father in a sacramental sacrifice and at the same time gave himself to the apostles in the sacrificial meal. He willed that they continue what he did at the Last Supper following his command (Luke 22:19). The Church, from the apostolic era on, has continued to obey this command in every generation as expressed in the Roman Canon of the eucharistic liturgy.[21]

The new dimension that Jesus introduced transformed the way the apostles would celebrate the Passover after his death, resurrection, and ascension. The apostles probably followed the order of the Last Supper they had with Jesus in their celebration of the Passover later in life (1 Cor. 11:23ff.). They would go to the temple for their Jewish prayers and would gather in the homes on the first day of the week to celebrate the meal of "thanksgiving." For the early Christians, Jesus' blood was the source of the forgiveness of sins (Rom. 3:25; Eph. 2:13; 1 John 1:7).

The early followers of Jesus gathered on the first day of the week to pray and to "break bread" (Acts 20:7). This is because they understood the command of Jesus to reenact what he did at the Last Supper in memory of him. All these were based on their understanding of the passion, death, and resurrection of Jesus as a sacrificial offering. As Paul the apostle puts it, "If Christ has not been raised from the dead, then our preaching is without substance, and so is your faith" (1 Cor. 15:14). Hence, liturgically, the breaking of bread is a time for Christians to reunite, relive, and renew the Paschal Mystery with the risen Lord.[22] It is an occasion of joy and brotherhood (Acts 1:4; 2:42).

---

21. Congregation for Divine Worship, *The New Roman Missal* (Totowa, NJ: Catholic Publishing Corporation, 2011), 491: "On the day before he was to suffer, he took bread in his holy and venerable hands, and with eyes raised to heaven to you, O God, his almighty Father, giving you thanks, he said the blessing, broke the bread and gave it to his disciples, saying: TAKE THIS, ALL OF YOU, AND EAT IT, FOR THIS IS MY BODY, WHICH WILL BE GIVEN UP FOR YOU." The Roman Liturgy narrates that Jesus did the same with the cup of wine saying: "TAKE THIS, ALL OF YOU, AND DRINK FROM IT, FOR THIS IS THE CHALICE OF MY BLOOD, THE BLOOD OF THE NEW AND ETERNAL COVENANT, WHICH WILL BE POURED OUT FOR YOU AND FOR MANY FOR THE FORGIVENESS OF SINS. DO THIS IN MEMORY OF ME."

22. According to the *Didache*, the early Christians gathered on Sunday, which they called "the Day of the Lord." The Lord's Day is the day of the resurrection, the beginning of the new creation, which looks forward to the consummation of all things in Jesus. See Joseph Ratzinger, *The Spirit of the Liturgy* (San Francisco: Ignatius Press,

The *Didache,* acclaimed to be the "Teaching of the Apostles," instructs as follows:

> On the Lord's Day of the Lord [*sic*] gather together, break bread and give thanks after confessing your transgressions so that your sacrifice may be pure. Let no one who has a quarrel with his neighbor join you until he is reconciled, lest your sacrifice be defiled.[23]

The early Christians called their celebration "a breaking of bread and giving thanks," which has become the technical term for Eucharist. The above text teaches that the early Christians also called the Passover a sacrifice, since it was only for those in good relations with each other. The Eucharist becomes real food and drink that binds believers to God. It abides in humans and joins humans to one another and to the Mystical Body of Christ. John Paul II explains this union with Christ:

> The Eucharistic sacrifice is intrinsically directed to the inward union of the faithful with Christ through communion; we receive the very One who offered himself for us, we receive his body which he gave up for us on the cross and his blood which he "poured out for the forgiveness of sins" (Mt. 26:28). We are reminded of his words: "As the living Father sent me, and I live because of the Father, so he who eats me will live because of me" (Jn. 6:57). Jesus assures us that this union, which he compares to that of the life of the Trinity, is truly realized.[24]

In the eucharistic meal, "the Church draws her life from Christ in the Eucharist; by him she is fed and by him she is enlightened."[25]

In his letter to the Philadelphians, Ignatius of Antioch called the Eucharist "the Bread of God, which is the Flesh of Jesus Christ, who was of the seed of David; . . . His Blood, which is love incorruptible."[26] There was no doubt in the

---

2000), 97. Ratzinger argues, "This is the orientation the Fathers wanted to express by calling the Day of the Resurrection the "eight day." Sunday looks not only backward but forward. Looking toward the Resurrection means looking toward the final consummation. With the Day of the Resurrection coming after the Sabbath, Christ as it were strode across time and lifted it up above itself."

23. William A. Jurgens, *The Faith of the Early Fathers: A Source-Book of Theological and Historical Passages from the Christian Writings of Pre-Nicene and Nicene Eras* (Collegeville, MN: Liturgical Press, 1970), "Didache," 4.

24. John Paul II, *Ecclesia de Eucharistia: On the Eucharist in Its Relationship to the Church* (Washington, DC: United States Conference of Catholic Bishops, 2003), art. 16.

25. Ibid., art. 6.

26. Jurgens, *Faith of the Early Fathers,* 22, "Ignatius of Antioch: Letter to the Philadelphians," 54a.

mind of the early Christians that their celebrations were a participation in the Paschal Mystery of Christ of which the "breaking of bread" was at the core.

The most revealing form of the celebration of the Paschal Mystery in the early Church is from Justin the Martyr. In his *Apology*, Justin explains the rite of the Sunday liturgy, which believers celebrated on the "Day of the Sun." There is a lengthy reading of the memoirs of the apostles, followed by a homily by the presiding minister and prayers.

> [W]hen our prayer is ended, bread is brought forward along with wine and water, and the president likewise gives thanks to the best of his ability, and the people call out their assent, saying the *Amen*. Then there is the distribution to each and the participation in the Eucharistic elements.[27]

In 96 CE, Clement of Rome called this celebration the fulfillment of all the Old Testament sacrifices (*1 Clement* 40:41). For Clement, only the bishop should celebrate the Paschal Mystery (*1 Clement* 44:4). He saw the inseparable link between the sacrifice of Christ and the gifts of bread and wine on the altar.

The theology of the early Church regarding the Paschal Mystery is in line with Paul's First Letter to the Corinthians, where he teaches that the sacrificial meal unites believers with Christ and with one another (1 Cor. 10:17), and it is the meal that announces the Lord's death until he comes again in glory. The Book of Revelation sums up the early belief in Jesus' Paschal Mystery, as John sees a vision of the lamb that was sacrificed sitting on the throne, receiving adoration, praise and honor from every creature (Rev. 5:13; 7:17). This vision of the Book of Revelation identifies Jesus crucified as the one who sits on the throne in heaven. Therefore, from the earliest period of the Church, the disciples of Jesus saw in him the fulfillment of the Suffering Servant of Isaiah and the prophecies about the Messiah.[28]

---

27. Jurgens, *Faith of the Early Fathers*, 56, "Justin the Martyr: Second Apology."

28. See James Muilenburg and Henry Sloane Coffin, "Isaiah 40–66," in *The Interpreter's Bible*, ed. George Arthur Buttrick (Nashville: Abingdon, 1980), 419–773. Israel is the servant of Yahweh. "In her degradation and misery, little as she suspects it, the Lord is baring 'his holy arm before the eyes of all the nations.' In her agonizing experience of national destruction and captivity 'all the ends of the earth shall see the salvation of our God.' The fourth Servant Song is a poem on the Servant of Yahweh through whom salvation and redemption would come to the people of Israel and to all nations. The Servant is introduced in 52:13 as exalted. From 53:14–15, he becomes the despised servant who suffers so terribly that 'he seemed no longer human.' The Bible also shows that he was wounded and pierced for the sins of humans and 'by his sufferings shall my servant justify many, taking their faults on himself' (Isa. 53:11). The early disciples of Jesus saw in the fourth Servant Song a fulfillment of Jesus' passion, death and resurrection. In 1 Peter, it is stated, 'Christ suffered for you and left an example for you. . . . He had not done anything wrong, and there had been no perjury in his mouth. He was insulted and did not retaliate with insults; when he was tortured he made no threats but

## 3.4 The Eucharist

### *3.4.1 The Eucharist: A Passover Meal*

In his discourse with his disciples at the Last Supper, the Passover meal, Jesus spoke of his own departure. "Poised between heaven and earth and already in the ascent to glory, the Johannine Jesus speaks both as still in the world and as no longer in it."[29] Brown's argument in the above passage portrays the Church as passing over to the kingdom of God, which is her ultimate goal. Jesus' sacrificial meal with his apostles was a Passover that culminated on the cross for the liberation of the world.

> By celebrating the Last Supper with his apostles in the course of the Passover meal, Jesus gave the Jewish Passover its definitive meaning. Jesus' passing over to his Father by his death and Resurrection, the new Passover, is anticipated in the supper and celebrated in the Eucharist, which fulfills the Jewish Passover and anticipates the final Passover of the Church in the glory of the kingdom.[30]

By uniting his Last Supper to his crucifixion, Jesus demonstrated that the Passover meal of the Last Supper would be the same sacrifice as the one on Calvary. In that Passover meal with his apostles, Jesus tells a new exodus story, which would be retold among believers in Jesus just as the old story of the Passover and exodus were told among later generations of Israel. Within that Passover meal with his disciples, "the hour of the exodus is repeated, here the freedom achieved is celebrated."[31] There is an anticipation of the coming deliv-

---

he put his trust in the righteous judge. He was bearing our faults in his own body on the cross, so that we might die to our faults and live for holiness; through his wounds you have been healed' (1 Pet. 2:22–24)." This passage has a remarkable similarity to the fourth Servant Song. It shows that, soon after the Ascension of Jesus, his followers believed and preached him to be the fulfillment of the prophecies. Hence, they believed in Jesus as the New Manna, the Bread of Life, and the new Passover lamb.

29. Brown, *Introduction to the New Testament*, 352.

30. Congregation for the Doctrine of Faith, *Catechism of the Catholic Church*, 2nd ed. (Washington, DC: United States Conference of Catholic Bishops, 1997), #1340 (hencforth cited as CCC). See also CCC #1323: "At the last supper, on the night he was betrayed, our Savior instituted the Eucharistic Sacrifice of his Body and Blood. This he did in order to perpetuate the sacrifice of the cross throughout the ages until he should come again, and so to entrust to his beloved spouse, the Church, a memorial of his death and resurrection: a sacrament of love, a sign of unity, a bond of charity, a paschal banquet in which Christ is consumed, the mind is filled with grace, and a pledge of future glory is given to us."

31. Joachim Jeremias, *The Eucharistic Words of Jesus,* trans. Norman Perrin (New York: Charles Scribner's Sons, 1966), 205.

erance Jesus would bring to humans in the new Passover meal. It is a deliverance wrought not by the blood of animals but by his own blood.

> For the sake of the Passover blood God revoked the death sentence against Israel; he said: I will see the blood of the Passover lamb and make atonement for you. In the same way the people of God of the End time will be redeemed by the merits of the Passover blood.[32]

What Jesus began in the Upper Room came to a conclusion on the cross of Calvary. Brant Pitre, citing Matt. 26:27–30 and Mark 14:24–26, argues that Jesus did not conclude the Passover in the Upper Room.[33] For Pitre, Jesus knew exactly what he was doing as he concluded the Passover on the cross of Calvary when he drank the fourth cup. If Pitre's logic is accepted, which seems right, it therefore means that Jesus united the Last Supper and the cross into one act that came to completion on the cross when he said, "It is finished" (John 19:30).

> By refusing to drink of the fruit of the vine until he gave up his final breath, [Jesus] joined the offering of himself under the form of bread and wine to the offering of himself on Calvary. Both actions said the same thing: "This is my body, given for you" (Luke 22:19). Both were done "for the forgiveness of sins" (Matthew 26:28). Both were done "as a ransom for many" (Mark 10:45). In short, *by means of the Last Supper, Jesus transformed the Cross into a Passover, and by means of the Cross, he transformed the Last Supper into a sacrifice.*[34]

Jesus was able to say, "It is consummated," after he drank the fourth cup (in his own case it was the cup of suffering) that concluded the Jewish Passover meal. Therefore, Jesus concluded his Passover meal through his cross (which was a means to his glory), and the apostles understood it that way (after the resurrection) as they continued the celebration in obedience to the command of Jesus. Therefore, I summarize the early Christian teachings on Jesus as the new Passover lamb with the words of Joachim Jeremias:

---

32. Ibid., 226.

33. Brant Pitre, *Jesus and the Jewish Roots of the Eucharist: Unlocking the Secrets of the Last Supper* (New York: Doubleday, 2011), 145–70. Pitre uses the Talmud, the Mishnah, and other rabbinic literature to point out that the Jewish Passover at the time of Jesus involved, among other things, the ritual of drinking four cups of wine. In the two biblical passages cited above, Jesus only drank three cups with his disciples when he said, "I shall not drink of the fruit of the vine until I drink it new in my Father's kingdom" (Matt. 26:30; Mark 14:26). He proceeded to the garden of Gethsemane, where he prayed that the cup should pass him by. Pitre questions, "To which cup is Jesus referring to here? The fourth cup? That I presume!" Pitre's work influenced this section.

34. Ibid., 167 (italics original).

The theme of this early Christian Passover is: on Good Friday the great Passover festival has begun. Therefore to be a Christian means: to live in the Passover, in the deliverance from the bondage of sin. This theme is developed in the text as follows: the Passover lamb is interpreted as the symbol of the Messiah who was sacrificed as the unblemished lamb.[35]

### 3.4.2 Eucharist: A Banquet

The Passover meal celebrated by Jesus with his apostles is a foretaste of the eschatological banquet promised by God. Jesus is the fulfillment of the expectations of the Israelites, whereby the Lord will prepare a banquet of rich food and the choicest wine for all peoples (Isa. 25:6–9; 55:2). "When it was evening he came with the twelve" (Mark 14:17). This meal is not just like any other meal; it is special, a Passover.

> It is the Passover meal, the table celebration of the whole people of God, the high point of the year. The solemn setting, the reclining on couches, the festal wine, the paschal lamb, the liturgy of the feast, mark it as a meal of rejoicing.[36]

The Passover banquet is, therefore, a meal of rejoicing in the sense that it gathers those who have been redeemed. The story of salvation from the Old Testament to the New Testament is to be viewed in totality. It is one story of God acting in the whole, in the life of his people called together. Jesus began this "in-gathering" by inviting and eating with the lame, the poor, tax collectors, and sinners (see Matt. 9:11; Mark 2:16; Luke 5:30; 14:13). This idea of calling together evokes a gathering that began in the exodus, the "in-gathering" from the Diaspora of all the children of God scattered among the gentile nations. It is also a sign of the gathering of the new chosen people of God, which is the beginning of the messianic era as proclaimed by the prophet Ezekiel.

> According to the Messianic expectation, the divine promises directly addressed to Israel would reach fulfillment when God himself had gathered his people through his Chosen One as a shepherd gathers his flock: "I will save my flock, they shall no longer be a prey. . . . I will set up over them one shepherd, my servant David, and he shall feed them; he shall feed them and be their shepherd. And I, the Lord, shall be their God, and my servant David will be prince among them" (Ez 34:22–24).[37]

---

35. Jeremias, *Eucharistic Words of Jesus*, 60.
36. Ibid., 205.
37. Pope Benedict XVI, *Jesus, the Apostles and the Early Church*, General Audiences, 15th March 2006 – 14th February 2007 (San Francisco: Ignatius Press, 2007), 14.

Christ becomes this true shepherd and leader of the new people of God. He is the true shepherd "who lays down his life for his sheep" (John 10:11). He feeds his flock.

In John 6, Jesus assumed the position of the new Moses, the promised Messiah, as the dialogue that transpired between him and the Jews indicates: "Our Fathers ate manna in the desert. What sign will you give us?" This was said because the Jews believed that, when the Messiah comes, he will give them the food of life, the new manna. Raymond Brown, commenting on John 6, writes, "Jesus did not come simply to satisfy earthly hunger but to give a bread that would nourish people for eternal life."[38]

Jesus becomes the last Adam who is to gather the chosen people of God and lead them to the kingdom of heaven, where he will feed them with the bread of angels.[39] Eating and drinking connote communion sacrifice, in which the community participates in the life of God, and this is manifested in the liturgy of the Holy Eucharist.[40]

In the liturgy, God gathers all and feeds them with the Bread of Life, a foretaste of the eternal banquet.

With the Eucharist, we enter into another dimension of time not subject to our measurement, in which the future, illuminated by the past, is offered to us as the unchanging present. In this way, the mystery of Christ, Alpha and Omega, the *telos* and *arche,* becomes contemporaneous to each person in every age and time. Humans begin to live in the eternity of God. Time grows short (1 Cor. 7:29), we await the resurrection of the dead and even now live the life of heaven. "This mystery makes heaven of earth."[41]

In the Eucharist, the earth becomes a place where God lives among men. Therefore, the eucharistic sacrifice of the Church joins the whole world to the timelessness of God. It always looks forward to the *eschaton* as it proclaims the "Lord's death until he comes again" (1 Cor. 11:26).

---

38. Brown, *Introduction to the New Testament*, 346.

39. Ibid.: "He is the eschatological shepherd who gathers the lost sheep of the house of Israel and goes in search of them because he knows them (cf. Lk 15:4–7; Mt 18:12–14; cf. also the figure of the Good Shepherd in Jn 10:11ff). Through this 'gathering together,' the Kingdom of God is proclaimed to all peoples: 'I will set my glory among the nations; and all the nations shall see my judgment which I have executed, and my hand which I have laid on them' (Ez 39:21). And Jesus followed precisely this prophetic indication. His first step was to 'gather together' the people of Israel, so that all the people called to gather in communion with the Lord might see and believe."

40. The eating and drinking are a real participation in God's life. This is what sets Christianity apart from all other religions.

41. Congregation for Divine Worship, *Lineamenta: The Eucharist: Source and Summit of the Life and Mission of the Church* (Washington, DC: United States Conference of Catholic Bishops, 2004), art. 11.

The Church, as she participates in the priestly actions of Jesus in her liturgy, continues the sacrifice of Jesus. On this, the Second Vatican Council states:

> [T]aking part in the Eucharistic sacrifice, the source and summit of the Christian life, they [the faithful] offer the divine victim to God and themselves along with it. And so it is that, both in the offering and in Holy Communion, each in his own way, though not of course indiscriminately, has his own part to play in the liturgical action. Then, strengthened by the body of Christ in the Eucharistic communion, they manifest in a concrete way that unity of the People of God which this holy sacrament aptly signifies and admirably realizes. (LG 11)[42]

The unity of the Christian faithful originates from Christ, who unites all in his Mystical Body. The unity is realized in a more sublime manner through the celebration of the liturgy, whereby humans acknowledge the love of God in the Bread of the Eucharist, which "shows the face of God" (Exod. 25:23–24; Leviticus 24). The acknowledgment of God's work in thanksgiving involves the mediation of the priest for it to be liturgical. In such a liturgical act, God communicates life to the individual as the person offers thanks. There is an exchange of energy. The person becomes the one whom he or she receives. The spirit of Jesus transforms and unites the person in the Mystical Body of Christ. The fruit of that meal is therefore rightly called "Communion," *koinōnia,* with the Blessed Trinity. The end product becomes the "divinization" of humans.

> Union with Christ is also union with all those to whom he gives himself. I cannot possess Christ just for myself; I can belong to him only in union with all those who have become, or who will become, his own. Communion draws me out of myself towards him, and thus also towards unity with all Christians. We become "one body," completely joined in a single existence. Love of God and love of neighbor are now truly united: God incarnate draws us all to himself.[43]

In the Old Testament, God manifested his presence to his people through various means, but in a special way in the *kābôd* ("glory"). When he revealed his personal name to Moses, he said, "'I AM' has sent you. . . . This is my name for all time" (Exod. 3:14–15). Though I do not wish to go into the intricacies of the tetragrammaton YHWH, the name denotes "One who is,"

---

42. Second Vatican Council, *Lumen Gentium,* "Dogmatic Constitution on the Church," in *Vatican Council II: The Conciliar and Post Conciliar Documents,* ed. Austin Flannery (Northport, NY: Costello, 1996), art. 11.

43. Benedict XVI, *God Is Love* (Washington, DC: United States Conference of Catholic Bishops, 2005), art. 14.

"the Ever Present One." He is the Being that subsists. The "I AM" of God means "Being" as opposed to "becoming." He is the Being which abides and persists in all that passes away.[44] Thus, God is present among all peoples. In a most sublime manner, he manifests his glory in the "Bread of the Presence" (Exod. 25:23–24, 29–30; Leviticus 24), which was called *lehem happānîm,* "the Bread of the Face." This bread indicates his presence.

In the New Testament, God manifested his presence in his Son, who is the image of the invisible God (see Col. 1:15; Heb. 1:3). He lives in those who partake of his flesh and blood (John 6:56). He is in the eucharistic species as real food and drink, hence the eating and drinking. His real presence is a fundamental eucharistic reality without which the sacrificial meal would be nonsensical.[45] Unlike when Jesus used parables, he was direct and did not use metaphorical language on the issue of the Eucharist. Saint John Paul II, explaining the reality of the presence and its salvific effect in relation to the Paschal Mystery, has this to say:

> The Eucharistic sacrifice makes present not only the mystery of the Savior's passion and death, but also the mystery of the resurrection which crowned his sacrifice. It is as the living and risen One that Christ can become in the Eucharist, the "bread of life" (Jn. 6:35, 48), the "living bread" (Jn. 6:51).[46]

Christians gain blessings from the Lord whenever they participate in the Paschal Mystery, especially the Eucharist. Saint John Paul II wrote:

> The saving efficacy of the sacrifice is fully realized when the Lord's body and blood are received in Holy Communion. The Eucharistic Sacrifice is intrinsically directed to the inward union of the faithful with Christ through Holy Communion; we receive the very One who offered himself for us, we receive his body which he gave up for us on the Cross and his blood which he "poured out for many for the forgiveness of sin."[47]

---

44. Joseph Ratzinger, *Introduction to Christianity*, trans. J. R. Foster (San Francisco: Ignatius Press, 2004; German original, 1968), 129.

45. *Lineamenta*, art. 12. "Christ is present in the Eucharist, Body and Blood, soul and divinity, giving himself and his life to all. In the Old Testament, God sent those who would point out his presence: in the cloud (*shekhina*), in the tent, in the temple. In the New Testament, in the fullness of time, he comes to live among humanity as Word-Made-Flesh (cf. Jn.1:14), becoming Emmanuel indeed."

46. John Paul II, *Ecclesia de Eucharistia,* art. 14.

47. Ibid., art 16.

### 3.4.3 Eucharist: Sacrifice of Reparation

By the words of Jesus at the Passover meal, "This is my body" and "this is my blood" (see Luke 22:19–21; Matt. 26:28ff.), he spoke of himself as the new lamb, the eschatological paschal lamb. "By comparing himself with the eschatological paschal lamb, Jesus describes his death as a *saving death*."[48] Jesus also used the language of sacrifice when he said his blood would be poured out "for you and for many" (Mark 14:24). This links his life, death, and resurrection to the sacrifice of reparation of the Suffering Servant (Isa. 53:12).

The apostles of Jesus preached the death and resurrection of Jesus as God's manifestation of his love for Jesus, who died for human sins and was raised for the justification of humans (1 Cor. 15:3; Rom. 4:25). Any first-century Jew who read 1 Peter on the suffering of Jesus would have understood that Peter was comparing Jesus to the Suffering Servant in Isaiah, who would bear the sins of many (Isa. 53:10). Hans Urs von Balthasar, commenting on both Isaiah and 1 Pet. 1:19, states that what was introduced in Isaiah as sacrificial through the blood of the "servant" emerges in 1 Peter as the most precious gift of God for many.[49] For Peter, then, believers are not redeemed with corruptible things such as silver and gold but with the precious blood of Jesus, a lamb unspotted and undefiled (1 Pet. 1:19). Jesus died for the forgiveness of sins, therefore making his death a sacrifice of reparation.

The teaching of the apostles on the Eucharist as a sacrifice of reparation was upheld by the Apostolic Fathers. Clement of Rome, in his first letter to the Church in Corinth, states:

> Let us fix our eyes on the blood of Christ and let us realize how precious it is to the Father, since it was poured out for salvation and brought the grace of repentance to the whole world. Let us go through all generations and observe that from one generation to another. . . .[50]

In the same line of thought, Ignatius of Antioch called the Eucharist "the medicine of immortality."[51] It is a medicine of immortality because the death of

---

48. Jeremias, *Eucharistic Words of Jesus,* 225.

49. Hans Urs von Balthasar, *Mysterium Paschale: The Mystery of Easter* (Edinburgh: T&T Clark, 1990), 98: "But if, in Isaiah 53, instead of an animal led to the abattoir there steps forth a representative man who shed his blood for our transgressions and 'poured out his soul to death' (Is 53,12c), and if this blood, belonging as it does to God, has such value in God's sight that 'it justifies many,' then the idea is already emerging that the 'precious blood' (1 Peter 1,19), reserved for God yet used by him for the good of many, might one day be made over to men as his most precious gift."

50. Cyril C. Richardson, ed. and trans., *Early Christian Fathers* (Philadelphia: Westminster, 1953), 47.

51. Ibid., 78.

Jesus gives life to believers. The act of reparation was effected through the perfect obedience of Jesus to God the Father. Jesus, as man, surrendered his will to his Father and it is in this surrendering that he bore the sins of the world (John 1:29), being "made sin for the sinful" (2 Cor. 5:21), becoming "a curse" (Gal. 3:13), and by being totally disposed to the will of God his Father. Hence, "by his wounds we are healed" (Isa. 53:11). He gave "himself up in our place as a fragrant offering and a service to God" (Eph. 5:2). This "giving up" is for reparation for humans. Paul states it in the most exquisite manner as follows: "He has . . . cancelled every record of the debt that we had to pay; he has done away with it by nailing it to the cross; and so he got rid of Sovereignties and the Powers, and paraded them in public, behind him in his triumphal procession" (Col. 2:14–15). In the ancient world, a triumphal procession was a way of displaying the victory of a king or a general over his enemies. Hence, for Paul, through the Paschal Mystery, Jesus conquered his enemies, paraded them openly for all to see, and set humans free. He accomplished this in the most unimaginable manner through the cross. Little wonder, then, that Hans Urs von Balthasar, reflecting on the Paschal Mystery, calls it a "theodrama":

> What is at stake in the theodrama is this: that God acts so as to take upon himself and make his own the tragedy of human existence even to the depths of that abyss, and thus conquering it without at the same time robbing it of its sting or going around the tragedy externally, overtaking it by avoiding it. [52]

The phrase "to take upon himself and make his own the tragedy of human existence even to the abyss" points to Jesus' identity with humans and to his sacrifice. Jesus really undertook the state of suffering humanity and really and truly died. From the Paschal Mystery, the Church was born. "For this very reason the Eucharist, which is in an outstanding way the sacrament of the Paschal Mystery, stands at the center of the Church's life,"[53] which is why the Church continues to celebrate it.

> Each Eucharistic sacrifice is a renewal and a re-enactment of the paschal mystery, that is, the death and resurrection of the Lord Jesus Christ, bread broken for the life of the world and blood poured out for the redemption of humanity and the liberation of the cosmos.[54]

---

52. Cited in Edward T. Oakes, S.J., *Pattern of Redemption: The Theology of Hans Urs von Balthasar* (New York: Continuum, 1994), 238.

53. John Paul II, *Ecclesia de Eucharistia*, art. 3.

54. John Paul II, *Instrumentum Laboris: Encounter with the Living Christ: The Way to Conversion, Communion and Solidarity in America* (Washington, DC: United States Conference of Catholic Bishops, 2007), art. 35. Pope Paul VI, in his Encyclical *Mysterium Fidei*, recalls thus: "Just as Moses with the blood of calves had sanctified

The Second Vatican Council proclaimed, "The deepest truth about God and the salvation of man shines forth in Christ, who is at the same time the mediator and the fullness of all revelation" (*Dei Verbum* 2). Alexander Schmemann, commenting on 1 Cor. 11:18 ("when you assemble as a church . . ."), notes that this is a gathering to reveal a person to oneself, to each other, and God to all, and it "is Eucharistic—its end and fulfillment lies in its being the setting wherein the Lord's supper is accomplished, wherein the Eucharistic 'breaking of bread' takes place."[55] The breaking of bread is to reenact the Paschal Mystery of Jesus in his Church, which is the source of life to believers. The life, death, and resurrection of Jesus therefore become a mystery of transformations because it transforms violence into love, and death into life.

The Apostolic Post-Synodal Document *Sacramentum Caritatis* teaches that Jesus accomplished his saving mission in the Paschal Mystery by sacrificing himself. The document states:

> On the Cross from which he draws all people to himself (Jn. 12:32) . . . in the mystery of Christ's obedience unto death, even death on a cross (Phil. 2:8), the new and eternal covenant was brought about. In his crucified flesh, God's freedom and our human freedom met definitively in an inviolable, eternally valid pact. Human sin was also redeemed once for all by God's Son. . . . In the Paschal Mystery, our deliverance from evil and death has taken place. In the institution of the Eucharist, Jesus had spoken the "new and eternal covenant" in the shedding of his blood (cf. Mt. 26:28; Mk. 14:24; Lk. 22:20).[56]

By drawing all peoples to himself, he begins the eschatological gathering where all who believe in him will be saved through the merits of his Paschal Mystery. Therefore, peoples, cultures, and nations are invited to accept the new priesthood with its sacrifice. It has replaced the old sacrifice of nations as the one sacrifice that is able to truly save.

---

the Old Testament, so also Christ Our Lord, through the institution of the Mystery of the Eucharist, with His own Blood sanctified the New Testament, whose Mediator He is. For, as the Evangelists narrate, at the Last Supper 'He took bread, and blessed and broke it, and gave it to them, saying: "This is My Body, given for you; do this for a commemoration of Me." And so with the cup, when supper was ended. "This cup," he said, "is the New Testament, in My Blood which is to be shed for you"' (Lk. 22:19–20)" (no. 28).

55. Alexander Schmemann, *The Eucharist: Sacrament of the Kingdom*, trans. Paul Kachur (Crestwood, NY: St. Vladimir's Seminary Press, 2003), 11.

56. Benedict XVI, *Sacramentum Caritatis: The Sacrament of Charity; On the Eucharist as the Source and Summit of the Church's Life and Mission* (Washington, DC: United States Conference of Catholic Bishops, 2007), art. 9.

### 3.5 Effects of the Paschal Mystery

#### 3.5.1 *Cosmic Redemption*

The Book of Genesis teaches that, with the fall of Adam, the earth was cursed. "Accursed be the soil because of you! Painfully will you get your food from it as long as you live. It will yield bramble and thistles" (Gen. 3:17). What followed was the banishment of Adam and Eve from the Garden of Eden and the killing of Abel by his brother Cain, which prompted God to banish Cain from the earth, which opened its mouth to receive the blood of Abel (Gen. 4:11–12). Then came the deluge, which wiped out all flesh except Noah and his family because wickedness was great on the earth and human thoughts fashioned nothing but evil all day long (see Gen. 6:6). The shedding of innocent blood continued to desecrate the earth. Very detestable in the Old Testament are the killing of Naboth (1 Kgs. 21:8–16) and the killing of Zechariah in the temple (2 Chr. 24:20–22). In the reign of Manasseh, king of Judah (687–642 BCE), blood flowed like water in Jerusalem. The world was inundated with sin and evil, which were exemplified in the infidelity of Israel. Therefore, the whole creation was in need of redemption and was groaning in labor pains waiting for redemption (Rom. 8:22). The long wait for redemption came to a stop by the coming of Jesus. By the incarnation of Christ, God stepped into human history. The incarnation is the καίρος (time) in history that ushers in the fulfillment of the prophecies of redemption and salvation. The Paschal Mystery becomes the culminating point in the step directly taken by God to re-create and restore the universe. It is the first sign and the beginning of the restoration of humanity by God. The Incarnation is the mercy of God made visible to the world. It is what binds God to humans.

> To believe in the Incarnation means to be bound to Christianity's origins, their particularity, and, in human terms, their contingency. Here is the guarantee that we are not chasing myths; that God really has acted in our history and taken our time into his hands. Only over the bridge of this "once for all" can we come into the "forever" of God's mercy.[57]

The Paschal Mystery of Christ is an event that happened "once and for all," but, at the same time, it was the decisive moment of mercy that continued in an eminent way the redemption of the cosmos. It was the beginning of transformations and renewal, for wherever/whatever the Lord touches, some changes occur. Jesus opens a new relationship with God and humans through his Paschal Mystery by giving humans to God. He redeems creation from the sin of Adam through his cross. "The arms, to left and to right, put to flight the enemy

---

57. Ratzinger, *Spirit of the Liturgy*, 104.

forces of chaos and re-gather the cosmos, while the lower part of the Cross, grounded in the depths, then, has cosmic dimensions."[58]

### 3.5.2 Forgiveness of Sin

At the Annunciation, the angel gave the name "Jesus" to the child to be born of Mary "because he will save his people from their sins" (Matt. 1:21). From the beginning of his earthly life, Jesus was portrayed as the savior. As Jesus began his public ministry, he frequently forgave sins: "My child, your sins are forgiven" (Mark 2:5). He also forgave the sins of the woman caught in adultery (John 8:1–11), and the woman considered a public sinner (Luke 7:48). The Pharisees and scribes questioned his authority to forgive sins (Luke 5:21). At the Last Supper with his disciples, Jesus referred to the cup of wine as his blood which will be shed for the forgiveness of sins (Matt. 26:28; Acts 13:38; Heb. 9:22). His death on the cross was the final moment, when he poured out his blood for the forgiveness of sins, making peace between God and humans (Col. 1:20).

Through these restorative acts of forgiveness, Jesus was giving life back to those who were dead in sin. "Just as all men die in Adam, so all are made righteous in Christ" (1 Cor. 15:22). He exercised his priestly functions through the Paschal Mystery and continues to do it through and in the Church. The Church thus becomes the Mystical Body of Christ on earth, which carries on the reconciliatory work of Christ, especially through the sacraments. Every celebration of the sacrament of the Eucharist is a participation and reenactment of an aspect of the Paschal Mystery.

In the Old Testament, the blood of animals was used for the forgiveness of sin (Lev. 4:20–26); in the new order of grace, humans gain forgiveness of sins through the blood of Christ (Eph. 1:7). Through the merits of the Paschal Mystery, humans can approach God. Those who are redeemed by Christ are in a unique relationship with God because their "sins are forgiven through his name" (1 John 2:12). They are invited to acknowledge humbly their weaknesses and to lean on the strength of Christ, through whom mercy, peace, and joy are bestowed on the world. Peace is restored through Jesus' death on the cross. Those who are forgiven constitute "a priestly people, a holy people, a royal nation and a people set apart to sing the praises of God" (1 Pet. 2:9).

### 3.5.3 New People of God

According to the recapitulation theology of Paul and according to the New Testament writers, God has made Jesus the head of all humanity through his Paschal Mystery (Col. 1:18; Eph. 1:22). God has fulfilled the promise of raising a faithful shepherd in Jesus, "the good shepherd" (John 10:11). Jesus is the

---

58. Von Balthasar, *Mysterium Paschale,* 58.

new shepherd who gathers the lost sheep of Israel. "We all had gone astray like sheep, each taking his own way, and Yahweh brought the acts of rebellion of all of us to bear on him" (Isa. 53:6). The prophet Ezekiel also takes up this theme to show how the shepherds failed in their responsibility of taking care of God's people and the promise by God to raise a true shepherd who would gather and unite all his people (Ezek. 34:23–24). The forming of the new people of God through the Paschal Mystery would become the channel through which the promises of old would be fulfilled and the grace of redemption and the restoration of the universe actualized. The choice of the Twelve is very significant, as it reflects the twelve tribes of Israel.[59] The Twelve had a specific mission, namely, to gather the lost sheep of the house of Israel (Matt. 10:5–6) and, later, to become witnesses of Jesus not only in Jerusalem but to the ends of the earth (Acts 1:8).

The new people of God are to be gathered in a new promised land of the already and the not yet. The already because this new people have a new high priest who leads them as the assembly of God in worship. It is worth noting that Adam was placed in the garden (Eden) by God (Gen. 2:8). He lost the privilege of living in God's presence through the tree of disobedience (Gen. 3:23–24). Jesus began the new creation in the garden (Gethsemane) so that the place of human's disobedience (the garden) would be the place of redemption. He completed his restoration on the tree of the cross, which has become the noble tree, the tree of life. In the new people, the Church becomes the first beneficiary through the Spirit given to her by Jesus.

> The first beneficiary of salvation is the Church. Christ won the Church for himself at the price of his own blood and made the Church his co-worker in the salvation of the world. Indeed, Christ dwells within the Church. She is his Bride. It is he who causes her to grow. He carries out his mission through her.[60]

---

59. Benedict XVI, *Jesus, the Apostles and the Early Church*, 9: "The number twelve, which evidently refers to the twelve tribes of Israel, already reveals the meaning of the prophetic-symbolic action implicit in the new initiative to re-establish the holy people. As the system of the twelve had long faded out, the hope of Israel awaited their restoration as a sign of the eschatological time (as referred to at the end of the Book of Ezekiel: 37:15–19; 39:23–29; 40–48). In choosing the Twelve, introducing them into a communion of life with himself and involving them in his mission of proclaiming the Kingdom in words and works (cf. Mk 6:7–13; Mt 10:5–8; Lk 9:1–6; 6:13), Jesus wants to say that the definitive time has arrived in which to constitute the new people of God, the people of the twelve tribes, which now becomes a universal people, his Church."

60. John Paul II, *Redemptoris Missio: On the Permanent Validity of the Church's Missionary Mandate* (Washington, DC: United States Conference of Catholic Bishops, 1990), no. 9. See also Karl Rahner, *The Church and the Sacraments* (New York: Herder & Herder, 1964), 15. Rahner notes, "But now in the Word of God, God's last word is uttered into the visible public history of mankind, a word of grace, reconciliation and

The liturgy becomes "a rehearsal, a prelude for the life to come, for eternal life."[61]

### 3.5.4 Adopted Sons and Daughters of God

Through the Paschal Mystery of Christ, believers become adopted sons and daughters of God. The believer is "born from above" (John 3:5). "All who were baptized are baptized into his death" (Rom. 6:3; Gal. 3:27). They become one in Christ as children of God. "There is no longer Jew or Greek, there is no longer slave or free, there is no longer male and female; for all of you are one in Christ Jesus" (Gal. 3:28). The believer becomes united to Christ and is initiated into the life of the Trinity through the power of the Holy Spirit.

The Council Fathers declared that "the Spirit dwells in the Church and in the hearts of the faithful, as in a temple. . . . In them he prays and bears witness to their adopted sonship" (*Lumen Gentium* 4). Believers acknowledge the "love the Father has lavished upon us by letting us be called His children" (1 John 3:1). They gather as a community to celebrate this memorial sacrifice as sons and daughters of God. Having united all in the Trinitarian life of God, the Church is seen as a people in the unity of the Father, the Son, and the Holy Spirit. Being children of the same father, all humanity can then call God with one voice "Father."

> The "*Our* Father" form of address is intended for the disciples, who say "we" as they pray as a community; it expresses the fact that those who belong to Jesus participate in Jesus' relationship to God through their community prayer, without blurring the difference between their respective modes of relationship to God. In the words of Jesus, this filial relationship shines through, ever-present, ever-creative.[62]

### 3.5.5 Pledge of Salvation

Through the merits of the Paschal Mystery, humans can attain salvation. If the blood of the Passover lamb could protect the household from the slaying angel (Exod. 12:13), how much more would the blood of Jesus do? Jesus leads creation in a new exodus from sin to a new life of grace, which will ultimately be brought to completion in the kingdom of heaven. The Paschal meal is, there-

---

eternal life: Jesus Christ. The grace of God no longer comes (when it does come) steeply down from on high, from a God absolutely transcending the world, and in a manner that is without history, purely episodic; it is permanently in the world in tangible historical form, established in the flesh of Christ as a part of the world, of humanity and of its very history."

61. Ratzinger, *Spirit of the Liturgy*, 14.

62. Joseph Ratzinger, *Behold the Pierced One* (San Francisco: Ignatius Press, 1986), 21.

fore, a sacrament of salvation because he who "eats this bread will live forever" (John 6:51). The Eucharist also bears the presence of the one it represents.

> Jesus gave this act of oblation an enduring presence through the institution of the Eucharist at the Last Supper. He anticipated his death and resurrection by giving his disciples, in the bread and wine, his very self, his body and blood as the new manna (cf. Jn. 6:31–33). The ancient world had dimly perceived that man's real food—what truly nourishes him as man—is ultimately the Logos, eternal wisdom: this same Logos now becomes food for us.[63]

### 3.6 Summary

This chapter studied the progression of the Passover from the Old Testament to the New Testament and how Jesus, the new priest, celebrated it with his disciples during his life and transformed the celebration into the mystery of his life, death, and resurrection. The apostles in turn continued this celebration as the source of liberation and salvation. The Passover was seen not just as a meal but also as a banquet and a sacrifice of reparation. Through the Passover of Jesus, God grants his forgiveness and love to believers and the world. Paul and the early Church use sacrificial and priestly language to describe the Paschal Mystery, thereby making the case for the new sacrifice and priesthood of Jesus.

Christians acknowledge and open up to the Spirit of God at the celebration of the Paschal Mystery in the liturgy so that oneness is achieved with God. Therefore, one who lives fully in the mystery of Christ, accomplished in a special manner in the liturgy of the Eucharist, which is a celebration of the Paschal Mystery, has hope of eternal life with God.

> The celebration becomes a constant synergy between him and us. That is why at the heart of each movement making up the Eucharistic liturgy we join him in a kind of two-step rhythm: the awakening of our faith and the faith event. The Spirit opens our eyes so that we may recognize the Lord; he gathers up our hearts so that they may receive the Word; he intensifies our hunger so that we may be filled with the Bread of Life; he makes us die to ourselves so that we may rise with Christ; he becomes our joy so that we may become the Father's joy; he breathes through us so that we may give life to our brothers and sisters.[64]

Eternal life, which the Igbos, like all peoples seek, comes through the Passover of Jesus. In the next chapter, I shall study how the Igbos, in their tradi-

---

63. Benedict XVI, *God Is Love*, art. 13.
64. Jean Corbon, *The Wellspring of Worship*, trans. Matthew J. O'Connell (San Francisco: Ignatius Press, 2005), 147.

tional beliefs, tried to resolve the issue of life through their priesthood and sacrifice. The next chapter will also show the need for a true shift based on the traditional belief of the Igbos as a way to guarantee effective Christianity. This is because the apostles and believers in Jesus came through the Passover with Jesus and emerged with a restructuring of their mode of worship based on the teachings of Jesus.

CHAPTER FOUR

# PRIESTHOOD AND SACRIFICE AMONG THE IGBOS

In the first chapter, I dealt with the history and development of priesthood in Israel. I also discussed how sacrifice was performed in Israel and examined those who presided over the rituals. This chapter deals with the priesthood and sacrificial rituals of the Igbo people. It will first give a brief explanation and analysis of the Igbo worldview for a better understanding of their priesthood and sacrificial system.

## 4.1 Igbos

### 4.1.1 Identity and Location of the Igbos

Igbo is one of the tribes of Nigeria, a country in West Africa. It is located in the southeastern part of Nigeria. Its territory lies "between latitude 5 to 7 degrees north and longitude 6 to 8 degrees east, occupying an area about 15,800 square miles."[1] The word "Igbo" defines the tribe, the language, and the territory. They speak a common language with dialectical variations that linguists believe originated from the *kwa* language group of the Niger-Congo.[2]

### 4.1.2 Igbo Worldview

Priesthood and sacrifice among the Igbos would be better appreciated and understood if one studies them in the context of the Igbo worldview. This is because the Igbo priesthood and sacrificial systems are not isolated events but are linked with the whole Igbo societal and religious structure in the Igbo tradition. Igbo religion permeates all aspects of the culture and life of the Igbos.[3]

---

1. Victor C. Uchendu, *The Igbos of Southeast Nigeria* (New York: Holt, Rinehart & Winston, 1965), 1.

2. Joseph H. Greenberg, *The Languages of Africa*, 3rd ed. (Bloomington: Indiana University Press, 1970), 6–41.

3. Rems N. Umeasiegbu, *Words Are Sweet: Igbo Stories and Storytelling* (Leiden: Brill, 1982), 3. For Umeasiegbu, "Religion permeates all aspects of life ranging from

Anthony N. O. Ekwunife offers an extensive definition of Igbo traditional religion as follows:

> Igbo traditional religion means those living institutionalized religious beliefs and practices which are rooted in the past Igbo religious culture; a religion that was transmitted to the present overt and covert votaries by successive Igbo forebears mainly through oral traditions (myths, folklores, songs and dances, liturgies, rituals, proverbs, pithy sayings and names), sacred institutions like sacred specialists and persons, initiation rites, festivals, sacred spaces and objects and religious works of art; a religion which is slowly but constantly updated by each generation in the light of new religious experiences through the dialectical process of continuities and discontinuities.[4]

It is along this line that this study focuses on priesthood and sacrifice in the Igbo religion.

The Igbos have a strong sense of the sacred. They are a people of rites, rituals, and cultic activities. The origin of cult in Igbo society is as a result of the religious organization and priestly duties. With so many priests and elders guarding the society and championing the cultural and social activities, cult becomes a daily affair of the Igbos, though at various levels, as circumstances demand. The priest and the community live in a cultic environment, and both are very conscious of that.

The Igbo idea of the community and the world as a cultic/sacred space was one of the elements that enabled the missionaries to penetrate into the life of the Igbos, though not without some resistance.[5] To think of the Igbos is to think of rituals and, consequently, priests. Their culture is very important to them.[6]

---

such major activities as procreation to minor ones such as storytelling." See also Ikenga Metuh, *African Religion in Western Conceptual Schemes: The Problem of Interpretation* (Jos, Nigeria: Imico Press, 1991), 167. Metuh maintains that in the Igbo worldview, "[t]he religious and the secular thus shade into each other."

4. Anthony N. O. Ekwunife, *Consecration in Igbo Traditional Religion* (Onitsha, Nigeria: Jet Publishers, 1990), 1.

5. Ogbu Kalu, *The Embattled Gods: The Christianization of Igboland, 1841–1991* (Trenton, NJ: Africa World Press, 2003), 21. Kalu, citing H. H. Dobinson, one of the early Anglican missionaries, noted that the Igbos then regarded the mission premises "as absolutely sacred ground, unto which they are on no pretext to enter. We hope to be able to break down this absurd idea." The missionaries called it an "absurd idea" because the Igbos had so much respect for the sacred that they found it difficult to approach. At the early stage of Christianity/evangelization, this caused them to withdraw from the missions so as not to defile or encroach into the realm of the sacred unworthily.

6. John L. McKenzie, *A Theology of the Old Testament* (Garden City, NY: Image Books, 1974), 39. McKenzie holds the same opinion about humans as a whole. He wrote,

Examples of cultural expressions include the reception of a guest, the presentation of the symbol of welcome (kola nut), the breaking of the same kola nut, their invocation of blessings and sending forth of family members to a distant land or for studies, comportment and composure before the elders, marriage, naming and burial ceremonies. These cultural expressions have their respective rituals accompanying them. By maintaining a cultic society, the Igbos still remember and keep retelling the story of the past and consequently make it present.

The cultic life of the Igbos means that they maintain a strong sense of the sacred place and are therefore in constant contact with the deity.[7] The rituals accompanying the cults are known to the priests and are observed by them faithfully and in great detail. The Igbos gladly perform these rituals because they believe that humans can court the relationship of the deities only through cultic activities, such as rituals and sacrifices, through which they hope to attract the blessings of the deity.[8]

The Igbos believe in the tradition handed down to them from their fathers. These traditions play a prominent role mostly when they are faced with mysteries or questions that defy easy answers. Hence the saying: "that is how our fathers did it." The Igbo worldview is therefore not different from that which their fathers held. The material world is linked to the spiritual, and therefore any destabilization of society through abominations or crime is to be utterly avoided, as this would interfere with the spiritual realm.[9] Interference with the spiritual realm causes the world to suffer the consequences of that misdeed. The Igbos strive to maintain a balance between the spiritual world and the

---

"The whole human life and experience is the object of cult. By ritual symbolism man symbolized his encounter with the deity in the whole of human life and experience."

7. Arnold Angenendt, "Holiness of the Person—Holiness of Space," *Studia Liturgica: An International Ecumenical Review for Liturgical Research and Renewal* 38: (2008): 53. Angenendt supports this idea of a person standing in the holy place thus: "Whoever stands outside the holy place, outside the boundary, cannot enter into contact with the gods or God, because heaven is not open there."

8. Millgram, *Jewish Worship*, 43. Millgram contends that primitive man saw his world as filled with the gods and so he needed to "feed" them for his own benefits. Millgram writes, "The gods were like men and women, but usually immortal. They possessed human frailties such as hunger, envy, and ambition. They loved and hated, fought and took vengeance, very much like human beings. . . . He [man] naturally tried to win the favor of the gods by offering sacrifices at the holy places in accordance with the hallowed procedures best known to the priests."

9. Kalu, *Embattled Gods*, 33. Kalu supports this idea by holding that "[i]n the encounter with the environment, the Igbo people have covenanted with over a thousand spiritual beings or gods. Some operate in the air or as water spirits, earth deities, guardians of professions, spirits in natural objects. Many are unbounded spiritual forces, which can be tapped to enhance or hinder the vital force of life; others serve as oracles and many as ancestral spirits." Their world is filled with spirits and deities.

material world, and they sometimes try to preempt events in the world through divination.[10] Igbos believe that the universe is full of spirits, good and bad; the invisible world contains the pure spirits (*mmuo*), and the visible world contains humans and the spirits of the dead (*Ndi mmuo*). "There is the world of man peopled by all created beings and things, both animate and inanimate. The spirit world is the abode of the creator, the deities, the disembodied and malignant spirits, and the ancestral spirits."[11]

The Igbos relate to God because of their belief in creation by *Chukwu*, God. *Chukwu* (God) gave man a *chi* (destiny) to guide each human. The *chi* is a divine spark that is distinct in each person and determines the destiny of each individual. Each person has his or her *chi,* and the *chi* is one of the means through which that person communes with *Chi-ukwu,* literally, the Great God. The *chi* is believed to be a gift of *Chukwu.* This divine spark constitutes the dignity of the human person, and the dignity corresponds to the fact that God created man and made him unique in creation by his *chi.*[12] Igbos believe that, once *chi* is allotted to an individual at birth, it remains a unique part of that person throughout his life. The *chi* directs the individual to keep *Nso-ala* (the sacred prohibitions of the land) and to avoid taboos. At any turn of event, an Igbo would exclaim *Chi m o!* (invoking his God/guardian spirit) to show surprises. The idea of a personal *chi* helps to fashion the notion of religion and the way the Igbos interact with forces in the universe.[13] This idea governs the belief

---

10. Uchendu, *Igbo of Southeast Nigeria*, 13. Uchendu supports this idea by stating that "the Igbo believe that these social calamities and cosmic forces which disturb their world are controllable and should be 'manipulated' by them for their own purpose. The maintenance of social and cosmological balance in the world becomes, therefore, a dominant and pervasive theme in Igbo life. They achieve this balance, for instance, through divination, sacrifice, appeal to the countervailing powers of their ancestors (who are their invisible father-figures) against the powers of the malignant, and non-ancestral spirits, and, socially, through constant realignment in their social groupings."

11. Ibid., 11.

12. John F. Thornton and Susan B. Varenne, *The Essential Pope Benedict XVI: His Central Writings and Speeches* (San Francisco: HarperCollins, 2007), 381. The essential point of departure is and remains the biblical vision of man, formulated in an exemplary way in the accounts of creation. The Bible defines the human being in his essence (which precedes all history and is never lost in history) with two distinctive features: man is created in the image and likeness of God (Gen. 1:26). The second account of creation expresses the same idea, saying that man, taken from the dust of the earth carries in himself the divine breath of life. Man is characterized by an immediacy with God that is proper to his being; man is *capax Dei,* and because he lives under the protection of God, he is "sacred."

13. Chibueze Udeani, *Inculturation as Dialogue: Igbo Culture and the Message of Christ,* Intercultural Theology and Study of Religions 2 (Amsterdam: Rodopi, 2007), 33. Udeani attests to this idea too by writing as follows: "Seen from the standpoint of his origin and final destiny, man is best understood in relationship to Chukwu, God,

in destiny in the Igbo religious and cultural life. What a person receives in life is allotted by God, but the individual is guided by his *chi* toward its realization. The individual does not have a priori knowledge of his destiny and, therefore, must work hard to achieve success. Hard work and belief are the basic characteristics of the Igbos because one can lose one's good fortune through laziness. Hence, the Igbo says, *"Onye kwe chi ya ekwe"* (If one acts, his *chi* supports him), but the deity is not obliged to respond positively.[14]

Igbos believe that their God, *Chukwu,* is the Lord of the sky, while *Ala* is the earth deity. This has led to some misconceptions on the issue of Igbo beliefs to the point that some imagine that the Igbos are dualists. Raymond Arazu, citing his oral interview with a traditionalist who was illiterate at the time, suggests this. The traditionalists insisted that *Chukwu* (the great Being) and Ana (the earth-goddess) are two supreme beings and must be invoked together. This is because humans rest on *Ana (ala)* and it gives them support, while *Chukwu* sends the rain from the sky and shields humans from the elements. If *Chukwu* lets go, the sky would fall on humans. Therefore, humans must hold on to the worship of *Igwe* (here with the meaning "sky") and *Ala*. Arazu explains:

> At this stage in the interview my missionary conscience got over my interest in Traditional Religion and I made an attempt to intimidate the old man to get off this dualism in the Supreme Being. I suggested to him that Chukwu and Ana (*sic*) could be one individual entity. He refused bluntly to my chagrin: "It is just what our ancestors invoked that we in our turn must invoke. We must not do a misinvocation."[15]

This theory is being challenged by some traditionalists, while W. R. C. Horton holds to the theory of a trinity. He writes:

> When invoking the Supreme Being, the people of *Ibagwa* frequently allude to the trinity Chukwu, Chi, and Okuke with the phrase Eze

---

and his creator. Man comes from God. He has a definite mission to fulfill in God's plan. Ontologically, man is a force in the universe full of forces."

14. Udeani (*Inculturation as Dialogue,* 37) argues in support of this proposition as follows: "They [Igbos] acknowledge the fact that resourcefulness may not always be rewarded. In one of the Igbo proverbs, it is said, 'Omelu ma chi ekweghi, onye-uta atakwana ya'—One who has tried, but Chi (destiny) did not consent, should not be blamed. The Igbo people try to emphasise the fact that human beings have chances of self-actualisation within the realms of human finite freedom. The human being must do something in order to receive the favours of the gods. But on the other hand, it dare not be understood as meaning that the gods are obliged to reciprocate."

15. Raymond Arazu, *Our Religion, Past and Present* (Awka, Nigeria: Martin-King Press, 2005), 115-16.

Citoke—Lord, chi, Creator. This trinity emphasizes at once the remote and the near aspects of the Ibo concept of God.[16]

Dualism, however, has no place among the Igbos; neither is the trinitarian idea meaningful to them. Horton, writing about the trinity and life in Igbo religion, approached the Igbo concept of God from a Western and Christian ideology. *Chukwu* is the Supreme Being who is the Lord of everything. That is indisputable among the Igbos. Chukwu, however, has delegated the earth-goddess *Ala* to take charge of the earth. *Ala* is therefore a subject of Chukwu, though she seems to be the most widely revered and spoken of, probably because of her perceived nearness to humans. The Igbos are therefore monotheists, and Equiano,[17] in his autobiography, notes as follows:

The natives believe that there is one Creator of all things, and that he lives in the sun, and is girded round with belt, that he may never eat or drink; but, according to some, he smokes a pipe, which is our own favourite luxury. They believe he governs events, especially our deaths or captivity.[18]

From Equiano's understanding in those early years and what is still practiced among the Igbos, Chukwu is the only God. However, Chukwu does not, as he noted, smoke, but because the clouds look like smoke, and with the people not very literate at the time, the Igbos then thought it was Chukwu's method of exhaling. Other spirits are lesser deities that operate according to the limits of authority given to them by Chukwu.

### 4.1.3 The Cult of Ala (Mother Earth)

Among the Igbos, the cult of *Ala* is very important. *Ala* is both the name of the earth-goddess and the earth itself. It is reverenced because the Igbos believe that *ala* gives humans their habitation and livelihood and that therefore all precautions should be taken in dealings with *ala,* the earth. For the Igbos, to honor and revere *ala* is a given, as she gives humans support and footing. *Ala* produces food for humans and provides support for living. Care is taken not to profane *ala* if one wishes to be supported by it.

---

16. W. R. C. Horton, "God, Man and the Land in Northern Ibo Village-Group," *Africa* 26 (1956): 18.

17. Equiano was a young boy sold into slavery at the age of eleven. He later regained his freedom by paying his ransom. He became a wealthy merchant later in life. In his autobiography, he recounts the Igbo beliefs as he understood them in the eighteenth century.

18. Vincent Carretta, *Equiano, the African: Biography of a Self-Made Man* (New York: Penguin Books, 2005), 12.

When someone commits an abomination that offends *ala*, it affects the entire community, and the spirit must be appeased and the earth cleansed. Without the cleansing, the Igbos believe that the repercussions of that act will reverberate on present or future generations. Hence, the necessity for the so-called cleansing men. These men act as custodians of traditions and help maintain law and order, thereby maintaining the sacredness of *ala*.

### 4.1.4 Basic Traditional Beliefs

There are some basic traditional principles that influence any Igbo, whether consciously or unconsciously, in his daily undertakings. These concepts will help one understand the reasons the Igbos value and appreciate their religious heritage. Oliver Onwubiko summarized these principles as follows:

i.   The concept of and an indigenous name for the Supreme Being—Invisible, Sovereign, and Benevolent.
ii.  A moral sense of justice and truth, and knowledge that there exists good and evil.
iii. The belief in the existence of the human soul and the belief that this soul does not die. . . .
iv.  The existence of spirits—good and bad—and the belief that communion with the Supreme Being is possible through the intermediation of these spirits and of the ancestors who are believed to be interested in the well-being of their living descendants.
v.   The existence of myths as rational and philosophic explanations to justify the continuance of some religious practices, the order they follow, and the use of specific symbolic objects as concrete means of strengthening the relationship between man and the transcendental realm of existence, the celebration of all these in feasts and festivals for the purpose of their continuity and culture transmission.[19]

The basic beliefs of the Igbos, as Onwubiko explains, are all good in principle, but their application sometimes leaves something to be desired. This is true, for example, in the case of the Igbo belief in the Supreme Being. The Igbos believe that it is difficult to reach God and that God has no direct "contact" with the world. God has delegated several lesser spirits to deal with the affairs of men. These numerous spirits are not worshiped as God but are revered as sacred objects of cult.[20] Bishop Joseph Shanahan, the great evangelizer of the

---

19. Oliver A. Onwubiko, *African Thought, Religion and Culture* (Enugu, Nigeria: SNAAP Press, 1991), 2:59–60.

20. George T. Basden, *Among the Ibos of Nigeria* (1920; repr., Gloucestershire, UK: Nonsuch Publishing, 2006), 179. Basden argues strongly that no object of worship is actually worshiped; rather, "it is sacred only as a habitation of a spirit."

Igbos, was of the opinion that the ideas and theology of worship of the Igbos needed to be guided and perfected. He wrote, "Many . . . ideas were not so much incorrect as incomplete, and required only completion and sublimation. Such for instance was the Ibo idea of God."[21]

The Igbos have a high sense of and belief in communality, which are exemplified in the way they live in clusters as well as in the names they bear. No one likes to live in isolation; every individual has links to the clan, village, or town.[22] The communal spirit permeates every aspect of their life, and when one person sins, the whole community believes that it will suffer the consequences of that sin. This implies that every adult in the Igbo society, particularly the elders, are seen as the custodians of customs and traditions; consequently, they do their best to hold on to what has been handed on to them. They try not to deviate from these customs and traditions even when they do not have a full understanding of them.

The Igbos have no written laws or books—hence, the oral tradition that has been handed down from generation to generation. These beliefs and practices handed down are preserved in their religion, which is woven together by custom.[23] These beliefs are held very sacred by everyone in the community. Every person is duty-bound to the community to protect one another and maintain equity and justice. Therefore, knowingly or willfully concealing an evil act or desecration of the land is a grave sin in itself and may have great consequences for the person as well as for the community. There is an old saying, "*otu mkpisi aka ruta mmanu, ozue aka nile,*" "when one finger is dipped in oil, it affects the other fingers." Therefore, every person sees it as a duty to guard the customs and traditions so that evil may not befall the community.

### 4.2 Priesthood among the Igbos

In Igbo traditional society, a priest is understood to be a religious specialist who has a culturally defined status and role and devotes himself to this role in a religious system. He is an acclaimed consultant in matters relating to the deity and religion, and his whole life is lived in contact with the deity he represents. He has a locale where his authority reigns, and he is widely respected and

---

21. John P. Jordan, *Bishop Shanahan of Southern Nigeria* (Dublin: Clonmore & Reynolds, 1949), 56–57.

22. Ambrose Chineme Agu, *The Eucharist and Igbo Communal Spirit: Towards a Solid Inculturation of the Christian Faith in Igboland* (Würzburg: Echter, 2004), 59: "Deep in the consciousness of every Igbo is then the belief that the journey of life or into the world is made in the company of others."

23. John S. Mbiti, *Introduction to African Religion* (London: Heinemann Educational Books, 1975), 29. For Mbiti, "Every African people has a set of beliefs and customs. Beliefs are an essential part of religion. Customs are not always religious, but may contain religious ideas. Religion helps to strengthen and perpetuate some of the customs; and in turn customs do the same to religion."

revered in the neighboring cities and villages, depending on the "power" of his deity. The priest in Igbo religion is a "servant of the deity" and is perceived as such by the people.[24] He is the one empowered by the particular deity to speak and act in his name. These priests are to oversee the affairs of the town or village and are the custodians of tradition and culture.[25]

The concept of traditional priesthood is very common and widespread in Igboland, and there is a hypothesis that all Igbo priests trace their origin to the priest-king *Eze-Nri*.[26] The *Eze* is widely believed among the Igbos to be the head and origin of all priesthood in Igboland. He is believed to have received his mandate directly from *Chukwu* (God) and has authority in the whole of Igboland. However, this hypothesis is yet to be proved.

The priesthood in Igbo traditional society has been a part of the life of the people from the time of their settlement.[27] The settlers had an innate idea of the place of religion in the affairs of the human person. Religion for the Igbos is

---

24. E. G. Parrinder, *African Traditional Religion*, 3rd ed. (London: Sheldon Press, 1974), 100: "The word priest is properly used of an official servant of a god, and he normally ministers at a temple. It follows that such priests are to be found in those places where there are gods worshipped with temples to which offerings are brought."

25. Joseph Okwor, *The Priesthood from an Igbo Perspective: A Theological Study Aimed at Improving the Formation of Catholic Priest in Igboland* (Enugu, Nigeria: Fulladu, 1998), 104. Okwor supports this view thus: "Christianity has not changed the mentality of the people towards religious priests. The natural desire of man to find transcendence in his life, and his attempt to find solutions to his earthly problems is central in Igbo religious practices. . . . This duty is fulfilled mostly by religious priests. Whether Christians or traditional, consulting priests is characteristic of religious life among the Igbos." See also John S. Mbiti, *Concepts of God in Africa* (London: Camelot, 1973), 220: "The reason for this feeling and practice derives mainly from the social and political life of different African societies." For Mbiti, the social and political life of the Africans are one and the same thing. Something that happens in one sphere has implications in the other. The African therefore tries to find solutions to his problems.

26. Metuh, *African Religion in Western Conceptual Schemes*, 6. Metuh writes that, with the excavations in Igbo-Ukwu, many motifs of artwork dated about 850 CE portray the burial of a purported "divine-priest/king." The "divine-priest/king" is traced as the beginning of all priesthood in Igboland.

27. Carretta, *Equiano, the African*, 12. Equiano the African wrote about priesthood among the Igbos as follows: "Although there were no 'places of public worship, we had priests and magicians, or wise men,' who 'were also our doctors or physicians.' The people revered them because they 'had . . . some extraordinary method of discovering jealousy, theft, and poisoning.' They also 'calculated our time and foretold events, as their name imported, for we called them Ah-affoe-way-cah, which signifies calculators, or yearly men, our year being called Ah-affoe.'" The words in single quotation marks are actual words of Equiano, the slave boy who was renamed Gustavo. It is significant to note that, though he claimed to have been sold at the age of eleven, he learned to write in England and was struggling to translate his traditional practices into English. To date, the Igbos still call the year Afor (Ah-affoe).

meant for instilling sacred order in the material universe, which is controlled by spiritual forces that are believed to have powers to bless or curse. Priests serve as mediators who attract divine favors for the people. E. G. Parrinder concurs with this view: "The sacred is dangerous to ordinary mortals, its demands are mysterious and perhaps its characters capricious, so that intermediaries are needed who themselves partake of the divine nature."[28] Women are excluded from the "priesthood," in the strict sense of the term, though they may be considered closer to the particular deity for belonging to the same sex.[29] For the Igbo people, the priest is a mediator between the people and their gods or God. Being a people with a culture that holds that the divine realm is so close to the human, they must have priests who mediate.[30]

Other religious specialists in Igboland who function as mediators are diviners, kings, medicine men, and seers. These are sometimes loosely referred to as "priests." Edmund Ilogu argues that their perceived mediation role results from the fact that they often work hand in hand with the priests of the deities.[31] People usually consult the mediators with their needs, and the mediators approach God through prayers, sacrifices, and offerings.[32] A special circumstance, when all other sacrifices and deities have failed, may warrant the direct approach to God, as in the case of *aja eze-elu,* sacrifice to the king of heaven.[33]

---

28. Parrinder, *African Traditional Religion*, 100.

29. Francis A. Arinze, *Sacrifice in Ibo Religion* (Ibadan, Nigeria: Ibadan University Press, 1970), 72.

30. Ibid., 62. For Arinze, "Sacrifice and priesthood stand and fall together."

31. Edmund Ilogu, *Christianity and Igbo Culture: A Study of the Interaction of Christianity and Igbo Culture* (New York: Nok, 1974), 53. Ilogu noted, "Such people sometimes combine three functions: those of medicine men with the knowledge of healing herbs, secondly divination and thirdly sacrificing priests. . . . In each village a priest is known to be specially related to one or more gods. When a diviner prescribes sacrifice he names the proper priest that should perform the function." See also Metuh, *African Religion in Western Conceptual Schemes,* 167–68. Metuh believes that people make vague, useless, and confusing comparisons between these cultic personnel: "A priest is called 'Isi-Mmuo,' head of spirit cult; a diviner is called 'Onye n'agba afa,' person who casts afa-divination; while a medicine-man is called 'Dibia,' healer. So the terms 'fetish priest,' 'juju priest,' 'witch doctor,' often used in anthropological writings and in books on African religion, are vague and confusing."

32. Mbiti, *Introduction to African Religion*, 62. Mbiti supports this view as pertaining to many African religions: "People feel themselves to be very small in the sight of God. In approaching him they sometimes need the help of someone else. Just as in the social life it is often the custom to approach someone of a high status through someone else. For that reason, some African people make use of helpers in approaching God, although they also approach him directly."

33. Chika Okpalike, *Ichuaja in Igbo Traditional Religion* (Bloomington, IN: iUniverse, 2008), 66–67. Okpalike writes that some Igbos call this sacrifice *Anyanwu-naezelu,* which is an issue of dialectical variations. Arinze (*Sacrifice in Ibo Religion*, 10) gives the reason for not approaching God because God is too good and does not

Aja eze-elu is offered directly to God to protect either a person or a family that is suffering chains of calamities. Chika Okpalike explains how a boy prone to violence in the family was restored through this sacrifice at the recommendation of a diviner.[34]

The traditional priest is called *Eze Muo* (King of spirits), and he offers sacrifice to the spirit and ministers at his or her shrine. A priest cannot serve two deities at the same time. It is acceptable, however, that sometimes one can be a priest and a *dibia* at the same time. A *dibia* is a medicine man, a doctor who heals with the use of herbs. It is believed that medicine men get their knowledge from the deities and by oral tradition after being an apprentice to a senior *dibia*. For Arinze, "many Igbo traditional priests are also '*ndi dibia*,' but a '*dibia*' is not always a priest. . . . For there are many Igbo *ndi dibia* who are not priests of any particular spirit and they are priests."[35] What Arinze is referring to here are *ndi dibia* (herbalists and medicine men), who are not priests, though they may at times be called priests in the loose sense. Their main specialty is the use of herbs for healing. Their services are required when one is sick. They are the equivalent of modern medical doctors. They are called *dibia ogwu* because they deal with medication and healing. On the other hand, there are those who specialize in soothsaying and divination. These are called *dibia afa*. Their primary responsibility is to find the causes of things: sicknesses, diseases, mishaps in the family or village, and so on. They are also invited to a family when there are series of untimely deaths or infertility. When a *dibia afa* performs his rituals, he prescribes solutions that may include the suggestion to go see a *dibia ogwu* if it is something that deals with health.

Because of the respected status the traditional priest holds in Igboland, men aspire to become priests because the priest is usually an important social figure and is highly honored. He is called upon at almost every celebration that involves the community, such as the enthronement of an *Eze* (king) and the installation of a chief. This is because the social, religious, and economic aspects of the life of the Igbos are interwoven. The office of the priest can either

---

trouble anyone. Why disturb him? "They are not sure how exactly to worship Him. His awe and majesty perplex them. He is entirely transcendent." It seems to me that the reason the Igbos do not approach God directly is because God has "delegated" these other lesser deities to see to the affairs of men and so, why go to God if you can get what you want through someone who is a part of your world.

34. Okpalike, *Ichuaja in Igbo Traditional Religion*, 66–67: "Okonkwo . . . narrated an incidence in his family in which one of his sons often inflicted wounds on other children in the course of playing. The frequency became so curious that he had to consult with *Afa* and was told that he needed to do Anyanwunaezelu for the little boy. The boy's *Afa-ije-uwa* (Astrological reading) revealed that he emanated from *Anyanwu* (the sun), the idea being that he was orientated [*sic*] from and destined for physical might and valiance, which could be corrupted to villainy if necessary *Itujuanya* was not done. The *Anyanwunaezelu* would serve the purpose of properly directing his destiny."

35. Arinze, *Sacrifice in Ibo Religion*, 63.

be through a special "call" or it may be hereditary. Arinze, however, contends that priesthood as we find it in Igbo society is strictly hereditary.[36] In either case, the candidate must prove his call by being possessed by the spirit of the particular deity that he will serve. I argue that priesthood in Igbo society is not strictly hereditary, in the sense that some are called to be priests by the elders of the community, while at times, others hold the office for someone who is still an infant until he assumes the responsibility as an adult. There are also occasions when one is deposed if one is not effective. It is an office that may be given to someone by a community. Inconclusive as the topic may be, this study will focus on the selection and types of priests. This will, it is hoped, clarify the issue.

### 4.2.1 Selection of a Priest

The Igbos believe that the deity chooses his or her priests through indications given in dreams, apparitions, mysterious phenomena, events, divination, incantations, or a combination of two or more of these. Some changes are expected in the behavior of the person, such as a trance, occasional loss of the power of speech, erratic anger, or unnecessary calmness, and these are believed to be indications of a call from the deity.[37]

Experiencing these changes in behavior is not enough, though, and confirmation by a diviner (*dibia afa*) is needed. When a person finds himself in such situations described above, the diviner is consulted to discern the will of the deity in relation to the phenomena. It is the diviner who gives the final verdict on who the candidate for the priesthood is according to the perceived will of the deity concerned.

It is believed that the deities often appoint the one in whom the spirit of the dead priest reincarnates. This explains why a priestly office could remain vacant for a long period waiting for a rightful person to be born. At times the duty will fall on an infant who is yet to come to the age of reason. In such situations, an adult relative takes up the office until the child comes of age.

Physical deformities or disabilities may not necessarily constitute an irregularity to the priesthood. Even one's disabled body can serve as an added advantage, for it is believed to help him mingle and interact with the spirits to the advantage of his people. In other kinds of priesthood, such as the *Eze-Ala*, disabilities such as dumbness, blindness, and lameness are not accepted, for

---

36. Ibid., 68: "The priesthood is *never by election*. It is hereditary; a person is a priest of a certain spirit because his father was the priest of that spirit" (emphasis added). There are arguments against Arinze's position because of cases in which there was no male child in the deceased priest's house and the community decides to localize a deity in their village. In those cases a person had to be nominated/elected and dedicated to the deity for services.

37. Metuh, *African Religion in Western Conceptual Schemes*, 170.

the *Eze-Ala* must be able to communicate the message of the earth-goddess to the people.[38]

### 4.2.2 Qualities for Priesthood

**Moral Integrity.** Generally, a priest is expected to be an upright person before and during his tenure of office. He must not have been involved in stealing (especially yams), be a drunk or a murderer, and he must not have committed adultery or incest. Any breach of these rules is believed to initiate a series of serious problems for the person from his deity.[39] Although in most cases one remains a priest till death, the enduring nature of the priest's office is guaranteed only by faithful observance of moral and traditional norms. Otherwise one would attract the wrath of the deity one serves. The priest, therefore, must be a good man.

In rare cases where the priest goes against the *Nso* (sacred prohibitions) of his deity, he may be removed from office. Offenses that may warrant his expulsion from office include some already mentioned (depending on the deity concerned) as well as the violation of a young virgin, abortion, and the refusal to undergo the rite of purification (*Ikwa ala, Ikpu aru*), to appease the earth-goddess. These crimes constitute a desecration of the *ala* (land). A priest who is found guilty of crimes against *ala* is dethroned and stripped of the office and may be excommunicated and exiled from the community.

### 4.2.3 Priestly Training

When a candidate for the priesthood shows signs that are ratified by a diviner, he usually begins his apprenticeship under a senior priest whom he will succeed. The manifestations for a priestly call may occur in infancy, thus affording the candidate ample time for training and maturing for priestly duties. Training of a new priest is not formal but rather is usually a simple affair. A designated priest successor learns on the job by assisting the incumbent in his priestly duties. He learns by being with the priest in office.

If the serving priest should die before his successor comes of age, the acting servant, *uko agbara*, who usually is someone in close association with the deceased priest, would assume the responsibility of directing the child. Given that the ritual functions of a priest are not extremely complex, the *uko agbara* is usually deemed competent enough to direct the successor well. Consequently, the complete training of the would-be priest is achieved without formal, organized training. In essence, training is strictly by observation. Arinze observes:

---

38. Arinze, *Sacrifice in Ibo Religion*, 72. Arinze sees deformities as a blessing to the office because they "are held as positive advantages in the case of a dibia to enable him 'see' the spirits more clearly."

39. Ibid., 76. See also Basden, *Among the Ibos of Nigeria*, 177.

The Ibos do not have a formal college for the education of their priests. There is nothing like highly developed "institution." From his childhood to his final initiation, the future priest must have gathered much of the priestly sayings and practices, especially with reference to sacrifices. In the case where the office is hereditary and the candidate is known, he gradually learns from his father as he helps him in his duties. He stays at his father's right hand during sacrificial rites and hands over to him those things which are to be offered. He is a servant and an apprentice. He is therefore called *Oje ozi* (messenger).[40]

### 4.2.4 Consecration and Investiture

The installation of a new priest varies from locality to locality and according to the status, nature, and influence of each deity. It involves some ritual sacrifices performed inside or outside of the shrine after which the priest will hold a feast for other priests. At the end of these, the priest will take possession of the shrine.

The rite of installation of a priest may be summarized in four important different rites.

#### 4.2.4.1 The Rite of Purification
The rite purifies and cleanses the individual for the responsibility he is about to assume. The essence of this rite is to make the candidate pure to approach the deity. This rite is done by rubbing one part of his body with *nzu* (white chalk) and the other part with *uhie* (dark red chalk). It shows the candidate's dual nature as half man and half spirit (mediator). The color white signifies his interaction with the spirits, and the dark red (*uhie*), his interaction with humans. He stands at a vantage point whereby he can "see" both the spirit and the human worlds. He officially becomes the middleman between the deity and the community and is recognized as such by all.

#### 4.2.4.2 The Rite of Consecration
In the rite of consecration, the candidate is officially dedicated to a deity for service. A goat or chicken (depending on the requirements of the deity) is slaughtered. The blood of the victim is sprinkled on the shrine as the *uko agbara* (presiding minister who is not a priest) offers the victim to the deity. He also touches the toes of the candidate with blood. This effects his bond with the deity and his consecration. In some situations, the candidate sleeps in the shrine for one market week (eight days) before the feast of the deity.

#### 4.2.4.3 Priestly Investiture
a. *The Garment*. The rite comprises putting on the priestly garb of the deity. It indicates the candidate's concrete participation in the world of the deity. He

---

40. Arinze, *Sacrifice in Ibo Religion*, 69.

becomes absorbed into the world of the deity as he becomes officially married to the deity, depending on the deity concerned. He is now a semihuman and is perceived as such by all in the community. The words from the priest after his installation are taken as official and authoritative words of the deity. The priest is acclaimed as the mouthpiece of the deity.

b. *The Anklet.* The priest next puts on the anklet (*ola muo*) of the deity. This rite establishes a special relationship between him and the deity. He is seen as one belonging to the deity and therefore sacred since the deity itself is believed to be sacred. Where the deity is a female spirit, the priest is conceived as being married to the deity. On particular feast days or market days dedicated to the deity, the priest of the deity does not sleep with his wife, as he spends the time with the deity instead.

### 4.2.4.4 The Outing Ceremony

The fourth rite is the processional outing to the market/square (*Ipu ahia muo*). The rite involves the carrying of the sacred symbol of the deity in the sacred pot or basket of the deity to the deity's market. The outing is the official public appearance of the new priest, and through the appearance he is openly acclaimed and recognized as the priest of a particular deity by the community.[41] The symbolism of the ritual is that the priest is officially the physical representative of the deity. He becomes the bearer of the seal of the deity. He is dedicated and honored as such.

One common factor that is present in every Igbo community during the installation and consecration of the appointed priest to his office is *nso*, which literally is translated as "sacred prohibitions." *Nso* in this instance comprises a number of "don'ts" that the candidate must observe to make him worthy of acceptance by the deity. Trespassing against any of the prohibitions is abominable. Some of the prohibitions include but are not limited to living in seclusion for a time, continence, keeping away from oil, and so on.[42] A common factor in the *nso* is the withdrawal of the candidate from the people to make him more

---

41. This section is influenced by Onwubiko, *African Thought, Religion, and Culture*, 77. See also Okwor, *Priesthood from an Igbo Perspective*, 141.

42. George N. Oranekwu, *The Significant Role of Initiation in the Traditional Igbo Culture and Religion* (Frankfurt: IKO-Verlag, 2004), 130: "i. He must leave his entire family and live in absolute seclusion, often in a special grove, which is normally dedicated to an Alusi. There in the woods, he spends the period in dry fasting and deep meditation. ii. He is to abstain from sexual intercourse until he has offered the final thanksgiving public sacrifice marking the end of his initiation and consequent installation. iii. He has to keep off from water and oil. If he wants to wash his hands, he does it with sand." See also Chika Justin Uzor, *Living between Two Worlds: Intrapersonal Conflicts among Igbo Seminarians; An Enquiry* (Bern: P. Lang, 2003), 50–53. Uzor says that the traditional priest does not sleep with his wife all through the execution of his function as priest on duty.

docile to hearing and understanding the voices of the deity and other spirits. With the installation and consequent fulfillment of the above procedures, the priest becomes recognized as the official guardian and chief of the cult of the particular deity.

### 4.3 Types of Priesthood in Igboland

Priesthood in Igbo may be grouped into the following categories.

1. The *Okpara*—firstborn sons who are priests of the ancestral family shrines.
2. The *Isi-muo*—priests of spirit cults who take charge of the village shrines.
3. The *Eze-Ala*—the chief priest of *Ala,* Mother-Earth (earth-goddess), who is the priest of the central shrine of Ala of each village group.
4. The *Eze-Nri*—the priest-king of Nri town, who is, as it were, the high priest of the cult of *ala* for the whole of Igboland.[43]

#### 4.3.1 The Okpara (paterfamilias)

The *Okpara* is the firstborn son and the male head of a family, or *Ezi n'ulo*. The *Ezi n'ulo* is a nuclear family composed of parents and their biological children. Within the nuclear family, the *Okpara* is next to the father. He is generally the one closest to his father in order to learn the history and tradition of the family. Being a patrilineal society, the *Okpara* inherits the family name, responsibilities, and assets. He presides at the ancestral shrine when his father dies but may not be called "priest" in the classical sense. While his father is still living, he is like an errand boy to his father and has a very unique relationship to his father. He gets to know the family secrets, if there are any, and he helps organize his brothers and sisters. He is the family priest, for cult begins at home. The *Okpara* is the nuclear family priest, though Metuh favors the idea that the family points to the smallest social group in the Igbo social structure called *Umunna*, or extended family.[44]

The *Umunna* is made up of the children from a common ancestor of several generations. In the gathering of the *Umunna* (gathering of all the *Okpara* from a common ancestor), their eldest male (*Okenye*) of the senior lineage

---

43. There is a debate about the legitimacy of the Eze-Nri as regards his claims to the rites, customs, and traditions of the Igbos, which he holds to be an offshoot of what the Nri people began. They are seen as the ancestors and progenitors of the whole Igbo race from recent excavations and research. See Metuh, *African Religion in Western Conceptual Schemes*, 6. Metuh notes that the Eze-Nri acquired the right of the priesthood for the whole of Igboland because it is believed that the Eze-Nri sacrificed his own son and daughter. He and his lineage are therefore the only persons who could fix or abrogate taboos and rituals connected with Ala.

44. Metuh, *African Religion in Western Conceptual Schemes*, 168.

becomes the priest of the *Umunna*, also called a clan. He is in charge of the ancestral shrine, the ancestral cult, and the ancestral staff, or *ofo*. This office is not by election or influence but strictly by heredity and is assumed by the eldest male of the clan. The office is given to the eldest because it is believed that he is closest to the ancestors and would be heard easily when he calls upon them for help. At his death, the next in line by age assumes the responsibilities with immediate effect. It does not require any ceremony, rites, or power struggle, as all in the clan know who he is. His duties include the offering of libations and prayers to the ancestors and to *Chukwu* during clan meetings and ceremonies. He offers sacrifices and intercedes for the *Umunna*. With his *ofo* (staff, which is a symbol of authority inherited from the forefathers), the *okenye-okpara* settles disputes and represents the *Umunna* religiously and socially in their dealings with neighbors. His priestly office is synonymous with leadership and authority.[45] The criterion for this position is that he has to be an elder, and the elder of the clan generally serves as on-the-spot priest.

### 4.3.2 Onye "Isi Muo" (Chief priest [of] . . .)

"Priests of the spirit cult" comprise the second category. This refers to priests who are in charge of the village shrine, and the priests of the spirit cults go by different names in different areas. A priest would be addressed as *isi* (head), plus the name of the deity or *alusi* of whose shrine he is in charge. In some parts of Igboland the priest is known as *Eze agbara* or *Eze muo*, chief priest of spirits; *Eze-Ala*, chief priest of earth-goddess; *Onye isi Amadioha*, chief priest of the god of thunder; and so on.

### 4.3.3 Oje na mmuo

*Oje na mmuo* literally translates as "one who travels to the land of the spirits" and refers to a priest sent by a community in difficult situations to go to the spirit world and get answers to their questions and the means to resolve their problems. He is believed to be "half spirit and half human." His "special nature" makes it easier for him to mingle with humans; at the same time, he is able to interact with the spirits.[46] He is believed to fulfill this function by means of divinations aided by herbs that put him in a state of ecstasy. Some-

---

45. Uzor, *Living between Two Worlds*, 192. Uzor calls the Okpara "the primary ritual leaders among the Igbo." This position is understandable because it is from the circle of the "Okparas" (first sons) that the chief priest of the community arises. See also Ilogu, *Christianity and Igbo Culture*, 52–53.

46. There is no proof that any human (apart from Jesus) has two natures. However, this tells us about what the Igbos believe in their culture and what they practiced in their religion. If this is the case with them, one can understand why it was easier for Christianity to spread the presentation of Jesus as having two natures—divine and

times he falls into deep slumber after taking his concoctions, and, in that state, he is believed to communicate with the deities or ancestors as the case may be. When he awakes he is able to communicate to the community or individuals his supposed interaction with the deities or ancestors. On some occasions he is sent to a more powerful deity outside the community to obtain information as requested by his people.

### 4.3.4 Eze-Ala (Chief priest of Ala)

The next category of priest is the priest of *Ala* (earth-goddess), who is in charge of the central shrine of *Ala* of each village group. Metuh stresses that the candidate for this office must be drawn from the most senior of the first settlers of the land.[47] Metuh's position is difficult to sustain, especially in the light of the uncertainty of knowing accurately the first settlers on the land. I would rather posit that the candidate must come from the freeborn in the society and not from the slaves or any of the lower classes that are still prevalent in Igbo society. He must be a bona fide son of *Ala*. *Ala* here means Mother Earth, who is the spirit next in rank to the Supreme Being, *Chukwu*. *Ala* is conceived as the mother of everything that lives, for life sprouts from the earth, living things are nourished by the fruits of the earth and finally committed to earth when they die. Therefore it is necessary to respect and reverence *Ala* so that "she" will receive humans when they die. Consequently, care is taken to observe the statutes and customs that come from the *Eze-Ala* so as not to profane *Ala*. Metuh writes about *Ala* as follows:

> *Ala* is always referred to as "she" and is the "queen of the underworld," the source and custodian of "*omenala*" (customs and traditions) and the morality of the populace. Laws are made in her name, oaths are sworn by her and she is treated with respect. The candidate for this office must be drawn from the most senior lineage among the first settlers of the land.[48]

The surviving elder in the hierarchy of settlers is believed to be nearest to the ancestors. Given his age and experience, he is believed to possess the requisite qualities of a reliable custodian of the land and priest of *Ala*. Among the duties of this type of priesthood is the right to perform purification rites for abominations and meting out determined punishments. He enacts all the laws and presides at oaths sworn before *Ala* to settle disputes.

---

human. Thus, Jesus may be perceived by the Igbos as being able to go to Chukwu (God) and then come back to humans to solve their problems.

47. Metuh, *African Traditional Religion in Western Conceptual Schemes*, 172.
48. Ibid.

### 4.3.5 *Eze-Nri (King of Nri)*

The *Eze-Nri* is the high priest for a large part of Igboland. One is called by the deity to this position. Genuine calls are confirmed by divination. When it is confirmed that one is called, he cannot refuse the call to serve the deity. If the person rejects the call, it is believed that there will be serious adverse consequences for him and his family. Misfortunes such as sickness and untimely death may befall his family as punishment for his refusal to serve the deity.[49] The *Eze-Nri* is accorded all respect as though a god. Like the deity he represents, *Eze-Nri* has no territorial bounds to his administration. His influence and power spread throughout the greater part of Igboland. He delegates the *Nri* priests to travel through different Igbo communities to provide services as needed and to perform sacrifices, to establish customs and traditions, and to cleanse abominations.[50]

Enumerated and described above are the official priests that are recognized throughout Igboland. There may be variations, however, with regard to particular deities in some localities.[51] Some localities have other functional personnel who perform duties that appear to be priestly and these persons are loosely called priests. Due to the fact that they are not strictly categorized as priests and lack the proper calling and investiture, I have not included them as priests. Already mentioned earlier in this discussion are the witch doctors, the herbalists, and the *dibia*.[52]

Igbo priesthood is ordered hierarchically, with each priest knowing his limits and capabilities. Usurping a priestly duty outside the competence of a given priest necessarily attracts the wrath of the deity. The delicate nature of the priest's role requires careful observance of the codes of conduct to avoid lead-

---

49. See Arinze, *Sacrifice in Ibo Religion*, 69. Arinze supports this view, saying that "pagan neighbours heap argument upon argument to persuade such people to accept the office, and above all warn the reluctant not to be surprised to contract a long chain of misfortunes if they dare say no to the spirit calling them."

50. Ikenga Metuh, *Comparative Studies of African Traditional Religion* (Jos, Nigeria: Imico Publishers, 1987), 207. Metuh supports my argument by writing thus: "The Nri priests are agents and delegates of the 'Eze-Nri,' who is believed to have received from God powers over mystical forces connected with the earth. Nri priests therefore have the prerogative of performing the purification rituals for offences believed to pollute the earth, like homicide, incest, suicide and theft of yams. Since only Nri priests may perform the cleansing rituals for these offences, many communities welcome some Nri priest families to settle among them to provide these services." See also Arinze, *Sacrifice in Ibo Religion*, 74–75.

51. An example is the chief priest of *Amadioha,* the god of thunder. Amadioha is the god that is believed to control thunder and lightning, and his priesthood is passed on by genealogy. I would prefer to include him under the second category of priests (*Isi muo*) because he is dedicated to a particular deity.

52. Arinze, *Sacrifice in Ibo Religion*, 62–79.

ing individuals, families, and communities astray and, consequently, attracting the wrath of the deity. The priest's instructions and advice influence the individual, family, and community. Given that the priest commands respect and authority in his locale, it is incumbent upon him to function with a high degree of rectitude.

### 4.4 Functions of Priests among the Igbos

The functions of a priest in Igbo society are as follows:

a. *The priest is sent to bless the people or community*. The Igbo priest, like all other priests, invokes blessings on those who consult him. It is his duty "to offer up man's worship and to bless man in the name of his object of worship."[53] He does this by using the symbols of his deity to touch the people on their heads, hands, legs, back, and chest, all depending on the particular case and circumstance. On some occasions, the priest uses the victim for sacrifice, for example, a chicken, to touch the petitioner as a sign of blessing while praying that all goes well with him.

b. *The priest instructs the community in the name of his deity*. Besides being an intermediary and a representative in religious matters in Igbo society, the priest serves as the repository of communal knowledge and traditions. Therefore he helps to maintain the equilibrium between the social and the religious life of the community, thus fostering unity and right order. His office demands that he have a vast knowledge of folklore, myths, idioms, and the priestly language necessary for rituals and liturgical ceremonies to teach the people rightly.

c. *The priest is an official representative of the community*. As such, he has influence on the society. Corroborating this view, K. A. Opoku asserts that, unlike magicians, who work independently, priests are officials of communities or organized and permanent institutions whose main objective is to win favors from the gods and ward off evil from humans. Priests, therefore, are not self-employed like magicians but are responsible to well-organized social organization, often not for economic purposes.[54] The traditional Igbo priest is endowed with special gifts and vocational qualities acquired through apprenticeship training. This helps him to enjoy considerable authority and the privileges accorded to respected men of traditional Igbo society. The authority and honor that the priests enjoy are geared toward the sustenance and renewal of the life of the communities they serve. "He is the man who leads the community in religious matters, and through rituals, sacrifices, prayers, etc. protects the community and removes obstacles for it in its dealings with spirit world."[55]

---

53. E. B. Idowu, *African Traditional Religion: A Definition* (London: SCM Press, 1973), 32.

54. K. A. Opoku, *West African Traditional Religion* (Singapore: Fep International, 1978), 75.

55. Onwubiko, *African Thought, Religion, and Culture*, 78.

## 4.5 Sacrifice among the Igbos

The Igbo worldview suggests that the invisible world and spirits, good and evil, are all converging around humans. Humans must be in constant communication with the good spirits that protect. Evil and bad spirits are to be repelled and appeased. Desirous of a life lived securely under the favor and protection of the good spirits and undisturbed by the influences of the bad spirits, offering of sacrifice is a frequent occurrence among the Igbos. Sacrifice is believed to be the most effective way to connect with the good spirits and to ward off the evil ones; hence, its importance and relevance in Igbo traditional culture cannot be overemphasized.[56] Given the importance of sacrifice in Igbo culture, this study will devote time and space to the clarification of major terms in sacrifice among the Igbos.

### 4.5.1 Meaning of Aja (sacrifice) and Ichu-aja (to sacrifice)

Sacrifice in Igbo is called *aja,* and "to sacrifice" is *ichu-aja.* Scholars have tried to unravel the meaning of *aja* and *ichu aja,* as they pose some difficulties. As a result, there are various opinions about sacrifice.[57] *Aja* is a term that means

---

56. Odo Casel, *The Mystery of Christian Worship* (New York: Herder & Herder, 1999), 19: "There is no religion without sacrifice.... God bends down to man, and man climbs up toward God; by his taking it and passing it into his possession God makes the sacrifice holy and consecrates it. If the offerer is stained with sin, and thereby retarded in his sacrifice, the act must become first of all one of reparation."

57. Okwor, *Priesthood from an Igbo Perspective*, 109. Okwor holds that ichu-aja is from two words: Ichupu (verb), "to chase away," and ija eze, literally, "to show the teeth" or "to mock." He claims that ija eze is from ajam eze ndi mmuo, which means that the spirits are mockingly showing their teeth to humans, implying that they are not happy with humans. Therefore, for Okwor, humans seek a way to appease the spirits, and to do it effectively they offer sacrifices. See also Okpalike, *Ichuaja in Igbo Traditional Religion*, xxxiii–xxxiv. The opinion of Okpalike is interesting because scholars in the Igbo Traditional Religion have long taken the idea of *ichuaja* as meaning "sacrifice to ward off evil." However, the Church in Igboland took *ichuaja* for sacrifice as a whole, that is, in the sense Okpalike portrays. Okpalike argues that *aja* (sacrifice) in the Igbo setting is twofold: *aja nchunyere* and *aja nchupu*. He goes further to say that *aja nchunyere* is that offered to the good spirits while *aja nchupu* is offered to evil spirits to send them away. Okpalike concludes by saying that *ichu-aja* (sacrifice) should be taken "as a proper translation of sacrifice." See also Basden, *Among the Ibos of Nigeria*, 182. Basden, who spent about thirty years in Nigeria and lived among the Igbos, commented on the sacrifice of the Igbos thus: "According to the Igbo, sacrifice is imperative in the case of 'strange' spirits only, i.e. other than those he has been accustomed to acknowledge; spirits shrouded in mystery whom he cannot manage, and whom he holds responsible for his present sickness or trouble. He cannot locate the spirits; he has no conception how or why they persecute him, yet he is convinced that they are the authors of all the evils that overtake him. In his distress he consults the dibia (medicine-man)

"sacrifice" in Igboland. The goal of sacrifice is not only to make peace with the deities but also to thank them. This study focuses more on the view that *aja* is a generic term for sacrifice in Igboland.

Sacrifice is a symbolic exchange of gifts with the divine. *Aja* is therefore widely accepted in Igbo culture as sacrifice but has some other negative and positive dimensions depending on the type of sacrifice. *Aja* is not a composite word. *Aja* as a noun is sacrifice, while the verbal form is *ichu-aja,* which may denote a sacrifice of petition, praise, or atonement. *Aja* is the generic term for sacrifice, which is any kind of animal or cereal offered to the deity as oblation, whether bloody or nonbloody. It is generally accompanied by words or prayers.

Metuh observes:

> The meaning of sacrifice should be sought in the totality of the sacri-
> ficial act, and not just in the significance of the gift. Sacrifice is indeed
> a gift to the God or gods, but more deeply, it is a prayer. In fact, the
> offering is only a means of expressing this primary purpose and mean-
> ing of sacrifice which is prayer.[58]

Metuh's view on sacrifice is not strange to the African idea as a whole, though Mbiti supports the notion of sacrifice as that which brings men closer to God.[59] Metuh goes a step further to offer another dimension of sacrifice. For him, sacrifice becomes clearer, meaningful, and comprehensible if it is seen in the form of prayer, that is, communication with God.

Metuh uses the broad definition of sacrifice, which distinguishes sacrifices as three kinds of prayer: vocalized prayer, materialized prayer, and corporal prayer. "Materialized prayer deals with the expression of the worshiper's basic disposition through manipulation of a material object, and corporal prayer is when communication with God is expressed through some actions."[60] In all, Metuh sees sacrifice as a form of material/corporal prayer. Therefore, sacrifice is a form of prayer which is a sacrifice of praise. There is a real distinction between pure prayer and sacrifice.[61] Strictly speaking, sacrifice has to do with the offering of a victim, and it is always accompanied by prayer.

Sacrifices are sometimes offered by the family head. Just as there are differ-ent types of priests in the Igbo society, so there are sacrifices according to one's

---

and, acting on his advice, endeavours to appease the spirits by performing *ichu aja*, lit. 'to drive out evil.'"

58. Metuh, *African Religion in Western Conceptual Schemes*, 84.

59. Mbiti, *Introduction to African Religion*, 20. For Mbiti, Africans offer their prayers and gifts at the shrines and sacred places. In such places they encounter God.

60. Metuh, *African Religion in Western Conceptual Schemes*, 84.

61. Sacrifice has to do with offering of a victim, either bread, wine, or animals to a deity while prayer is a dialogue between humans and the deity. Sacrifice is often com-posed of prayer and vice versa.

rank in the hierarchy of the priesthood. The family head, who is the oldest member of the kindred, offers sacrifices for the kindred he represents. In addition, the family head of each nuclear family conducts the daily morning devotion sacrifice. This he does every morning as he wakes from sleep. This type of offering is not considered sacrifice in the strict sense of the word because it is primarily a prayer to God for guidance and assistance all through the day's journey for himself and for his family. Occasionally he nonetheless offers kola nut and pours libations as part of the morning devotion. Every Igbo prayer is accompanied by some sort of offering. The morning prayer is strictly prayer but includes offerings. In this sense, it is a sacrifice of some sort.

Sacrifice may be generally classified into two major groups: *aja nchunyere* (positive) and *aja nchupu* (negative).

a. *Aja nchunyere* is a sacrifice that gives glory to the deity or wins blessings and favor from him. It is always a joyous celebration. *Aja nchunyere* comprises *aja ekele* (thanksgiving sacrifice), *aja otito* (sacrifice of praise), and all the sacrifices that have to do with happiness. They are offered to God or the good spirits. The victim for sacrifice depends on the disposition of the offerer and, in some instances, is suggested by the oracle or by a diviner.

b. *Aja nchupu* is directed against evil spirits to ward them off from the human domain. Arinze, however, believes that this is the only sacrifice.[62] *Aja nchupu* is offered to the evil or malignant spirits, known or unknown, who prowl around to inflict pain and sorrow on individuals and families. There are usually no shrines involved; the sacrifices take place near a forest or market square or at a road junction. This is because the evil spirits are not honored with shrines, as no one wants to have these malignant spirits around.

### 4.5.2 The Rite of Sacrifice

All sacrifices in the traditional context have virtually the same structure, which always starts with purification of the petitioner, acknowledgment of one's inadequacy before the deity, and confession. Hence, one with good moral standing is better placed to offer sacrifices than one with a dubious life. Igbo sacrifices more or less follow the following rite:

#### 4.5.2.1 Salutation and Confession

At the appropriate time, the individual or family or community gathers at the shrine. If the sacrifice is a joyous one, for example, the celebration of the new yam festival, all gather in festive attire with musical instruments ready to party at the end of the sacrifice. The community waits in expectation of the appearance of the chief priest (*Eze Mmuo*). The elders of the different villages all assemble close to the shrine as the chief priest approaches the shrine. The chief priest begins incantations as he enters the shrine, saluting the deity as he pours

---

62. Arinze, *Sacrifice in Ibo Religion*, 33.

libations on the shrine. The priest then welcomes all present in the name of the deity and reminds them why they are gathered. He salutes the deity again praising the deity with glorious titles with the community acclaiming with cheers of *Ise* ("so be it").

### 4.5.2.2 Dedication/Immolation

At this point, the priest kills the victim if it is an animal and pours the blood on the image of the deity and on the four corners of the shrine. While the priest is smearing the blood, he prays for the community, for the good health of all, for rain, for rich harvest, and for protection. The priest invites the elders representing the villages to come forward and rededicate themselves to the deity. Each comes forward and pledges loyalty to their deity as may be directed by the priest. Sometimes the priest touches the toes and forehead of the elders with the blood of the victim as a sign of protection and dedication. The priest then touches each representative elder with his staff of authority as he venerates the deity.

### 4.5.2.3 Sacrificial Meal in Joyous Sacrifices

After slaughtering the victim, the carcass is roasted by the priest servants. The priest takes his portion, which is the heart, liver, and thigh of the animal. The elders are invited to take a piece of the meat each as a communion with their deity. The elders approach the shrine in a hierarchical form according to each one's status and dignity in the community. The titled men are the first to have their share, followed by the kindred heads and the family heads. As each head takes a piece, he calls on the rest of the family to behold their share, at which point they cheer and clap. The entrails are cooked and given to children. The members of the community sit according to their kindreds and families to share and eat their meat. As they eat, members of the cultural music group hurry over theirs to prepare for the dance that follows.

### 4.5.2.4 Dances and Departure

Having participated in the sacred meal, the community is thrown into a jubilant mood for the opportunity they have had in eating with their deity. Flute players, drummers, and dancers all begin to entertain the community. The women dance in circles to the melodies and beats of the drums while the titled men and elders wave their multicolored hand fans as they walk around the dancers majestically. The community jubilates and dances until nightfall. There is no official closing ceremony, as the chief priest leaves the arena whenever he wishes. The people stay as long as they wish before making their way to their respective homes.

The sacrifices may be subdivided into bloody and nonbloody sacrifices. In bloody sacrifices, sometimes the victim is either killed, pierced, and left half-dead, or it is left to live, as in the case of consecratory sacrifice. Arinze distinguishes between the general and the particular, the internal and the external sacrifices.[63] In his opinion, sacrifice is composed of two basic elements: oblation and immolation. Oblation does not have to be bloody, while immolation is the act of killing a victim and presenting it to God. It should be said, however, that not every sacrifice is bloody.

Herbert Anyanwu, commenting on sacrifice, points out a distinction between oblation and immolation:

> Immolation or what can be identified as pure sacrifice is one which claims life of birds or animals. Oblation identified as offering is one which involves the offering of edible food stuffs other than animals. In oblation there is no bloodshed while in immolation there is the shedding of blood.[64]

Unbloody sacrifices are composed of cereal offerings, yam festival, libations, and morning prayer offering by the *Okpara*. For instance, the new yam festival is a joyous sacrifice that is nonbloody, while the *eghu-ukwu* (sacrifice to the goddess of childbearing) is a joyous sacrifice but involves the killing of a goat. In the strict sense, prayer is different from sacrifice, but it is rare to find an Igbo praying without something tangible to offer alongside his prayer.

### 4.6 Types of Sacrifice

Igbo scholars are of different opinions as to the number of sacrifices in the Igbo religion and culture. There are so many sacrifices at every point in life as the need of the individual demands. Arinze lists five types of sacrifices in Igbo traditional religion:

1. Expiation
2. Sacrifice to ward off molestation from unknown evil spirit
3. Petition
4. Thanksgiving
5. Interior sacrifice[65]

Metuh presents four types of sacrifice:

1. Sacrifice of consecration (*Igo mmuo*)
2. Propitiatory sacrifice (*Ilo mmuo* or *Imeria mmuo*)
3. Purificatory sacrifice (*Ikpu Alu*)
4. Sacrifice of exorcism (*Ichu Aja*)[66]

---

63. Arinze, *Sacrifice in Ibo Religion*, 31–32.

64. Herbert Onyema Anyanwu, *African Traditional Religion from the Grassroot* (Uyo, Nigeria: Minders International, 2004), 151–52.

65. Arinze, *Sacrifice in Ibo Religion*, 34.

66. Metuh, *African Religion in Western Conceptual Schemes*, 74–79.

This study groups the various sacrifices in Igbo into five:

1. Sacrifice of purification
2. Sacrifice of thanksgiving
3. Sacrifice of petition
4. Sacrifice of consecration.
5. Sacrifice of exorcism *(Aja nchupu)*

### 4.6.1 Purificatory Sacrifice

Sacrifices of purification are offered to reestablish a right relationship with the deity and with fellow humans. Such sacrifices are necessary because humans do not want to incur the wrath of the deities. The Igbos want to restore right order when things go wrong between them and the deity and offer sacrifices of purification and atonement. Offenses that demand this type of sacrifice fall into the category of those called *ajo ihe* (evil deed). They are evil in themselves but to a lesser degree, such as trespassing onto another's farmland, assaulting a titled man, or defying the orders of an elder.

There is a strong belief among the Igbos that any bit of *ajo ihe* (evil deed) that is not atoned for by the person or family will definitely affect the individual in question or his family or posterity. If an individual transgresses the taboos, the repercussions will affect every member of the kindred. This is not debated among the Igbos. According to Anyanwu, "[I]f abominations are not atoned for, the penalty is sure to descend on the culprit or his relations and descendants. Therefore to stop the descending of any penalty on the culprit a sacrifice of expiation is made to atone for the abominations."[67]

There is a cosmic and corporate dimension of sin among the Igbos. Everyone tries to be a custodian of the tradition in order not to be affected by the sin of any member of the community, as that will pollute the land. Metuh argues that purificatory sacrifice is necessary because *ajo ihe* (evil) threatens the peace and safety of the community.[68] Since the Igbo man vehemently believes that *ajo ihe,* known or unknown, brings upon him sanctions that will anger the deities, purificatory sacrifice is offered to cleanse himself and his people that they may be in good standing with their deity.

There are other offenses *(mmeru)* that affect the offender and his kindred, such as adultery, stealing of yams, a woman climbing the palm tree, and so on. When these sins are committed, a cleansing or purificatory sacrifice becomes necessary. Arinze's contribution on this issue is helpful:

> [T]here is no question of hiding such a crime or trying to omit the sacrifice. The Ibos believe firmly that if such abominations are not atoned

---

67. Anyanwu, *African Traditional Religion*, 153.
68. Metuh, *African Religion in Western Conceptual Schemes*, 78.

for, be they ever so secretly committed, the penalty is sure to descend on the culprit's head or on his relations and descendants. If the culprit in the major abomination is known, he is cut off from social communication, he is ostracized from the market, and if he dies he is not given full burial rites. To hide one's crime or to refuse to sacrifice is to lead a dangerous life, to walk a tight rope, to play with fire. Once, however, he offers the necessary sacrifice, the erstwhile wrong-doer is regarded as cleansed and any ensuing death is given another interpretation.[69]

The Igbos predominantly believe that sacrifice of expiation is necessary also when someone, whether an indigene or a foreigner, or the community has transgressed the *Nso Ala* (sacred taboos/prohibitions of the earth) and the ancestors because they threaten the community as a whole.[70] *Aru* are those things that are evil in themselves and at the same time an abomination. It is a transgression against the sacred prohibitions that are the worst form of evil. These *Aru* include suicide by hanging, murder, and incest, and the purificatory sacrifice is performed by special priests from Nri. They perform the ritual by *Ikpu Alu* (*Aru*), literally, "dragging away abomination."

> The ordinary victim is a sheep. The Earth Spirit, Ani, and the ancestors are involved to forgive the culprit. Sometimes the offender is required to say out his abomination aloud before the shrine and to smear his body with ashes. The Nri priest takes a great part of the sacrificed sheep together with a fat fee. Very few people, never the culprit, are allowed to eat of the rest of the sheep. After this cleansing sacrifice, the offender once more regains full association with others.[71]

### 4.6.2 Thanksgiving Sacrifice

Thanksgiving sacrifices are offered only to good spirits and the ancestors for favors received. It is a mark of appreciation for blessings on a family or a community. Basic courtesy teaches people to say "thanks" for favors received. In God's case, it is not simply an act of courtesy but a duty to God that may not be overlooked for fear that God may not send his blessings to an ungrateful person. Igbos offer gifts to their ancestors in appreciation for favors received and to show their good disposition and love to them. For Arinze, "[w]hen the Igbo man obtains his heart's request, he often makes a sacrifice of thanksgiving, which is almost always mixed up with hopes for future protection and favour."[72]

---

69. Arinze, *Sacrifice in Ibo Religion*, 35.
70. Metuh, *African Religion in Western Conceptual Schemes*, 78.
71. Arinze, *Sacrifice in Ibo Religion*, 36.
72. Ibid., 42.

Sacrifice is offered when a child is born, especially when the child is the result of the request of the parents. The parents would often present a sacrifice to the deity, and the gender of the child determines the present they offer in sacrifice. According to Arinze, "the couple offers a sacrifice of thanksgiving to the spirit of *Omumu* [spirit responsible for childbearing], to whom the woman had made a special request for a child. If the baby is a boy, a cock is the accepted victim, while a hen is given in the case of a baby girl."[73]

A sacrifice of thanksgiving is offered for a good harvest. The Igbo man would not taste the first fruit until it is offered to God, and it is celebrated in the *Ahia-njoku* ceremony, *Njoku* being the spirit or god of yams. *Ahia-njoku* is a harvest of thanksgiving to the Yam spirit or god of yam. Through this celebration God is thanked for making the year's planting season a fruitful one, and request is made that a similar and even greater harvest would occur the next planting season.

Thanksgiving sacrifices are also offered after an epidemic, recovery from sickness, triumph in war, winning a land case, and return of a family member after a long absence. Examples are innumerable, these being only a few. It can therefore be said that the Igbo offer sacrifices for anything they perceive to be a blessing.

### 4.6.3 Sacrifice of Petition

To have a quick and favorable solution to his problems, the Igbo man presents items for sacrifice. Arinze notes that "the Ibo believes that his many desires can be obtained if he has the proper recourse to the ancestors, the spirits or God in rare cases . . . the Ibo wants to give something to make his prayer more expressive, more touching, more efficient."[74] The Igbos desire to offer something that will assure them that their prayers are more effective and their petitions granted. They bring offerings confident that the gifts will move the spirits or God to grant their requests.

Of these petitions, top on the list is life. It is no wonder that the Igbos give names to their children that manifest the attachment to life such as *Ndukaku* (life is more than wealth), *Ndudiri* (may life abide), *Ndubuisi* (life comes first), and so on. In sacrifice of petition they present all their needs to God of life and hence they pray for life, health, protection, wealth, and children.

### 4.6.4 Sacrifice of Consecration

The sacrifice of consecration is known in Igbo as *Igo mmuo, Ilo mmuo*. The determining word is the verb *Igo,* which means "to consecrate," "to dedicate" a thing to a spirit or a deity or ancestors. In most cases, the victim is not

---

73. Ibid.
74. Ibid., 38.

destroyed but is left to live to be in the service of the deity. The victim, human or animal, is usually given a little mark on the body, either the ear, hand, or feet and the blood that flows is allowed to drop over the deity's shrine as the priest pronounces words of consecration or dedication to the deity. Metuh observes as follows:

> The sacrifice is effected the moment the victim is consecrated to the deity, with or without the killing of the victim. The Igbo in fact have such bloodless sacrifices, in which the offering, an animal or even a human being, is consecrated as a sacrifice to a deity and kept to live around the shrine.[75]

In such cases the person or animal victim is left to wander about without any molestation, as people are afraid of harming or killing the victim even by accident for fear of the wrath of the deity. This sacrifice can be offered directly to the Supreme Being, to deities, or to any of the many spirits. Consecratory sacrifice is always a joyful sacrifice because it is a part of a solemn celebration that deepens the relationship between the deity and the community. The victim becomes the living symbol of the covenant between the deity and the people.

### 4.6.5 Sacrifice of Exorcism (Aja nchupu)

*Aja nchupu* is a sacrifice to drive away malevolent spirits. In this sacrifice, the offerer begs the spirits to leave the family member or clan or village because the unwanted or evil spirits prowl around humans to cause misfortune, sickness, disease, or even death. It is never a joyous sacrifice. Often the sacrificial rite is performed with no specific ritual. This is because the offerer does not gladly or willingly perform the sacrifice. It is to ward off the evil spirits from his family and from himself. Since the Igbos believe that no one appears empty-handed before someone from whom a favor is sought, the sacrifice of expiation is offered to pressure the evil forces to depart, to go away quietly without harming anyone. Things used for this type of sacrifice are useless or rotten food, and the plates on which the food is served to the spirits are broken plates or leaves. Given that the malevolent spirits are believed to be blind or greedy or mean, and that anything, no matter how bad, is good enough for them, the materials used for this sacrifice reveal the pain and sentiments of the individual or family offering the sacrifice. The belief is that foul-smelling and rotten things will not entice the wicked spirits to stay around them but would rather ward them off quickly.

In addition, the sacrifice ends informally and hurriedly, because such a sacrifice is considered a necessary evil. No one partakes of the victim, not only because it is worthless but primarily because no one wants communion with

---

75. Metuh, *African Religion in Western Conceptual Schemes*, 75.

those evil spirits. This is the reason that the sacrifice is offered by roadsides, crossroads, or near the evil forests.

## 4.7 Summary

Sacrifice is a part of Igbo life and culture from birth to death. Every major event, activity, success, and even failure calls for sacrifice. It is at the very heart of Igbo life and culture. This was the major reason they accepted the Catholic faith when the missionaries came to their land, believing in the efficacy of the sacrifice of the Church. Looking at the different types of priests and sacrifice in Igboland, one comes to the conclusion that, in the Church, the Igbos are missing some of the elaborate rituals of their tradition. This accounts for their occasional recourse to the traditional priests when certain events or problems seem to defy conventional solutions. In such cases, a spirit may have caused it, and there is need for one form of sacrifice or another. Such belief shapes how Igbos participate in the Church's liturgy and how they live.

# III

# THE CHURCH IN
# IGBOLAND TODAY

# CHAPTER FIVE

# THE CELEBRATION
# OF THE PASCHAL MYSTERY
# IN IGBOLAND

## 5.1 The Advent of the Church

A brief history of the Church in Igboland is of paramount importance, as it will show how Christianity gradually stripped the traditional priests of some of the powers and control they had over the people. The history will also furnish the reader with information on how the Igbo religion and sacrifice contributed to the openness of the people to the new religion: Christianity. With the new religion, the sacrifices offered by the traditional priests began to be limited, as the number of adherents to the local religion was gradually waning. This also meant that the priests' means of livelihood were gradually being limited, as the office of the priest demands remuneration.

The Portuguese and the Spaniards were among the first to have missionary contact in Nigeria, starting in the fifteenth century as a result of the "Accord of Patronage" (Padroado), granted by Pope Martin V (1417–1431) to the king of the Iberian Peninsula. This gave him authority to appoint bishops and missionaries for the missions. Pope Alexander VI, by the famous "Bull of Demarcation" (1493), handed full ecclesiastical authority and control of Africa and the West Indies to the Portuguese missionaries.[1] With authority and commissioning given by the Holy See, evangelization of West Africa started in full force. The efforts of the first missionaries were short-lived, as all attempts by the Catholic missionaries to establish missions in the then Benin Empire through the *Oba* (king) did not have the desired effect.[2] One reason for the lack of success in the then Benin Empire of Nigeria was lack of Portuguese missionaries to train the

---

1. A. F. C. Ryder, "Portuguese Mission in Western Africa," *Tarikh* 3 (1969): 1.

2. A. F. C. Ryder, "The Benin Missions," *Journal of the Historical Society of Nigeria* 2 (1961): 231–319. See also J. F. Ade Ajayi, *Christian Missions in Nigeria, 1841–1981,* ed. K. O. Dike (Evanston, IL: Northwestern University Press, 1969), 1–4.

indigenous clergy. The slave trade flourishing in Africa and southeastern Nigeria was also a major factor. Evangelization was therefore carried out to win souls in numbers in this early stage.

It was only in the year 1885 that the second tier of Catholic evangelization began in Igboland. Father Joseph Lutz, a native of Dauendorf in the diocese of Strasbourg (then a French diocese), spearheaded the missionary work. He was accompanied by Brother Johann Horne, Brother Hermas, and Jean-Gotto. With the English seaman Townsend steering them on the sea, they sailed from Brass in the southern part of Nigeria on 26 November 1885 and arrived in Onitsha in the heart of Igboland on 6 December 1885.[3] The missionaries established Christian villages and drilled the residents in Catholic doctrine as well as Western education. The Congress of Malines, Belgium, in 1909 permitted liturgical texts to be translated into the vernacular. Father Joseph Lutz, then Prefect Apostolic of the area, responded to the yearnings of the people by interpreting the liturgical texts into the vernacular with the help of the first graduates from the schools.[4] This made a huge impression on the people because they could read and sing in the vernacular. It enabled the Igbos to understand the readings and celebrate the sacraments.

When the young and dynamic Father Joseph Shanahan (later Bishop Shanahan) took over the mantle of leadership from the French missionaries, it ushered in a period of radical evangelization and consolidation in Igboland.

## 5.2 Period of Intensification and Consolidation

Despite the death toll of the missionaries, sometimes within two weeks of their arrival, they nevertheless embarked on intensive evangelization by learning the local language and building schools and hospitals. As Ogudo points out, "what the Igbo faithful needed at this early stage was a solid base of formation in the Catholic faith, and of infrastructure and communication of the life of grace as realized through the liturgical celebrations of the sacred mysteries."[5] The

---

3. Celestine A. Obi, ed., *A Hundred Years of the Catholic Church in Eastern Nigeria, 1885–1985* (Onitsha, Nigeria: Africana-FEB Publishers, 1985), 1–30. Archives, Congregation du Saint-Espirit (CSSp, Paris, Bulletin, 14, 1887–1888), pp. 459–60. Lutz and company left Liverpool, England, on 8 October 1885 and arrived in Akassa on 20 November 1885. See also Catholic Archdiocese of Onitsha, "Know Our Chief Shepherds," http://www.onitsha-archdiocese.org/farinze.htm (accessed April 12, 2013).

4. Augustine Okwu, *Igbo Culture and the Christian Missions, 1857–1957* (Lanham, MD: University Press of America, 2010), 184: "With the penetration of the Spiritans into the heart-land of Igboland the use of the Catechist-Teachers increased even more enormously. In 1906, there were 33 Catechist-Teachers, 24 schools, 10 Reverend Fathers and 8 Reverend Brothers."

5. Donatus E.O. Ogudo, *The Catholic Missionaries and the Liturgical Movement in Nigeria: An Historical Overview*, vol. 1, *The Holy Ghost Fathers and Catholic*

early missionaries offered these as they built schools and published catechetical books.

The missionaries intensified their efforts in evangelization through catechetical texts in the vernacular. They published the first Catechism in Igbo. It was a summary of the Church's doctrine drawn from the teachings of the Fathers and Sacred Scripture. It was called *Katekismi nke Okwukwe* or *Katekismi Igbo* (A Catechism of Faith or Igbo Catechism). An example is Father Aime Ganot's Catechism of 1901,[6] which contained daily morning and evening prayers, devotional prayers and prayers for Mass in Latin with vernacular commentaries. The catechism of Fathers Vogler and Lejeune contained two major parts: Catechism and Prayers. One catechetical work followed another, and before long there were many such texts available to the people. A text worthy of mention is the Catechism by Ephraim Agha, who was one of the graduates of the missionary schools and an outstanding teacher. He and his group interpreted the "Penny Catechism"[7] into the Igbo language. Hymns and prayers in the Igbo language followed, such as *Akwukwo Ekpele na Ukwe ndi Katolik N'Onu Igbo* (Catholic Hymn and Prayer Book in Igbo) in 1932, *Katekisma nke Umuaka* (A Catechism for Children) in 1940, *Ekpere Missa Maka Umuaka* (Mass Prayers for Children) in 1948, *Ekali Chukwu Uka: Akwukwu Ekpele maka Ndi Katolik* (Conversing with God: Catholic Prayer Book) in 1949, *Igbo Hymnal* put together by Fr. William Doolin in 1951, and the contributions of Monsignor Joseph Nwanegbo, one of the first indigenous priests of Igboland, to music and the liturgy. These texts and hymns contributed to the Igbo understanding of Christianity and the practice of the same, and they helped the Igbos to adopt the foreign religion as their own. It was the foundation of the faith that the Igbos have nurtured until the present day.

### 5.3 The Igbos and the Liturgy

The Igbos, like all peoples, are aware of the double dimension of human existence. They have a firm understanding that they came from the earth but at the same time have the breath of God. One often hears sayings like these: *Chinwendu* (Chi has life), *Ume si na Chi* (Breath is from God), *Anyi bu ndi obia n'uwa* (We are visitors/aliens in the world), *Onye nwe uwa* ("One who owns the world," referring to God). Consequently, Igbos owe their existence and loyalty

---

*Worship among the Igbo People of Eastern Nigeria* (Paderborn: Bonifatius, 1988), 65. Ogudo's idea influenced the above subtitle.

6. Ibid., 67.

7. Igbos use this term for the text, probably because it is a small pamphlet. It is titled *"A Catechism of Christian Doctrine,"* approved by the Bishops of England and Wales, first published in 1899 and revised in 1971 by the Catholic Truth Society, UK.

to God because of breath that comes from God. The one thing that synthesizes their worldview and relationship with God is their mode of worship.[8]

An area that is worthy of mention is the Igbo conception of weeks. The Igbos have four days in a week or eight days (as some interpret it) consisting of four great market days and four minor market days.[9] What is ordinarily counted as *Eke nta* (the small market day on *Eke*) or *Orie nta* (small market day on *Orie*) is in the strict sense the minor market day following the great market day. Communities use such appellations to differentiate their market days from other days.[10] When one is referring to the major market days one simply says *Eke* or *Orie*, and the message is understood. In some cases, to emphasize the day, one could say *Eke ukwu*, meaning the big *Eke*. Following this line of thought, J. O. Ukaegbu explains the Igbo calendar as follows:

> The Igbos have a calendar consisting of a week or izu made up of four days; a lunar month or onwa, of 28 days comprising seven native weeks or izu; . . . a year . . . made up of 91 weeks or izus, or 13 lunar months. . . . The lunar months dictate major feasts and celebrations in Igbo land.[11]

Every Igbo town has some sacred days of rest. These days regulate liturgy, religious life, and events. In most of the traditional Igbo society, the *Eke*[12] is believed to be the first day of the Igbo week. It is a sacred day, on which farm work or any unnecessary labor is prohibited. In most areas even a funeral is not performed on an *Eke* day. It is a solemn day dedicated to the deity of the community. For the Igbos, a sacred day, which often is a village or town's market day, is believed to be a day the local deities leave their shrines to visit the community. It is a day on which deities communicate with their priests and a day on which the deities do their own work. As such, no human is expected to be at the farms on the day. It is a day to honor the deities. It is a day of peace at all

---

8. Joseph Ratzinger, *God and the World: A Conversation with Peter Seewald* (San Francisco: Ignatius Press, 1986), 77. The belief of the Igbos is not isolated from the rest of the world. Ratzinger puts it in another form: "Man has within him the breath of God. He is capable of relating to God; he can pass beyond material creation. He is unique. He stands in the sight of God and is in a special sense directed toward God."

9. This means that each market day is duplicated within the Igbo week. There is *Eke, Orie, Afo*, and *Nkwo*. These are the four major days, while the minor ones are *Eke nta, Orie nta, Afo nta*, and *Nkwo nta*. The word *nta* means "small," and it is used to refer to the lesser market days. This means that every community celebrates its market day after every seven days.

10. In the Western sense it is the equivalent of "every other week."

11. J. O. Ukaegbu, *Igbo Identity and Personality vis-à-vis Igbo Cultural Symbols* (Salamanca: Universidad Pontificia de Salamanca, 1991), 57.

12. The *Eke* is believed to be a male deity and, as such, is given primacy in the solemnity of the days.

levels.[13] With the above information, it is easier to understand how the Paschal Mystery is celebrated and lived out among the Igbos and the esteemed status the priest occupies in Igboland.

On any given Sunday, Christian families, following the tradition of keeping one of their market days "solemn," rise early and prepare for the Sunday's liturgy. It is rare for any member of the family to abstain from the Sunday liturgy. This is because the Igbo believes that in going to worship God, one asks pardon for one's offenses, gains forgiveness of sin, and makes peace with the highest deity, God. They also believe that they pray for blessings on the family—long life, health, protection, and guidance for the work of their hands, whether farming, trading, business, or embarking on a journey. Hence, homes, community squares, and marketplaces are deserted on Sunday morning, as Sunday has replaced the solemnity of the market day. It was easy for the Igbos to accommodate this practice on Sunday because they realized the sacredness of such days from their traditional religion.

### 5.4 The Sunday Liturgy

Bishop Joseph Shanahan, one of the early missionaries in Igboland, whose name is almost synonymous with the Catholic faith in southern Nigeria, describes the piety and reverence of the Igbos at Mass in those early years of Christianity.

> The joy of offering the Holy Sacrifice in these . . . stations cannot be estimated. . . . The children kneel or sit on the hard, beaten, mud benches they use as desks during school hours. There are generally up to 200 of them, because they come from up to six or seven miles away when they know that Mass is being said. . . . They keep their hands joined very fervently all the time, and answer the prayers before and after the Mass. . . . There are grown-ups present too. . . . How wonderful, when the time for Holy Communion approaches, to hear the Christians moving up behind me to receive . . . with the greatest reverence. . . . They are wonderful, God bless them![14]

The observations Shanahan made more than a hundred years ago are still valid today. The same reverence is still observed on the part of the priest and the people in their celebration of the Paschal Mystery; the same faith, but in a

13. Oliver A. Onwubiko, *African Thought, Religion, and Culture* (Enugu, Nigeria: SNAAP Press, 1991), 52. Onwubiko wrote that a festive day is a day when "custom forbids fighting or quarreling at all levels. Creditors are not allowed to collect debts. Anyone who dies at this period is said to have died at the wrong time and is ignominiously thrown into the evil forest and is not afterwards entitled to a decent burial. All types of conflicts are suspended during festivals."

14. John P. Jordan, *Bishop Shanahan of Southern Nigeria* (Dublin: Clonmore & Reynolds, 1949), 84–85.

new, modern setting. Despite the change of times, the Igbos still remain Igbos, clinging to the Church and observing their revered traditions, which shape their way of worship.

Sunday begins with the faithful trooping out *en masse* to the church. Everyone dresses in festive, colorful garments. The beauty of the day is radiated in the joy of the faithful as they exchange pleasantries within the church's premises. Men, women, youths, children, and even infants all assemble in church for the liturgy. In nonparochial centers, sometimes the congregation waits for quite some time before the priest arrives. This is partly due to the distance between communities, the bumpy roads, or both. Yet in all these situations, the faithful wait patiently for the priest, as they do not want to miss out on the opportunity of communing with God that week. As they wait, the catechist uses the opportunity to catechize the faithful in the faith, and new songs are learned, as time permits. The language of the liturgy is Igbo, but in the cities where many Masses are celebrated on a Sunday, one of the Masses may be celebrated in English for the benefit of non-Igbos, with Latin used sometimes for the Common of the Mass.

The liturgy in Igboland is performed according to the Roman Rite with the entrance song by the choir, joyfully taken up by the congregation. The mood in the church is a very joyous one, as people exude happiness, manifested in the manner in which they sing. Traditional instruments are used in the liturgy such as drums, gongs, xylophones, flutes, and occasionally foreign musical instruments such as the piano, organ, and guitar, according to the resources and personnel of the community. The members of the congregation move their bodies to the melodies with a few really dancing. Years ago, before the Second Vatican Council, men sat on one side of the church and women on the other. Today, families usually sit together. Sometimes children sit in the front seats, or if there is not enough space, they sit around the sanctuary and at kneelers on the altar rail.

The priest begins the eucharistic celebration with the congregation responding accordingly. The Common of the Mass is invariably sung. The readings are proclaimed, and the cantor or choir with the congregation chants the Responsorial Psalm. The Mass goes on as prescribed by the Roman Rite, but there is much singing when appropriate. The Gospel is proclaimed by the priest or a deacon where there is one. At the homily, the priest explains the readings of the day, educating the people in the faith. It is usually lengthy, as he takes some time to interpret the Scriptures. During this period, those who are late for Mass are not allowed into the church until the homily is over to avoid distractions, though they stay at a place from which they can listen to the homily.

The Offertory is a time for the congregation to offer themselves and their gifts to God, and it is a time to sing many hymns. This is symbolized by everyone going before the altar to offer their gifts, singing and dancing all the while. Everyone tries to present something to God at this time, even the very poorest of the community. It is a special opportunity to offer their possessions, as they believe and hope to win divine favors. Ogudo offers an interesting picture of the celebration of the Sunday liturgy in mission outposts at the time of the missionaries. For him, the Sunday liturgy had an atmosphere of joy: "The faithful, for their part, were inserted into the celebrating mood through their proper responses, hymns, gestures and body-movement as directed by the celebrant through the teacher-catechist-interpreter."[15] The major point of Ogudo's narrative is that all participate in the singing with their whole heart. This is because they know and believe that they are participating in the Paschal Mystery, which is a source of blessings. During the Offertory, as the oblation is presented, the families with the special intention for the Mass process to the altar with gifts ranging from domesticated animals to groceries to any other gift deemed appropriate. Farmers bring animals and crops, while traders bring their wares. The priest, as God's representative, accepts the gifts and presents them to God.

The Liturgy of the Eucharist is a time of total concentration and intense prayer for the Igbos. The congregation kneels as the priest begins the Eucharistic Prayer. At the end, there is a resounding "Amen" to the "Great Doxology" from the congregation as they acclaim their faith in the prayer. Participation in Holy Communion is believed to be a true sharing in the body and blood of Jesus. The congregation receives the sacrament with total reverence and devotion. The ushers guide them toward the sanctuary where they kneel to receive the eucharistic species on the tongue. Occasionally, one or two who are known to be public sinners such as those living in concubinage or under sanction from the Catholic women or men are pulled out of the communion line as a reminder to all that the Eucharist is only for those in good moral standing in the local community and in the Church. The sense of being a brother's keeper is still strong in the community, and it is borne out in the liturgy. This accounts for the concern of some parents who become upset with their children for perceived bad behavior that could lead to their being barred from going to Holy Communion. Friends and neighbors who do not come for the Sunday liturgy are checked upon to find out if all is well with them.

The Church becomes another avenue of strengthening the brotherhood that the community offers. It becomes the gathering of the new community of brothers and sisters in Jesus with the priest leading them more into the mysteries of faith. Gatherings in the Igbo context could be social, religious, or political, depending on who convokes them and for what purpose. In the case of the Eucharist, it is God who convokes the gathering. Thus, it is called *Nzuko ndi Katolik*, A Gathering of Catholics.

The above section highlights the worshiping community of the Igbos. It shows how the priest and the community are closely held together. At the apex of the community are the priests, led by the chief priest. In the past, they con-

---

15. Ogudo, *Catholic Missionaries and the Liturgical Movement*, 8.

trolled the affairs of the community until the Christian religion challenged their authority through the conversion of many of their subjects. It has generated some problems for the Church in Igboland, which has lingered till the present. Some of these problems have militated against the growth of the Church in Igboland. These problems are studied below.

### 5.5 Areas of Concern for the Church in Igboland

#### 5.5.1 Use of Images

The use of images in Catholic worship is not foreign to the Igbos. As a people who have images in the form of *Mbari* (a sculptured pantheon of their deities) and *ikenga* (a personal or family guardian), the Igbos have no problem accepting the images of the Catholic religion. These images in the traditional religion are a constant reminder of the role of the deities in their lives, as their help is sought incessantly. The issue at present is whether the Igbos have truly and completely abandoned those traditional images. Some Christians still hold onto the images passed on to them by their ancestors and revere them as sacred. It is still a subject of serious controversy, as the Church has not devoted the required time and resources toward studying these images. Some of these images are not bad in themselves, but there may be some problematic histories behind them. The present generation may not really know what their ancestors did with them and what use they served, but because they were passed from one generation to the next, the people prefer to keep them. The possibility looms that some images like the *ofo*, the symbol of justice, drums, gongs, and so on might have been used for traditional rituals and may have been dedicated to evil forces. A cleansing is therefore required of these images by the Church to clear any doubts about them. Often priests do not pay attention to families who may be traumatized by perceived powers latent in some of these objects. Whether it is a fact or not that there are powers in these images, the Christians are yearning for attention, counseling, and prayers to give them solace. When the Church does not pay attention to the people's problems, the alternative for some is to go back to the traditionalists, who would pretend to be offering solutions by leading people through the traditional rituals. This is an area where the people need urgent pastoral care.

#### 5.5.2 The Ancestors

Since ancestors are believed to have a keen interest in the affairs of their living family members, just as they did when they were alive, Igbos keep their memory alive. The ancestors are regarded as "saints" for the Igbos, and every person hopes to join the ranks of the ancestors in the next life. Reverence of the ancestors brings blessings and good fortune. They were close to family members while they lived with them and, at death, are with *Chukwu* (God) because they led good lives on earth. They occupy a mediatory role between the living and the dead. Some of the dead who have not fully joined the fold of the ancestors because of some misdeeds or breach of *nso* by the living members of their families depend on the prayers and sacrifices of the living to join fully in the fold of the revered ones. This means there is reciprocity between the living and the dead.[16] The major issue is that the dead are believed to be not really dead; they are still alive somewhere, and those of them who lived well on earth are at peace. This accounts for the extra care taken in funeral rites, as the dead are sent forth in a fitting manner to the world of the living-dead. Azu K. Oko narrates how people from Abiriba (a town in Igbo land) bury their men in the living room and women in the kitchen.[17] These traditional burial rites affect worship in the Christian Church. While extra care is taken in the planning and burial of departed faithful, unfortunately, undue and unnecessary attention and money are directed to ostentatious funerals performed on some occasions. Such a showy funeral plunges the bereaved family into debt after the death of a loved one. Sometimes the dead are kept for months, and in some rare cases up to a year, as the family prepares for the funeral. The Church has stepped in already in this area, but only at the diocesan level. Some bishops have introduced measures in the form of diocesan regulations to check this practice. Hence, if a Catholic dies and is not buried within a certain number of days, or a month in some areas, the Church will not accord the departed a burial presided over by the clergy. To some extent this is good, but, on the other hand, the departed Christian is penalized as a result of the decision of the family members. I am advocating that proper catechesis in this area will help to educate the people. They should be taught to forgo expensive funerals, as the money spent on funerals or the elaborate traditional rites do not help the dead in the next life. In catechizing the people, the ancestral belief could be used as a basis for more elaborate teaching on the doctrine of purgatory, that is, that people who do not live good Christian lives may not immediately join their ancestors in the kingdom of heaven and therefore will need to be purified before being reckoned as saints.

---

16. Victor C. Uchendu, *The Igbo of Southeast Nigeria* (New York: Holt Rinehart & Winston, 1965), 14. He commented on the reciprocity of the living and the ancestors by writing that the "principle of reciprocity demands that the ancestors be honored and offered regular sacrifice, and be 'fed' with some crumbs each time the living take their meal; it also imposes on the ancestors the obligation of prospering the lineage, protecting its members, and standing with them as a unit against the machinations of wicked men and malignant spirits."

17. Azu K. Oko, *Ancestor Worship, Roots/Biblicity* (Aba, Nigeria: Enuda Video House, 1992), 13.

### 5.5.3 Liberation from Evil and the Role of Priests

The pragmatic views of the Igbos often affect their practice of the faith and the celebration of the liturgy. In search of ready-made answers to the problems they experience in daily living, some Igbos have come to believe that through the celebration of the Paschal Mystery in the liturgy, they will be freed from sickness, possible curses inherited from their ancestors, and all life hazards. Being a people who believe strongly in the efficacy of rites, some have unwittingly arrived at a conclusion that the Christian rites work like magic. Hence, some have the expectation that the sacraments should not only instantaneously afford them purification from and atonement for their sins and those of their ancestors but also render them immune from the struggles of daily life occasioned by the mystery of evil in the world. Families with a history of adolescent deaths attribute such occurrences to the deities or to some evil people or forces. Those who have difficulty in their trade or business try to find solutions to their apparent failings. Having accepted Christianity, the Igbos seek the assistance of Catholic priests, believing that their prayers and rituals will free them from their foes, known or unknown, seen or unseen.

Since the Igbos still believe in the visible and invisible forces that manipulate positively or negatively the activities of humans, they pray to God (*Chukwu*) to tame or expel the evil spirits and, in turn, to bless them. The role of the traditional priest (*Eze Agbara*) in such instances of great need has been transferred to the Catholic priest. The danger here is that some priests have developed private, makeshift rituals for such occasions for which the Church's Book of Rites and Blessings has made no provision.[18] This development most often places the priest on the path to syncretism, as he devises his own rites to satisfy the yearnings of the faithful for possible help. Some priests who are losing focus capitalize on the weakness of the faithful by using them in making more money.[19]

---

18. There are situations in which the priest blesses his own oils and sells them. In some of the rituals the priests perform, they sometimes bless salt, citing 2 Kgs. 2:20–21, and pour salt around houses or places that are believed to be plagued by evil spirits. On some occasions, the crucifix is buried to deter evil, and prayers are fashioned to suit the particular need.

19. I was visiting with a priest in his parish and he requested me to celebrate a weekday Mass for him, which I agreed to do. The priest, to my greatest surprise, brought some olive oil he had blessed, and he instructed me to use it and anoint the people as they came for the Offertory. I rejected the idea, questioning him on the rationale and rite that the practice stands for. He merely responded by saying: "it is how we do it in this parish." I refused to do it, and he came up after I had celebrated Mass to anoint the members of the congregation. I realized after inquiries that he would anoint the people as they came to offer their gifts before the altar. As one puts money in the collection basket, the priest would anoint the person. Hence, it will have a negative effect on those who have no money or do not feel like giving at that particular Mass. Therefore, they will be moved to respond by desiring the anointing "oil of good fortune and protec-

A rite with proper catechesis should be developed to address such situations. Given that the Igbos will not rest until they find a solution to the problem, the local Church should use the theology of the cross in teaching the people that problems and hazards are part of human life and are often unrelated to holiness or curse (John 9). Jesus did not come to take all suffering away but to teach humans the royal way of the cross through the Paschal Mystery.

### 5.5.4 Influence of the Community

In his missionary exploits in Igboland, Bishop Shanahan narrated the following to buttress the communal nature of the Igbos as he tried to persuade a chief to accept Christianity. It shows how the community influences decisions of individuals.

> The chief listened gravely to a rough-edged exposition of heaven, and what it meant. He heard me through and through, and then said seriously: "That is heaven, you say. But tell me, will all the other chiefs be there too? You see . . . if I go to heaven and they all go off somewhere else . . . I'd be up there in heaven all by myself . . . while all my brother chiefs would be down in this other place you speak of. . . . No! I'd rather be with my own!"[20]

If one looks at this statement positively, one notes that the Igbo would want to be where his brothers and sisters are. In the Catholic Church in Igboland today, the faithful are conscious of the need to help one another in their faith journey. They remind those who do not go to the sacraments of the need to do so and check on those they do not see at Sunday liturgy. This is the result of their belief that it is preferable to belong to a community than to be individualistic. The negative aspect of the community is that sometimes one who inherited a shrine or deity from his father finds it extremely difficult to let go of it for Christianity, especially if it is his main source of income.[21] There is a constant tension for him between the demands of the Church and those of the community. Because of the tremendous influence and pressure of the community, indi-

---

tion," and go to the altar to receive their anointing. To be able to receive the anointing, one has to put money in the collection basket!

20. Jordan, *Bishop Shanahan,* 31.

21. I had an awful experience in one of the pastoral internships I did as a seminarian when I spoke to a traditionalist of the need to accept Jesus and the Church. The old man was very interested and accepted almost all I told him. He was ready to let go of polygamy and be baptized and married in the Church. There was one problem, though, as he asked the following question: "If I left this practice which is a source of my income, how would I be able to take care of my family?" It was a difficult question for a young seminarian to answer because neither the Church nor the state has any structure in place to help people like this man who yearned for Jesus.

viduals and families that are not strongly grounded in the faith tend to sway in the direction of the community. A balance should be struck in this aspect of the life of Igbos. I am proposing grassroots evangelization through small prayer groups that will keep the clans together. These groups are to gather within the families or at a designated place. The aim would be to bind the members together religiously and foster a more brotherly community of believers in the eucharistic assembly. In such gatherings, the members would seek to aid other members of the community in need of help.

### 5.5.5 Lack of Awareness in the Liturgy

I attribute the problem of lack of awareness in the liturgy to poor catechesis. When awareness of the importance of the Paschal Mystery of Christ is lost, it may lead the assembly to a bored and dull celebration. Adequate catechesis is required to promote faith and participation in the liturgy. It is desirable that there be interaction between the clergy and the laity in order to promote greater appreciation of the mysteries celebrated. Though Christianity is a little more than a hundred years old in Igboland, if serious effort and structures are not put in place during these early years, Christian faith may not be properly grounded. The priest or catechizers of the present time should be ready to study the culture and find a meeting ground with the Christian doctrine for a way forward. The bishops' collaboration is very important, too. The bishops need to encourage the priests and the laity to dig deep into the culture and find those elements that will enhance the liturgical celebration and, it is hoped, deepen the faith among believers.

### 5.5.6 Syncretism

This word was used by Plutarch as a "political alliance in which mutual differences were overlooked in the face of threat to all."[22] The term has been used from the nineteenth century in comparative religion as a fusion of different godheads, cults, and religions. It is the mixture of two incompatible religions in such a manner that it makes it difficult to decipher the difference between the two. Syncretism undermines the Church in her efforts to promote orthodoxy. It is not difficult to find the reasons behind such a trend among the Igbos. According to the Igbo mentality and worldview, answers are sought by all means; the Igbos are lured to anyone who promises quick solutions to problems. This has led to a few priests going purely charismatic in their celebrations of the liturgy, appearing like healers to retain their congregations. An example is when a priest blesses salt or olive oil and directs the Christian in question to pour

---

22. John Charles Maraldo, "Syncretism," in *Sacramentum Mundi: An Encyclopedia of Theology*, ed. Karl Rahner et al. (New York: Herder & Herder, 1970), 6:201-3.

them on the farms to ward off dangers, or to put some drops of the blessed olive oil into water and bathe with the water for unfailing protection and assured safety.[23] This cannot be ignored, as it undermines the true identity and mission of the Church. Many such practices are still going on, and I believe it is time for the Church in Igboland to address these issues. Some reasons for syncretism among the Igbos may be the following:

"Back to Sender" oil

_____

23. I was surprised to see in one of the Catholic churches an oil sold to believers to ward off dangers and evil. The oil pictured is called "Back to Sender" oil. This implies that one who has rubbed this oil on his/her body is protected all day from the attacks of the enemy, whether temporal or spiritual. This is an example of a personal rite for the purpose of helping a situation. See also Christopher Ejizu, "The Influence of African Indigenous Religions on Roman Catholicism: The Igbo Example" (Lecture, University of Port Harcourt, Nigeria, 2010), 7, http://www.afrikaworld.net/afrel/ejizu-atrcath. htm. Ejizu witnesses to this incessant development of rites by priests as follows: "Innovative pastors feel sufficiently challenged and are able to create rites in the Church to respond to felt-need. This appears to be the case for funeral/burial rituals, naming of babies, churching of women after child-birth, marriage practice, new yam ritual, widowhood practice, outing of a new dance, etc." He goes on to say, "Currently, some pastors I know are seriously concerned with how to respond to the serious threat they feel among the flock from the indigenous religio-cultural practices."

a. Attachment to culture or worldview
b. Tenacity of the Igbos
c. Attraction to novelty
d. Desire of priests to prove themselves.

These aberrations are found in bits and pieces, especially in the celebration of the Holy Eucharist, where some priests turn the liturgy into a "healing service," thereby keeping the congregation for three to five hours. Aberrations and syncretism also creep in, which suggests that some Igbo Christians have not completely let go of their attachment to the personal or family deities. The aberrations come in the form of burying crucifixes or statues around the home, or hanging a holy water bottle in the barns, on door posts, and at farms, apparently believing it to ward off evil spirits or scare evildoers. An atmosphere of uncertainty suggests a yearning for definite solutions to the problems of everyday life to which Christianity has not yet, to the satisfaction of some Igbo Christians, given an answer. The phenomenon suggests that more effort should go into catechesis and inculturation. The aberrations can be curbed if adequate measures are taken to develop a rite that will accommodate the suggestions this study gives.

### 5.5.7 *Westernization*

The world is fast becoming a global village, and therefore it is much easier, with the Internet and technological advances, to see within minutes what happens in any other part of the world. These things affect people in Igboland, as in any other part of the world. Some Igbos, though a minority, when they return from the first-world countries to their homeland sometimes look down on others, sometimes challenging the faith that is practiced among the people. They come back with Western influence and ideas that are not always orthodox, which those at home quickly tend to copy. This has somehow affected the formation of future priests, as African theology is not yet developed. Seminarians are occasionally trained according to Western categories and worldview. I am not implying that these teachings or trainings are bad in themselves, but, given that these young minds will become priests and work among their fellow Igbos, more emphasis should be given to their cultural realities. African theology should be developed and made a required course all through the seminary formation to help seminarians be at home with what obtains in their immediate environs. This should guide all the disciplines taught. So what I have proposed so far on the liturgy of the Eucharist should serve as a guide for the advancement of an Igbo rite of worship, for it is in line with their cultural values and mode of prayer.

### 5.5.8 Poor Quality of Life

Sickness, disease, hunger, and poverty affect the way people worship God. Sickness is believed to be a negative force among the Igbos, and because the Igbos interpret things in a mystical and mythical way, sickness is a diminution of life and a hindrance to progress. The influence of the medicine men and sacred prohibitions of the land *(nso)* are still in force in many communities, and they affect the Christians. Dioceses, parochial churches and individuals should not lose sight of the fact that the early Church had a special place for the poor (Acts 4:32). Priests and pastors of churches should pay more attention to the weaker and poorer members of their congregations, as they are the most vulnerable. In addition, priests should be encouraged to devote more time to knowing and listening to their parishioners as a way of drawing them closer to God in their spiritual journey.

### 5.6 Summary

As a deeply religious people, the Igbos received Christianity with joy from the missionaries. Despite their openness to the gospel message, to which the missionaries attest, there seems to be something missing in the faith with which the Igbos need to connect. This chapter studied the beginning of Christianity in Igboland through the missionaries and the problems they met as they tried to pass on the message of Christ. I discussed the liturgical life of the Igbos as they are guided by the priests in their daily life. Looking at the yearnings and desires of the people and at their celebration of the liturgy, one notices that there are major areas to revise in the Church in Igboland. This chapter has addressed problems that affect the ministry of priests. The next chapter will study ways to reposition the Church in the light of Vatican II.

# CHAPTER SIX

# THE PASCHAL MYSTERY IN THE CHURCH IN IGBOLAND: A LITURGICAL SYNTHESIS.

## 6.1 Repositioning the Church in Igboland in the Teachings of Vatican II

It is historically indisputable that Christianity is a religion that was brought to the Igbos in colonial categories as the early missionaries sought followers.[1] The creed was memorized in catechism classes but was not truly internalized. This is partly because certain words could not be translated by the few indigenous teachers at the time and partly because certain aspects of the tradition were not appreciated by the missionaries. The status quo was left to be the "norm," and the local clergy have continued in some of the same "traditions" because the hierarchy is slow to initiate changes. The result of such a stance is that many aspects of the Igbo traditions condemned by the missionaries are

---

1. Chibueze Udeani, *Inculturation as Dialogue: Igbo Culture and the Message of Christ,* Intercultural Theology and Study of Religions 2 (Amsterdam: Rodopi, 2007), 88. Though Udeani speaks of the Africans in general, he adds another dimension to support my argument. "There was no substantial communication between the African world and Christianity . . . there was only monologue. Even where some of the missionaries made efforts to understand the indigenous or native spirituality and the religion and culture of the people in question, no effort was made to establish a dialogue." See also Okwu, *Igbo Culture and the Christian Missions,* 111: "The scramble for missionary territory between Protestants and Roman Catholics with the advent of the Spiritans in 1886 made the European evangelizers of two Christian denominations both desperate and unscrupulous in their tactics for winning members for their missions in Igboland. . . . The Protestants interpreted as self-serving bribes and ingratiating deeds the Catholic missionaries' charitable and humanitarian services such as their distribution of free clothes, victuals, and medicines to the sick, the building of schools and feeding the children *gratis.*" The above passage is a reminder of the apparent "conflict" between the two leading missionary churches in their quest to win souls for God through the new religion.

suspect by the present hierarchy, for example, *nso* (taboos), *mbari* (a cultural symbol of deities), and some masquerades and dance groups. However, I have tried to show throughout this work that Christianity does not mean a repudiation of one's cultural heritage. "The Church, therefore, urges her sons to enter with prudence and charity into discussion and collaboration with members of other religions" for a better liturgical awareness and practice (*Nostra Aetate* 2). Sometimes comments such as, "Igbos are more Roman than the Roman Church" are heard. By implication, this purports to show that the Igbos are continuously stripping themselves of their true identity to accept Christianity. The *ummunna*, or clan, which the Igbos held so closely to the heart in the past is also fading away, and this failure is attributed to the influence of Western culture and urbanization. The new wave of evangelical Christianity is also fast affecting the Catholics, as evangelicals present a "feel good" Christianity—a Christianity rooted in Lutheran theology. "Miracle manufacturing centers" are also thriving in Igboland. These pose constant threats to the Catholic religion, as the faithful are caught in a triangle of the Church, cultural values, and evangelical Christianity. I therefore propose an inculturation that will have to come from the Igbos within the common culture of Catholic religion "because each culture is unique" (*Sacrosanctum Concilium* 1).

A look at the teachings of the Second Vatican Council concerning religion, worship, and cultures at this point will help in repositioning Christian worship in Igboland. In article 1 of *Sacrosanctum Concilium*, it is unequivocally stated that the main goal in the restructuring and renewal of the liturgy is "to foster whatever can promote union among all who believe in Christ; to strengthen whatever can help to call all mankind into the Church's fold" (*Sacrosanctum Concilium* 1). The document goes on to state that "it is the liturgy through which, especially in the divine sacrifice of the Eucharist, 'the work of our redemption is accomplished'" (*Sacrosanctum Concilium* 2). Hence, *Sacrosanctum Concilium* has singled out in a special manner "the divine sacrifice of the Eucharist" as a way in which redemption is accomplished. It therefore justifies the time and energy invested in this study and research into how the celebration of the eucharistic sacrifice among the Igbos can help them participate more fully and actively in the mystery of Christ's sacrifice. This is also echoed in *Sacrosanctum Concilium* 2: "The Liturgy, then, is rightly seen as an exercise of the priestly office of Jesus Christ. It involves the presentation of man's sanctification under the guise of signs perceptible to the senses and its accomplishment in ways appropriate to each of these signs."[2]

It is these signs that I am advocating, hoping their use will not only obviate the apparent meaninglessness of some signs in the Church, but more positively, bring deeper configuration to Christ. These signs are exemplified in a more

---

2. See also *Sacrosanctum Concilium* 7: "Every liturgical celebration, because it is an action of Christ the Priest and of his Body, which is the Church, is a sacred action surpassing all others."

sublime way among the Igbos through sacrifice, priesthood, and the celebration of the Paschal Mystery. By use of signs and symbols perceptible to the Igbos, the liturgy would be able to realize the goals of the Second Vatican Council, which may be summarized as the renewal of God's people, the adaptation to the times, ecumenism, and evangelization. To achieve these goals, *Sacrosanctum Concilium* suggests that participants in the liturgy "attune their minds to their voices" (*Sacrosanctum Concilium* 11). This is because in the liturgy, participants are expected to open up to God and offer their hearts as a sacrifice to God. The liturgy is therefore not a private but a communal function. It is hoped that through the actions of the priest, the faithful are led to a more intimate union with God. *Sacrosanctum Concilium* therefore welcomes and respects the priesthood of the baptized but also insists on the special role of the ministerial priesthood over it (48, 53). The ministerial priests, having been conformed to Christ by ordination, are leaders of the faithful. Just like the traditional priesthood in Igbo religion, the biblical priest leads and directs a group of people in his care. This role takes this book to the similarities and dissimilarities of the priesthood and sacrifice in the Bible and in Igbo religion.

### 6.2 Biblical Priesthood and Sacrifice and the Igbo Priesthood and Sacrifice: Similarities and Differences

Having discussed the Catholic priesthood and the Igbo priesthood and sacrifice in detail, I turn to their similarities and differences.

1. Both priests represent the deity they serve. The biblical priest is called by God to minister to him. He is the representative of God before the faithful. The priest in Igbo religion, on the other hand, represents the particular deity he serves. The biblical priest mediates the presence of God to his people. Given that the Igbos have many deities, they have many priests, too, representing their numerous deities for the people. There is no priest representing the Supreme God in the Igbo traditional religion, as God has no shrine among them. Therefore, no priest represents God for the people directly, but through the intermediary of some lesser deities they serve.

2. Both priests bless the community. One of the functions of the priest is to bless the people. A priest, whether biblical or Igbo, blesses the people. The difference here is that the biblical priest blesses in the name of God, while the Igbo priest blesses in the name of the particular deity he serves.

3. The priest, whether Igbo or biblical, is a leader. As a leader of the people, the biblical priest heads the liturgical assembly and guides the faithful as they offer sacrifice. The Igbo priest guides the community by revealing the mind of the deity to them. He wields more authority in his community than the Catholic priest, because the religious and social life of the Igbos are linked. Both, however, have the governing power over a certain group.

4. The priesthood in ancient Israel developed over time, and at first the head of the family performed the function of priest. Similarly, the Igbo priests

have the head of the family as priest. Just as in ancient Israel the family head and the tribal heads offered sacrifice (Passover), the head of the family in Igboland is a priest who does the daily morning prayer/sacrifice for his family. However, the family head in Igboland is not a priest in the strict sense of the word but assumes that role in some family functions. Being the oldest male in the clan, he is believed to be close to the ancestors and so his prayers would be heard by them.

5. Both priests, biblical and Igbo, are consultants in religious matters. The priests are expected to be men of knowledge who can help the people to choose right from wrong. The priests guide the people and instruct and teach them the way that will bring peace to them. The Igbo priest differs a little here, because he is also believed to be a healer of spiritual and bodily ailments. Hence, people go to him with virtually all their problems, and he is expected to have answers. The biblical priest always has recourse to God, and certain problems that defy solutions are accepted as a share in the cross of Jesus. In contrast, for the Igbo, there must be a solution—if not with one priest, then with another. Such belief among the Igbos created the many sacrifices they offer as a way of proffering solutions to their problems or gaining the blessings of the deity.

6. Both the biblical and Igbo priestly and sacrificial systems believe that sacrifice has atoning power. Ancient Israel had the Day of Atonement set aside for the atonement of sins, whereas the Igbos have sacrifices of purification and expiation. These sacrifices serve to appease God or the deities and to reestablish peace.

I therefore surmise that the biblical priesthood and sacrifice are a prolepsis to the reception of Christianity in Igboland, judging from the similarities between them. For a better appreciation of the liturgy through the priesthood and sacrifice, the following should be reconsidered in Igboland in light of the Second Vatican Council.

### 6.3 Sacrifice

The Church's teachings on the Eucharist, Holy Communion, and sacrifice were major issues that captivated the Igbos in their encounter with the Christian religion. I have noted that the Igbos are a people who strongly believe in the efficacy of sacrifice and communion; they widely accepted these ideas from Christian theology. John P. Jordan comments on this as he recounts the conversion of the Igbos through Bishop Shanahan's preaching among them.

> He pointed out that the Mass is a sacrifice to propitiate God on account of sin; that a deputed priest was the right person to offer it; and that Holy Communion at the end was a spiritual feast partaken of only by those who had been fully reconciled to God through forgiveness.[3]

---

3. Jordan, *Bishop Shanahan*, 119.

Shanahan understood to an extent the belief of the Igbos on sacrifice and used it effectively in evangelization in Igbo communities. Following what Shanahan and other missionaries taught the Igbos in the early 1900s, it becomes easier to understand how Christianity attracted the Igbos, who were very familiar with sacrifice and communion. Since their life is characterized by sacrifice and communion, they favored the new form of sacrifice in Christianity as richer than what they had. Their faith was never doubted by the missionaries.

> Our African converts often remind me of our Irish fore-fathers in their love of the Mass. I wonder will our Ibos preserve the little chalices that . . . travel in our humble bush-boxes and that rest during the Holy Sacrifice on tables of beaten mud . . . ? If they do not, it will not be through lack of reverence. They are full of reverence for the Mass and everything connected with it.[4]

Nevertheless, one must acknowledge that there exists an inadequate understanding and impatience among some Igbos concerning some realities of the Christian faith and life. The impatience and incomplete understanding of the Christian faith are evident in the lack of humility with which some Igbos approach prayer. In search of answers, some Igbos view the Mass as a magical rite that should provide immediate answers to their problems. Such people, though they believe that the Mass is a better and a more efficacious means of sacrifice to God without the terrors and demands of the traditional deities and priests, nevertheless, do not have the necessary patience that goes with worship. Those, however, who take up the Christian message and understand the mystery of the cross manifest a lively faith that defies the heat of the day and the wetness of the rains to participate in the eucharistic celebration. The same faith also guides the people's relationship to Jesus, whom they believe is the new Priest, the family head, *Okpara* (firstborn), who inherits the authority of the Father. As such, he is the new Priest who prays and intercedes for his people through the ordained ministers who are his servants.

### 6.4 Priesthood

Prior to the coming of Christianity in Igboland, the Igbos already had a developed idea of the priesthood, as portrayed in this study. The word "priest" in Igbo is *uko*. When it refers to the Christian priest, it acquires an expansion to become *uko-Chukwu,* describing the Great God whom the priest serves. It is a combination of two words: *uko,* meaning "the go-between," "middleman," and *Chukwu*, meaning "God." The priest is therefore the go-between of *Chukwu,*

---

4. Ibid., 120. In a similar story, another missionary priest recounted how three women traveled for miles to participate in the eucharistic celebration.

*Chi ukwu*, the great Being, and humans. In the traditional religion the word *Uko* precedes the name of the deity or the person the individual mediates. It is the name of the deity that follows that indicates the type of priest one serves.

Igbo converts to Christianity found it intriguing that priesthood in their new religion was not significantly different from their original idea of priesthood in the traditional setting. For the Christians among the Igbos, the word has not changed in meaning but acquired a new dimension and interpretation. They perceive the priest as a man who connects them with the Supreme Being. Furthermore, the role of the priest as one who stands before the deity and offers gifts for himself and for the people was already known to the Igbos. Yet response to prayer is aggressively sought by the Igbos. Delays in answer to prayers signal nonperformance and unreliability on the part of the priest or the deity to whom prayer is addressed.[5] Therefore, for the priest to be valued and to continue to hold primacy of place among them, he should be able to be a powerful intercessor. He is expected to be very effective in his intercessions with God.

Igbo Catholics view their priest as a leader, a firstborn (*Okpala*), and a bearer of blessings in the same light as the traditionalists view their priests in the Igbo traditional religion. The traditional priest alone leads prayers, while others respond. He offers sacrifices for the family or the worshiping assembly.[6] In Catholic theology, Jesus occupies the position of the firstborn in God's household (Col. 1:15). As the firstborn, he is the leader, and prayers are offered by him and through him, the priest. The priest in the new assembly of God's people, among the Igbos, leads the community in prayers, oversees the different religious prayer groups, Bible study, and, above all, leads in the liturgy of the Eucharist. The faith of the Igbos is shown in the popularity of Adoration of Jesus in the Blessed Sacrament. Adoration chapels spring up steadily in parishes where a number of the faithful throughout the day and often at night visit to adore, worship, and praise God, laying their problems at the feet of Jesus, their God.

---

5. George T. Basden, *Among the Ibos of Nigeria* (1920; repr., Gloucestershire, UK: Nonsuch Publishing, 2007), 176. Basden commented on how a community had withdrawn all sacrifices and devotion to their deity Ngenne because "he had no power to avert disaster, or he was of such a sour disposition that nothing would satisfy him." They begged him [the chief priest] to destroy the deity, since he had "no power over one who prayed to Chukwu [the Supreme Being]" (brackets original). In some cases involving individual deities, the person in question destroys his *ikenga,* communities expel their deity and burn the shrine as a result of nonperformance and unreliability. Basden also echoed this idea during his sojourn in Nigeria even when communities were untouched by Christianity.

6. Ibid., 187. Basden wrote about the faith and solemnity with which the Igbos approached their local deities and their effects on the people.

Catholics to this day revere their priests, visit with them, and call upon them with their problems. They hold priests in high esteem and consult them in almost all aspects of their lives. When they are sick or when women are unable to conceive a child or are pregnant, when they are building a house, receiving a chieftaincy title, engaging in a trade, setting out on a journey, they always seek the blessing and assistance of their priest. For them, the priest is God's representative and, as such, should be involved in every aspect of their lives. It is not difficult to see how Catholic priests in Igboland inherited such prestige from the past. The priest has become the new *paterfamilias* of the local community and is accorded all the respect and support due his position. It is therefore disheartening for the people to make their petitions through the Catholic priest and realize that there is no perceived positive result, because, for the Igbos, sickness and diseases are contrary to life. They diminish life and therefore indicate divine displeasure. Therefore, the priest should be able to do "something" to help alleviate these problems. However, there are some gaps in the rites of the Church that the Christians are seeking a way to fill. When the Church does not fill this vacuum, they are left to do it themselves. It is right to say that such practices delight the weak Christians while the ardent and strong ones are caught in the middle.

Vatican Council II has replaced the royal emphasis of the priesthood with a more pastoral emphasis, projecting Jesus Christ as the Good Shepherd (*Lumen Gentium* 20, 21). Christ is the Good Shepherd who is close to his people. He is in their midst as the shepherd of souls and goes after the lost sheep (cf. Luke 15:4-7; Matt. 18:12). It is important that the Church's priests in Igboland are conscious of this shift and try to remain close to their people in their problems. Being close to the people will help to actualize the goal of Vatican Council II and instill the conviction in the people about the priest as a true shepherd. The Church in Igboland, however, is still basking in the glories of kingly priests and bishops. A reorientation is therefore required to help reposition the Church. It may not be possible to realize the goal of nearness to the faithful in their problems if the competent ecclesiastical authorities do not address the problems discussed in this book.

In the traditional religion, when one appeals to a priest for help and none is forthcoming, he searches for other priests and deities to help. That temptation is very real among the Igbos, for they want to go back "to do as their fathers did," because *awo anaghi agba oso ehihe n'efu* ("the toad does not run in daylight for no reason!," meaning "every effect has a cause"). This situation pushes some to invite evangelical/Protestant pastors who carry Bibles in one hand and a staff in the other. They make incantations and pour some liquids, dig around the house, and sometimes, to one's greatest surprise, unearth coins, locked padlocks, pins, and so on—and they are the only ones capable of explaining how those things got in there. To liberate a family from a curse or bondage, as they claim, they perform rituals with animals or any object and are paid huge sums as they leave.

This being said, the inherent problem of today is: What went wrong despite all the testimonies of the missionaries? Where did the Igbos or the missionaries miss the track, if they did at all? I still believe that certain areas in the traditional rites and customs are still in need of "redemption" by the Paschal Mystery of Christ. To help achieve this, there has to be a clear understanding of the Paschal Mystery of Christ in salvation history and the place of the cross of Christ in the life and ministry of both the priest and the faithful.

### 6.5 Configuration with Christ through a Theology of the Cross for the Igbos

Configuration with Christ addresses the issue of suffering for the Igbos. Those of them who have accepted Christianity are called to follow in the footsteps of their Master and Lord, Jesus, who willingly accepted the cross for the salvation of all. "If anyone wants to be a follower of mine, let him renounce himself and take up his cross every day and follow me" (Luke 9:23). Jesus also said, "Anyone who does not take up his cross and follow in my footsteps is not worthy of me" (Matt. 10:38). Witnessing to Christ, even unto death, is part of the life of the Church. The apostles and the great men and women of the faith in the past went through the cross. Paul exhorted the Christians in Corinth on suffering as follows:

> We are in difficulties on all sides, but never cornered; we see no answer to our problems, but never despair; we have been persecuted, but never deserted; knocked down, but never killed; always, wherever we may be, we carry with us in our body the death of Jesus, so that the life of Jesus, too, may always be seen in our body. (2 Cor. 4:7–10).

Christianity can never be separated from the cross, as the founder, Jesus, brought forth the Church from his pierced side as he hung on the cross. "For it was from the side of Christ as he slept the sleep of death upon the cross that there came forth 'the wondrous sacrament of the whole Church'" (*Sacramentum Concilium* 5). "Christ and the Church, according to St. Bede, had 'one nature.' The Church had come from the side of Christ, just as Eve had been taken from the side of Adam."[7] Believers in Jesus bear the cross patiently, hoping that a day will come when God will wipe away all tears (Rev. 21:4) and give them joy (Matt. 5:5). It will be joy for those who faithfully follow Jesus in this

---

7. Jaroslav Pelikan, *The Christian Tradition: A History of the Development of Doctrine*, vol. 3, *The Growth of Medieval Theology (600–1300)* (Chicago: University of Chicago Press, 1987), 43. John Chrysostom, *Catechesis* 3.13–19.

life through all the toils and rigors of being a true Christian without asking for a truce. Therefore, Christianity will not be much different for the Igbo. Suffering is part of the created order. In every age and among all races, none can be found that has not had his fair share of suffering. The Igbo should not hope to escape the lot and destiny of humanity. Jesus, good and loving though he is, did not remove suffering; rather, he sanctified it through his Paschal Mystery.

The cross remains a constitutive element of Christianity even for the Igbos. Christians live with suffering but offer it up as sacrifice to God (see Rom. 12:1–2). Proper integration of the theology of the cross and the Paschal Mystery with the practical realities of life will enable the Igbos to approach Jesus in faith with their spiritual and material problems. Though the believer is constantly saddled with doubts, uncertainty, and suffering, perseverance in Jesus will lead to salvation (see Matt. 24:13). In the light of the above, the Igbos should be "content with weaknesses, and with insults, hardships, persecutions, and agonies . . . for Christ's sake" (2 Cor. 12:10), believing that they are aiming at a higher goal. Priests, teachers, and catechists should embark on a more thorough catechesis of the cross to better understand and live the Christian message.

## 6.6 The Need for an Igbo Theology and Rite

One of the things that would help the Igbos in their celebration of the liturgy is the inculturation of theology and ritual. It is important that the basic concepts of Christianity be translated, not by a mechanical translation, but with apposite attention to linguistic expressions that reveal the true meaning of the gospel to the people. So far, the categories and thought patterns used hitherto are Western, which is foreign to the Igbos.[8]

Translation is a basic element in the transmission of the gospel. Inculturation of words and actions of the gospel will help the Igbos perceive the liturgy as their own, in union with Christ. Inculturation in liturgy is about lifting up of the particular to a universal value. The actions, signs, and symbols the priest uses should be such that the people would be able to understand. On the necessity for in-depth inculturation of the Christian message, E. B. Idowu encouraged theologians to "use African spiritual values with the African mind and at the same time, have a requisite knowledge of the Christian articles of faith which they seek to interpret in indigenous expressions."[9] Certain theological concepts, for example, "Person" in the doctrine of the Trinity, are often merely transliterated without any corresponding terminology in Igbo created to fit-

---

8. There is no doubt that it is important for Africans to listen to European theologians and translate their ideas into the terms of their own culture, but if it is admitted that the cultural formulation is secondary, there is absolutely no justification whatever for the process of translation going only one way.

9. E. B. Idowu, *African Traditional Religion: A Definition* (London: SCM, 1973), xi.

tingly make them understandable to everyone. The result is that the richness of the thought is lost to the people. Alien structures that surround the Church in Igboland have prevented a meaningful discussion. Sometimes new ideas in African categories are rejected simply because they have roots in Igbo tradition and culture.[10] Sometimes ideas with African originality are rejected by ecclesiastical authorities on the assumption that they are not understood and are not relevant. Belief in the universality of the Church does not preclude the interpretation of the message of Jesus in the cultural values of the Igbos. I surmise that, if the Igbo context is not considered, Christianity will remain a foreign religion to many Igbos. Accordingly, the desire of the Church that the gospel message of today must respond to the needs of the particular Church will be defeated.[11] The need of the Church in Igboland currently is to engage the faithful actively in their lives, so that they are totally attuned to the gospel of Jesus Christ.

This book calls for a genuine reexamination of the rites of worship and the liturgical theology of the Church in Igboland, so that the faithful may attain fulfillment through local self-expression. In this way, Christian liturgy may become an authentic "locus of vital self-expression."[12]

### 6.7 A Rite of the Eucharist for the Igbos

Given that the sacrifice of the Mass is the central act of worship of the Catholic community, my proposals will center on the celebration and actions within the Mass. The liturgical actions of the priest in the sacrifice of the Holy Mass should be reevaluated in a manner that will reflect the traditional values of the Igbos. The Mass should begin in the usual manner according to the Roman Rite but with the following modifications subject to the approval of competent ecclesiastical authorities, in the light of the Second Vatican Council.

1. The Greeting
2. Elaborate Penitential Rite
3. The Kiss of Peace
4. The *Gloria*
5. The Opening Prayer

---

10. Joseph Okwor, *Priesthood from an Igbo Perspective: A Theological Study Aimed at Improving the Formation of Catholic Priests in Igboland* (Enugu, Nigeria: Falladu Publishing, 1998), 181. Okwor presents a scene in the seminary where a non-Catholic professor's teaching appointment was terminated because he taught ideas that "did not go down well with the then seminary authorities. . . . The whole idea of African thought was questioned."

11. John Paul II, *Pastores Dabo Vobis* (Washington, DC: United States Conference of Catholic Bishops, 1992), 10.

12. Raymond Vaillancourt, *Toward a Renewal of Sacramental Theology*, trans. Matthew J. O'Connell (Collegeville, MN: Liturgical Press, 1979), 2.

6. Readings
7. Solemn Procession with the Book of the Gospel
8. The Homily
9. Prayers of the Faithful
10. The Offertory/*Oblatio*
11. The Liturgy of the Eucharist/The Anaphora
12. Holy Communion
13. Dismissal

1. *The Greeting.* In the eucharistic celebration, the Igbos gather on any given Sunday or Holy Day of Obligation. As a sign of welcome and to inculturate the good elements of their culture into the liturgy, the kola nut,[13] which is a sign of welcome, acceptance, and brotherhood, should be the first thing to be shared among the gathered community. The Igbos believe that one who has shared a lobe of the kola nut with another will not harm that individual or think evil against his person. He is believed to have a good disposition and be free of rancor and bitterness. I recommend that kola nut be allowed to be shared among the gathered assembly. By so doing, the gathered assembly is welcomed in terms and customs familiar to them. Since the Igbos value the community, the priest should pray for their welfare and their families as a way to open their hearts to the liturgy. A welcome greeting in Igboland is usually followed with a cordial extension to one's family. A Catholic assembly gathered in a church in Igboland is a form of the Igbo extended family. This ceremony may be done while people are still outside in small groups or as soon as they enter the church. Just as the Sign of the Cross with the words accompanying the action reveals the relational dynamics of the Trinity, so the sharing of kola nut shows the love and family orientation of the Igbos. They gather in worship as one family in God.

2. *Elaborate Penitential Rite.* At the penitential rite, I suggest an elaborate ritual whereby Igbos can fully express themselves and ask forgiveness from God and from one another. The Igbos have a deep sense of the gravity of sin. Sin brings conflict and alienation among individuals and families. One who is not at peace with a neighbor does not share a meal with him. Consequently, the person cannot be at peace with God either: "Anyone who says, 'I love God,' and hates his brother, is a liar" (1 John 4:20). Jesus also teaches, "So then, if you are bringing your offering to the altar and there you remember that your brother has something against you, leave your offering there before the altar, go and be reconciled with your brother first, then come back and present your offering" (Matt. 5:23-24). As a result, the Igbos are always asking for pardon,

---

13. One must note that the kola nut is the first thing that is presented before any visitor in any Igbo home. Without the presentation of the kola nut, one is believed not to be welcome in that family. It carries so much importance that the guest is not satisfied with other things given to him if kola nut is not among them. It is the first sign of hospitality.

trying to have a good relationship with God, as well as with the living and the dead. They believe that abundant blessings flow to them when they are at peace with all. Confession of sins and reconciliation with God and neighbor should be the starting point of the liturgical worship.

Igbos could use this rite to avail themselves of the opportunity to open up and be reconciled to God and to one another. They could use a local penitential formula of asking for mercy. Igbos like repetition as a means of emphasis and conviction. This may be incorporated into the rite too (*Sacrosanctum Concilium* 110). I am proposing that the congregation stand at this time and that the priest or deacon lead by guiding them through a rigorous examination of conscience drawn from their life situations and culture. Inquiries could be such as: Have I transgressed any of the taboos? Have I wished another evil? Have I done harm to another's property? Have I stolen? This is necessary because the Igbos are people who love to say the same thing in different ways as a way of getting the message across. A refrain at the end of each examination could have words like, *Chukwu ebere, gbaghara anyi,* "God of mercy, forgive us." This will give them a greater sense of participation. At the moment in the liturgy in Igboland, some *Kyrie eleison*s are so lengthy when sung by the choir. They are also a sign and a reminder that the people are yearning for something deeper. The Church can help a little more on this following my suggestions.

3. *The Kiss of Peace.* After the penitential rite, the kiss of peace should follow. The greeting of peace is important at this point because, having made peace with God and with their neighbors, the parishioners can have more meaningful communication with one another. It is the belief that one who is not at peace with a brother or sister cannot offer a worthy sacrifice. If such person participates in a sacrifice, the person violates the very principle of communion and desecrates the sacrifice (*Oriko*).[14] With reconciliation having taken place, all can then exchange the kiss of peace, which is traditionally given by hugging relations and friends and exchanging handshakes with the elders and others.

4. *The Gloria.* The celebrant calls on the people to sing the *Gloria*. When the *Gloria* is sung, the people should be allowed to be expressive through clapping

---

14. In one of the communities in Igboland, there was a man who was a public sinner in the traditional view but was given the privilege of being a catechist in the Catholic Church by the missionaries. Toward the final blessing at Mass, he would stand to make some announcements. As soon as he stood up, many people in Church left without waiting to hear anything from him. When asked why they left, their reasons were that the man was so bad in the community that his presence alone or any word from him was considered evil. The fear of *oriko* (unworthy communion), eating with one who is not reconciled with the community, can make one decide not to participate in a sacrificial offering. Generally, Igbos believe that, without the proper rituals, one may incur evil or untimely death to the family.

of hands and movement of their bodies to the melody. Evangelical Protestants seem to understand the phenomenon of dance in Igboland better and have used it as a medium to attract to their fold Catholics who perceive the Church's liturgy to be cold and lifeless. Although dancing in evangelical Churches is often done in excess, appropriate liturgical dance in the Catholic liturgy would not affect the solemnity of the celebration. It is, on the other hand, obedience to the call of the Council Fathers to people who have their own musical traditions to use them in the liturgy in "adapting worship to their native genius" (*Sacrosanctum Concilium* 119).

5. *Opening Prayer.* The opening prayer should introduce the readings, intentions of the Mass, and the needs of the community. Intentions for the Mass vary in Igboland and could indicate prayer for good harvest, for success in business, for protection of family, and for healing from diseases and illnesses. Currently, the Collect recalls only the needs of the universal Church and the central ideas in the readings of the day. Incorporating the needs of the faithful will influence positively the participation of the people in the Paschal Mystery they celebrate and bring the event of redemption closer to their hearts.

6. *Readings from the Old and New Testaments.* During this time, all sit and listen to the readings as they are proclaimed. The reading from the Old Testament unites Christians with God's people of the past (ancient Israel) because they are one people of God. God is One, both in the Old Testament and in the New Testament, and the Psalmist captures it as we proclaim with him: "O Lord, you have been our refuge age after age. Before the mountains, before the earth or the world came to birth, you were God from all eternity and forever" (Ps. 90:1–2). God is therefore the same God of Israel, of the Igbos, and of Christians. The congregation assents to the Responsorial Psalm by singing the response, acclaiming the song of the ancestors of Christians in the faith. The Psalm reminds Christians and Igbos of the pains, the sorrows, and the joys of the ancestors and should also serve as a source of encouragement to the Igbo Christians to persevere.

7. *Solemn Procession with the Book of the Gospel Reading.* A solemn procession with the Book of the Gospel accompanied by melodious hymns and dance is an appropriate way of emphasizing the importance of the Good News brought to the people. The Deacon of the Word should solemnly carry the Book of the Gospel from the narthex of the church through the central aisle to the sanctuary. Children in dance costumes could be selected to accompany the deacon as he carries the Book of the Gospel through the nave to the sanctuary. In some parishes where this is possible, the congregation sings *Ozioma, Ozioma, Ozioma Chineke abiago,* "The Good News, the Good News, the Good

News of God is here," as the refrain while the choir sings the verses.[15] After the proclamation of the Gospel by the deacon, the priest gives the homily.

8. *The Homily.* The priest explains the readings and the mysteries, using familiar examples and stories known to the people in folklore, idioms, and sayings drawn from the wisdom of their ancestors. Songs relevant to the message may be used to emphasize and not detract from the message.

9. *The Prayer of the Faithful.* The Igbos love to voice their prayerful concerns personally in the assembly. Spontaneous prayers could have their advantages and disadvantages in the liturgy. When people are allowed to voice their prayers spontaneously, they feel a sense of real participation as they pray from the heart. They use expressions that depict their personalities, concerns, and deep feelings. The words of the Gospel that they have heard move them to respond in sincere prayer. One disadvantage is that spontaneous prayers could give some members the leverage to employ inappropriate or offensive language in their prayers. There should be guidelines put in place by the competent authority.

10. *The Offertory/Oblatio.* During the Offertory, the members of the congregation offer to God from their trade, as mentioned earlier. They jubilate and dance to the altar with their offerings. This is already being practiced and should be continued. At this point the members of the congregation should know that they offer primarily themselves and only later their gifts.

As the Liturgy of the Eucharist continues, I recommend that altar servers carry incense in wooden bowls and present them to the priest, who will accept them with the gifts of bread and wine and other items presented. The minister would move to a large pot of hot coals placed at the foot of the altar and pour incense into it. As he does this, the congregation would acclaim with a suitable song. So far, this is practiced in some parochial churches but needs the approval of competent authorities for adoption into the local church.

11. *Liturgy of the Eucharist/Anaphora.* The celebrant should pray the Eucharistic Prayer with the acclaim of the people. The anaphora could be divided into sections or stanzas so that people would have the opportunity to voice their support and consent through a refrain. An example will serve to illustrate the idea:

---

15. The point I am conveying in all these elements is that some of these practices are done in bits in different parishes without any guidelines. Individual priests devise and use whatever they think is best for their parish. This gives room for confusion and disorderliness. If a regulation is put in place and the Conference of Bishops decides to adopt all or some of these suggestions, it will enhance uniformity and improve the participation of the people.

P = Priest
C = Congregation

C. *Nna, idi nso ezie, so gi na-edo ihe nile aso.*
    You are indeed holy, O Lord, the fount of all holiness.
C. *Ka anyi tobe ya.* (May we adore Him.)
P. *Anyi na-ario ka idoo onyinye ndia nso.*
    Make holy, therefore, these gifts, we pray,
C. *Ka oree* (May it be as you have said.)
P. *Site na ihukwasa ha mmuo Gi, ka ha wee ghoro anyi Ahu na Obara nke
    Onyenweanyi Jesu Kristi.*
    by sending down your Spirit upon them like the dewfall.
C. *Ka oree* (May it be as you have said.)

Such a format should be developed and used, subject to the approval of the competent authorities. Its implementation would offer the people a more confident and proper participation whereby they will accept the Mass as their own prayer in union with Christ, the high priest. At the end of the Eucharistic Prayer, the people acclaim with a resounding *Amen* by saying in their vernacular, *Isee!* (Amen). The Our Father and the embolism will follow as usual without any modification.

12. *Holy Communion*. During Holy Communion, the Igbos always say a prayer for Communion together. After the prayer, those who have prepared for the reception of Holy Communion process to the altar. So far, Communion is given by the priest or deacon, and it is placed on the tongue. The communicants receive the Eucharist with the greatest reverence and would not even touch the sacred Host. This is because they strongly believe that they receive Jesus in the eucharistic species. The hymns at Holy Communion remind the faithful of the blessings of Holy Communion and the dangers of making unworthy communion. Their reverence is commendable and should be continued.

13. *Dismissal*. After the closing prayer, the priest should invite those with special needs such as farmers, the sick, those setting out on a journey, or those plagued by misfortune, for special prayer and blessings. This will give them the assurance and confidence that God is with them, and that the Church has their interest at heart. It may also be an occasion for one or two minutes of catechesis to help the people realize that they are having a share in the passion of Jesus. With this done, the priest should give the final blessing and dismiss all in the peace of Christ. Such a rite would be more meaningful to the people when they see the priest dressed in traditional fabric and designs, accompanied by some of their revered and sacred signs, and praying in a manner that truly engages and involves the people.

## 6.8 Evaluation

### *6.8.1 Inculturation of Worship in Igboland*

For an effective liturgical activity and for the growth of the Church in Igboland, the first thing that should be done is inculturation of worship. The Igbos should worship God as he made them. Worshiping God through their God-given traditions and customs would be beneficial to the community of faith and to the Church on a much larger scale. Until valuable cultural elements are studied, or what I have proposed so far is implemented and incorporated into the liturgy, Christianity may not be solidly grounded among the Igbos. Edward Fischer follows this line of thought:

> That ritual fit the time and the place is necessary for good communication, and there may also be a moral dimension involved. . . . To force a man into a ritual is a form of cruelty. Physical or moral, such force treats man as less than man. If there is one thing that should be done with an open heart and embraced with both arms, it is the way in which one communicates his reverence for God.[16]

Christianity bears the stamp of all races and cultures and, at the same time, retains its uniqueness. The danger of not making the Catholic faith firmly rooted in the culture of the people makes the Church's future bleak despite the flurry of activities of priests and the Christian faithful. In light of the Second Vatican Council, changes appropriate to the way of life of the people are required.

> The goal which should guide the inculturation of the Roman rite is that laid down by the Second Vatican Council as the basis of the general restoration of the liturgy: "Both texts and rites should be so drawn up that they express more clearly the holy things they signify and so that the Christian people, as far as possible, may be able to understand them with ease and to take part in the rites fully, actively and as befits a community. [73][17]

With gradual change, I am optimistic that the gospel will take root in the hearts of the people. Changes especially in liturgical expressions will enable the natives to make the faith a part of their everyday life, and not just one of

---

16. Edward Fischer, "Ritual as Communication," in *The Roots of Ritual,* ed. James D. Shaughnessy (Grand Rapids: Eerdmans, 1973), 165–66. Fischer argued that "one must know the audience in a liturgical assembly to be able to get the best out of them in worship."

17. Congregation for Divine Worship and the Discipline of the Sacraments, "Inculturation and the Roman Liturgy" (March 29, 1994) no. 35, http://www.adoremus.org/VarietatesLegitimae.html (accessed September 1, 2010).

the ways in life. Change will create an evangelization of Igbo culture and shed the light of Christ on the people. Only then will Christ be the real light of the nations and the glory of all peoples. By recapitulating everything in Christ, a *nova patria Christi* (new homeland for Christ) will be born for the Church in Igboland.

### 6.8.2 Active Participation

The liturgy is the Mystical Body of Christ in worship. It is not the act of an individual; it is the Church at prayer with Christ the high priest leading the worship in the person of the minister. Those at worship should be encouraged to see the liturgy as "their own" and so actively engage in the rites led by the priest. There is a current trend in societies whereby people misunderstand active participation as activism. Inasmuch as passivity is to be discouraged, people are called to allow the mystery of Christ that is celebrated to touch them with reverence and occasionally in silence. The expression *participatio actuosa,* used by the Second Vatican Council, implies maximum attention of the worshipers in a liturgical celebration. It means allowing oneself to be engrossed with the liturgy. The sense of total attention is what is implied when the people respond to the priestly dialogue, "*Sursum Corda*" (Lift up your hearts), with the answer, "*Habemus ad Dominum*" (We life them up to the Lord). It is a lifting up of the spirit to God the Father through Jesus, in the Holy Spirit who unites all in the sacrifice of the Cross that is reenacted at the Eucharist.

### 6.8.3 The Notion of God

Though the Igbos have a strong belief in the existence of God, they should realize that God is actively involved in every event in the world. The idea that some saints and ancestors act on behalf of *Chukwu* (God) should be purified. God is one and the Creator of all. He is guiding the world as his divine will decides, and it is for the good of all. The priests of the Church are his delegates and should unite themselves with the sufferings of Christ, which will be a model to the faithful. Only a total self-denial on the part of priests will transform the genius of Igbo pre-Christian religiosity and culture into an authentic priestly people, kingly people, and a holy nation for God. Such a unity and transformation are realized most effectively at the eucharistic table, as Christians unite with Jesus.

> At the Last Supper . . . Our Saviour instituted the Eucharistic Sacrifice of His Body and Blood. He did this in order to perpetuate the Sacrifice of the Cross throughout the centuries until He should come again, and so to entrust to His beloved spouse, the Church, a memorial of His death and resurrection, a sacrament of love, a sign of unity, a bond of charity, a paschal banquet in which Christ is consumed, the mind

is filled with grace, and a pledge of future glory is given to us. (*Sacro-sanctum Concilium* 47)

The Church's liturgy serves this purpose: a gathering under a new and eternal high priest, Jesus Christ, the Lord, who leads all God's chosen people in worship through his Paschal Mystery and into the kingdom of God.

### 6.9 Summary

This chapter shows how the Igbos experience the liturgy in their day-to-day activities. It has also portrayed the problems facing the Church in Igboland and the efforts the priests are making to solve these problems. Their solitary efforts are leading some of them and the faithful away from the true worship of God within the Catholic religion. The areas of concern are major issues that need urgent attention for the fruits of the Paschal Mystery to be realized in Igboland. It is my wish and hope that adequate time and attention be given to these issues as a means of restoring and strengthening the faith among the people.

### 6.10 Conclusion

The study has tried to prove from the Old Testament, the New Testament, and traditional Igbo religion that sacrifice and priesthood, as important aspects of worship, are more effective and meaningful to peoples and cultures when people are helped to worship God according to their values and cultural setting. The Israelites received the Torah at a moment in their history and received their sacrificial worship with individuals, family heads, and priests presiding as occasion demanded. Family heads, priests, and kings led the nation during national sacrifices and feasts and in periods of crises (Gen. 4:4; 31:54; Exod. 24:5; Lev. 8:1–8; Num. 3:1–10; Deut. 10:8–9; 2 Sam. 24:24). The priest is the mediator between God and his people. Among the many functions of the priest was the offering of sacrifice. Sacrifice could either be a holocaust, votive, expiatory, or reparatory offering. In all these, one common thing is that it was offered to God. In sacrifice, humans ask for forgiveness and seek the blessings of God.

In the New Testament, Jesus instituted a new form of sacrifice through his actions at the Last Supper. His actions brought a new dimension to the Passover. This was introduced by Jesus when he called the bread his "body" and the wine his "blood" and commanded his disciples, "do this in memory of me" (see Luke 22:19–20; 1 Cor. 11:24). He performed the ultimate sacrifice by his death on the cross, which is the high point of his Paschal Mystery. The Twelve continued that mission by reaching out to the nations. They gathered on the first day of the week for the "breaking of bread" (Acts 2:46). They continued in the tradition of breaking bread within a family meal and attending to the temple sacrifices until the final separation from Judaism. It was within the Jewish milieu that the Church was born.

The ministry of the early Church spread throughout the world with missionaries reaching out to peoples, cultures, and nations. It was in the same faith in the Paschal Mystery that evangelization reached Igboland in the southern part of Nigeria. Though the Igbos had their traditional religion at the time, they joyfully welcomed the new religion. This is manifested in their way of life and worship. They have love for the Church and her priesthood but find it difficult at times to let go of some aspects of their traditional religion. Only a true Christocentric shift based on the Paschal Mystery will help transform their pre-Christian religiosity. Above all, the different cultures are united under one Eucharist, which is the common culture of the Church. The Church becomes the new people of God convoked by God the Father to celebrate the mysteries of Jesus by the power of the Holy Spirit. They are to "sing the praises of God who has called them out of darkness into his wonderful light" (1 Pet. 2:9; cf. Exod. 19:6).

When the Church gathers to celebrate this memorial sacrifice, she gives thanks to God for the love he has lavished on humans by allowing his Son to die for sinful humanity. What the Church does in her liturgy is a response in thanksgiving to the saving act of God in Christ. Hence, the Church participates in the heavenly liturgy where Christ eternally intercedes for all and presents his sacrifice to the Father. "To the one who sits on the throne and to the Lamb be blessing and honor, glory and might, forever and ever" (Rev. 5:13). As the *Catechism of the Catholic Church* teaches, "By the Eucharistic celebration we already unite ourselves with the heavenly liturgy and anticipate eternal life, when God will be all in all" (no. 1326). This is made possible through the Paschal Mystery of Christ, and in the Church. "When in her liturgy the Church proclaims the *Sanctus* she echoes on earth the song of seraphs as they worship God in heaven."[18] In her liturgical celebration, the Church does not simply remember an event in history, rather, through the mysterious action of the Holy Spirit she reenacts these mysteries in the eucharistic celebration of the Lord's Paschal Mystery. The mystery is made present and contemporaneous to his spouse the Church.

Thus far, I have attempted to show through this work that priesthood and sacrifice, ancient as they may be, are valid for all ages. However, just as the Israelite priesthood was elevated to an institution and perfected in Jesus Christ through his Paschal Mystery, so the Igbos should allow the mystery of Christ to permeate and transform their life. For the Igbos to be actively engaged in the liturgical and sacramental life, I wish to use the following methods and apply them to Christianity in Igboland. They are: (1) inculturating the rituals, (2) reinterpreting the rituals, and (3) internalizing the rituals.[19]

---

18. United States Conference of Catholic Bishops, "The Real Presence of Jesus Christ in the Sacrament of the Eucharist: Basic Questions and Answers," http://www.usccb.org/prayer-and-worship/the-mass/order-of-mass/liturgy-of-the-eucharist/the-real-presence-of-jesus-christ-in-the-sacrament-of-the-eucharist-basic-questions-and-answers.cfm (accessed May 12, 2007).

19. Stephen Finlan, *Problems with Atonement* (Collegeville, MN: Liturgical Press,

### 6.10.1 Inculturating the Rituals

The Igbos are attempting to internalize the message when it has not been made to take root in the culture and there is no authentic internalization. Though there is one common Christian culture, the Igbos should worship God according to their way of life. The theologians and liturgists of the Church in Igboland with competent ecclesiastical authority should be ready to make changes where necessary to inculturate some revered traditions and culture into the liturgy. Igbos themselves should be involved in the decision in light of the Paschal Mystery and, with their knowledge of the traditions, determine what cultural changes are to be made. To buttress my point, I give the following example.

*The Igbo Naming Ceremony.* The rite for the naming of a child is celebrated in the home, which is the focal point for the Igbos. People are identified with their families and communities. Anyone who cannot identify his home or family is nobody and has no identity. The name gives the child identity and a place in the community. After childbirth, the woman stays at home for about a month. During this period, she does no strenuous work, as relatives and her mother, if she is still alive, help her with household chores. It is always a daily celebration during this month following childbirth, as relatives and friends keep coming to see the newborn child. On an appointed day, the relatives and neighbors gather and the woman presents the child to the husband, who in turn presents the child to his clan. The child is officially presented to all and is eventually given a name by the father in that gathering. It is followed by celebrations and merriment. The Church in Igboland could develop a rite that will incorporate this rite as a first step in the rite of infant baptism. The issue is that after the naming ceremony, the parents of the child still have to take the child to the Church for baptism. It is obvious that the two ceremonies are not the same, but if my suggestion is implemented, it will help in giving the naming ceremony a Christian background and identity. This is important because baptism initiates one into the Paschal Mystery. It is the first step to establishing a Christian relationship with God.

In the words of Stephen Finlan, "Rejection of rites seems to imply a repudiation of tradition, and so of the society that preserved the tradition."[20] To preserve their culture and tradition and still be authentic Christians, Igbos have a duty to make a few necessary changes to enhance their mode of worship and life.

Another aspect that requires attention is the *anaphora*. In the Eucharistic Prayer of the Mass, the Igbos will appreciate it more if it is celebrated with a

---

2005), 24. Finlan proposes altering the rituals, reinterpreting the rituals, and internalizing the rituals. I differ from his first point because altering the ritual is an aberration in liturgy and does not fit into liturgical worship. Once it is altered, the goal and meaning of the ritual stand in danger of being lost. I therefore use "inculturating" instead of "altering."

20. Finlan, *Problems with Atonement*, 24.

refrain, as earlier suggested, so that the congregation will acclaim at the end of each segment of the prayer. It could be laid out in a way that the priest says the prayers, as directed by the Church, with the people intermittently acknowledging with a refrain quite as they do when an elder is presiding in religious rites. In this case, it could be their usual way of concurring to a prayer by saying, "*Ise!*" ("So may it be"). The *memento* should incorporate the ancestors without mentioning any particular person, since canonization of saints is celebrated by the Roman Pontiff. This will help lift up the spirits of the living to lead a good life, knowing that they will also be incorporated into the rank of the ancestors of the new community, of brothers and sisters in Jesus and be remembered in the eucharistic celebration. This is important because the saints we mention in the Canon of the Mass are people unknown to the Igbos. These names mean so much to the Church, which is why they are used. I am advocating for a situation where we find space within the liturgy, subject to approval, to remember the distinguished people of the past in Igbo society.

### 6.10.2 Reinterpreting the Rituals

In their traditional setup, Igbos have signs and symbols that enhance their way of life. Liturgical inculturation through these meaningful signs and symbols in their culture will help give more meaning to their liturgical celebrations. The cross of Jesus has summed up all other sacrifices of the Igbos both at the crossroads and the shrines, and he invites all, including the Igbos, to this one supreme sacrifice on the cross in the Paschal Mystery. A positive interpretation of the rituals will also help to promote the people's faith in God and enhance worship.[21] When they use some of those sacred symbols in Catholic ritual, it would enhance their liturgical life and keep them from falling back to traditional practices outside the liturgical setting. The Igbos should retain their noble and good traditions as they strive to worship God in spirit and truth. A people without a tradition is heading fast toward extinction.

### 6.10.3 Internalizing the Rituals

This third point, internalization, is to a large extent the outcome of the first two: inculturating the rituals and reinterpreting the rituals. When the ritual is inculturated to suit the life, culture, and traditions of the people as deemed necessary by their liturgical theologians and reinterpreted according to their way of life, it becomes easier to internalize the message of Jesus. There comes a fusion between the teaching of the Church and the life of the community.

---

21. *Catechism of the Catholic Church*, no. 2441. The puts it in a different form: "An increased sense of God and increased self-awareness are fundamental to any *full development of human society*. . . . It makes for growth in respect for cultural identities and openness to the transcendent."

This is where the priests are most needed, as their constant instruction based on the reinterpreted and inculturated rituals will help the people to internalize the message.

In the ancient religions, humans search for God, but Christianity is a religion where God searches for humans and offers them a possibility of a new life that is higher than the old. God has visited the Igbos in a unique way with the Christian faith. The uniqueness of Jesus' priesthood and sacrifice lies in the fact that both the movement of humans toward God and God's condescension to humans converge in the person of Jesus Christ, who is God incarnate.

The sacrificial death of Jesus abolishes all other sacrifices and becomes the sacrifice that is capable of restoring and leading men and women back to God. For an effective liturgy and meaningful sacramental life, the Igbos and all peoples are therefore called upon to embrace the cross of Jesus, understanding its mystery especially in moments of trial and hardship as it gives hope of a resurrection. It is not only a bodily resurrection Christians hope for, but a spiritual one as well. The sacrificial death of Jesus did not end on the cross but continues to the resurrection, which is the goal of Christian life—to live on Easter day until the Lord Jesus comes again with full recompense for full transformation.

Transformation begins with what is known: its practice should be Christocentric. Only an authentic Christocentric shift, based on their traditional values, will help the Igbos understand the true meaning of the ritual of sacrifice practiced by the Church as a true sacrifice replacing their traditional ones. It will also help them make meaning of their sufferings and pains by uniting their trials to those of Christ, as Jesus identified with humans in all things but sin.[22] Both culture and theology should coexist in a mutual relationship, nourishing and empowering each other for the salvation of souls. Therefore, for an effective liturgical celebration, the liturgy should think, speak, and worship according to the way of life of each culture without losing what binds the Church together—Christ. In the words of Bishop Shanahan, "Mere churchgoing or observance would make little change in them. What they needed [and still need] as a preparation for faith, and as a safeguard for it after its reception, was a new orientation of mind, based on the acceptance of Christian standards

---

22. Brian D. McLaren, *A Generous Orthodoxy* (Grand Rapids: Zondervan, 2006), 105. McLaren argues that Jesus absorbed all our sorrows and pains in order to save us. He notes, "This is a window into the meaning of the cross. Absorbing the worst that human beings can offer—crooked religiosity, petty political systems, individual betrayal, physical torture with whip and thorn and nail and hammer and spear—Jesus enters into the center of the thunderstorm of human evil and takes full shock on the cross. Our evil is brutally, unmistakably exposed, drawn into broad daylight, and judged—named and shown for what it is. Then, having felt its agony and evil firsthand, in person, Jesus pronounces forgiveness and demonstrates that the grace of God is more powerful and expansive than the evil of humanity. Justice and mercy kiss; judgment and forgiveness embrace. From their marriage a new future is conceived."

of judgment."[23] It is obvious that the words of Bishop Shanahan pronounced more than a century ago are still valid.

In this way, the Igbos will remain true to their tradition and culture and also be faithful to the Catholic religion. They will accept the grace of Christianity without losing their identity, since "grace builds on nature." This will imply participating in the liturgy not as "Father's Mass" or as an idle worshiper but as someone who worships in sincerity and truth (John 4:23–24). I therefore conclude with the words of Hans Urs von Balthasar:

> What the formal concept of nature tells us is that everything touched by grace retains its natural side: grace is always a grace in a nature and for a nature. It remains modal to nature and is never itself substantial. But while this is all true, so is the converse: grace so radically transforms, exults and irradiates nature with the divine reality that no aspect or corner of nature can escape its impact. Yes, even the most apparently God-forsaken realm—where sin took hold and reigned— was chosen as *the* site for God's revelation of grace in Christ![24]

Grace has touched the Igbos, and they are called to live out this grace in full without compromising the Catholic faith, so that the fruits of the Spirit may be made manifest in their lives. When the fruits of the Paschal Mystery shine forth in their life, culture, liturgy, and priesthood, then will they be true and authentic Catholics.

Therefore, I state the following:

1. Igbo traditional religion through its priesthood, sacrifice, and elaborate liturgy prepared the grounds for the reception of Christianity.
2. There is an urgent need to assimilate the good elements in the culture of the people into the liturgy as a way of enhancing their liturgical life.
3. I hope that the competent ecclesiastical authorities and theologians of the Igbos would see reasons in the points raised in this book and decide how best to inculturate the traditional values of the Igbos into the liturgy, in light of Vatican Council II (*Sacrosanctum Concilium* 40).

By so doing, the Paschal Mystery will be lived out through the priestly and sacrificial activities of the Church in Igboland to the greater glory of God.

---

23. Jordan, *Bishop Shanahan*, 37.
24. Hans Urs von Balthasar, *The Theology of Karl Barth*, trans. Edward T. Oakes (San Francisco: Ignatius Press, 1992), 287.

# BIBLIOGRAPHY

Agu, Ambrose Chimeme. *The Eucharist and Igbo Communal Spirit: Towards a Solid Inculturation of the Christian Faith in Igboland.* Würzburg: Echter, 2004.

Ajayi, J. F. Ade. *Christian Missions in Nigeria, 1841–1981.* Edited by K. O. Dike. Evanston, IL: Northwestern University Press, 1965.

Anyanwu, Herbert Onyema. *African Traditional Religion from the Grassroot.* Uyo: Minders International, 2004.

Arazu, Raymond. *Our Religion, Past and Present.* Awka, Nigeria: Martin-King Press, 2005.

Archdiocese of Onitsha. "Know Our Pastors." http://www.onitsha-arch diocese.org.

Arinze, Francis A. *Sacrifice in Ibo Religion.* Ibadan, Nigeria: Ibadan University Press, 1970.

Ashley, Benedict M., O.P. "The Priesthood of Christ, the Baptized, and the Ordained." In *The Theology of Priesthood,* edited by Donald J. Goergen and Ann Garrido. Collegeville, MN: Liturgical Press, 2000.

Averback, Richard E. "*'ašam.*" In *New International Dictionary of Old Testament Theology and Exegesis,* edited by Willem A. VanGemeren. Grand Rapids: Zondervan, 1997.

———. "*Kalil.*" In *New International Dictionary of Old Testament Theology and Exegesis,* edited by Willem A. VanGemeren. Grand Rapids: Zondervan, 1997.

———. "*Minḥah.*" In *New International Dictionary of Old Testament Theology and Exegesis,* edited by Willem A. VanGemeren. Grand Rapids: Zondervan, 1997.

———. "*Zbḥ.*" In *New International Dictionary of Old Testament Theology and Exegesis,* edited by Willem A. VanGemeren. Grand Rapids: Zondervan, 1997.

Balentine, Samuel E. *Leviticus.* Interpretation: A Bible Commentary for Teaching and Preaching. Louisville: Westminster John Knox, 2002

Balthasar, Hans Urs von. *Mysterium Paschale: The Mystery of Easter.* Translated by Aidan Nichols, O.P. Edinburgh: T&T Clark, 1990.

———. *The Theology of Karl Barth.* Translated by Edward T. Oakes. San Francisco: Ignatius Press, 1992.

Barclay, William. *The Gospel of John*. New Daily Study Bible. Louisville: Westminster John Knox, 2001.

———. *The Gospel of Mark*. New Daily Study Bible. Louisville: Westminster John Knox, 2001.

———. *The Letters to the Philippians, Colossians, and Thessalonians*. 3rd rev. and updated ed. New Daily Study Bible. Louisville: Westminster John Knox, 2001.

Basden, George, T. *Among the Ibos of Nigeria*. 1920. Reprint, Gloucestershire, UK: Nonsuch Publishing, 2007.

Benedict XVI, Pope. *Sacramentum Caritatis: The Sacrament of Charity; On the Eucharist as the Source and Summit of the Church's Life and Mission*. Washington, DC: United States Conference of Catholic Bishops, 2007.

———. *God Is Love*. Washington, DC: United States Conference of Catholic Bishops, 2005.

———. *The Yes of Jesus Christ*. Translated by Robert Nowell. New York: Crossroad, 1991.

———. *Jesus of Nazareth*. Translated by Adrian J. Walker. New York: Doubleday, 2007.

———. *Jesus, the Apostles and the Early Church: General Audiences, 15th March 2006 – 14 February 2007*. San Francisco: Ignatius Press, 2007.

Black, Jeremy, et al., eds. *A Concise Dictionary of Akkadian*. Santag 5. Wiesbaden: Harrassowitz, 2000.

Boadt, Lawrence. *Reading the Old Testament: An Introduction*. New York: Paulist, 1984.

Bosman, Hendrick L. "Passover." In *New International Dictionary of Old Testament Theology and Exegesis*, edited by Willem A. VanGemeren. Grand Rapids, MI: Zondervan, 1997.

Bright, John. *A History of Israel*. Old Testament Library. Louisville: Westminster, 1952. 4th ed., 2000.

Brown, Raymond E. *An Introduction to the New Testament*. Anchor Bible Reference Library. New York: Doubleday, 1997.

———. *Priest and Bishop: Biblical Reflections*. Paramus, NJ: Paulist, 1970. Reprint, Eugene, OR: Wipf & and Stock, 1999.

Brueggemann, Walter. *Theology of the Old Testament: Testimony, Dispute, Advocacy*. Minneapolis: Fortress, 1997.

Carretta, Vincent. *Equiano, the African: Biography of a Self-Made Man*. New York: Penguin Books, 2005.

Casel, Odo. *The Mystery of Christian Worship*. New York: Herder & Herder, 1999.

Cody, Aelred. *A History of Old Testament Priesthood*. Analecta Biblica 35. Rome: Pontifical Biblical Institute, 1969.

Corbon, Jean. *The Wellspring of Worship*. Translated by Matthew J. O'Connell. San Francisco: Ignatius Press, 2005.

Daly, Robert J. *Sacrifice Unveiled: The True Meaning of Christian Sacrifice.* New York: T&T Clark, 2009.

Denzinger, Heinrich. *Enchiridion symbolorum definitionum et declarationum de rebus fidei et morum, Latin-English.* 43rd ed. Edited by Peter Hünermann. San Francisco: Ignatius Press, 2012.

DomNwachukwu, Peter Nlemadim. *Authentic African Christianity: An Inculturation Model for the Igbo.* American University Studies: Series VII, Theology and Religion 210. New York: Peter Lang, 2000.

Duke, Rodney K. "Priests, Priesthood." In *Dictionary of Old Testament: Pentateuch,* edited by T. Desmond Alexander and David W. Baker. Downers Grove, IL: Intervarsity Press, 2003.

Dunn, Patrick J. *Priesthood: A Re-examination of the Roman Catholic Theology of the Ordained Presbyterate.* 1990. Reprint, New York: St. Paul Publications, 2007.

Ejizu, Christopher. *The Influence of African Indigenous Religions on Roman Catholicism: The Igbo Example.* Lecture, University of Port Harcourt, Nigeria, http://www.afrikaworld.net/afrel/elizu-atrcath.htm.

Ekwunife, Anthony N. O. *Consecration in Igbo Traditional Religion.* Onitsha, Nigeria: Jet Publishers, 1990.

Eliade, Mircea. *Cosmos and History: The Myth of the Eternal Return.* Translated by Willard R. Trask. New York: Harper, 1959.

Finlan, Stephen. *Problems with Atonement.* Collegeville, MN: Liturgical Press, 2005.

Fischer, Edward. "Ritual as Communication." In *The Roots of Ritual,* edited by James D. Shaughnessy. Grand Rapids: Eerdmans, 1973.

Galot, Jean. *Theology of the Priesthood.* Translated by Roger Balducelli. 2nd ed. San Francisco: Ignatius Press, 2005.

Goergen, Donald J., and Ann Garrido, eds. *The Theology of Priesthood.* Collegeville, MN: Liturgical Press, 2000.

Gordon, Cyrus H. *Ugaritic Manual: Newly Revised Grammar, Texts in Transliteration, Cuneiform Selections, Paradigms, Glossary, Indices.* Analecta Orientalia 35. Rome: Pontificium Institutum Biblicum, 1955.

Grabbe, Lester L. *Priests, Prophets, Diviners, Sages: A Socio-Historical Study of Religious Specialists in Ancient Israel.* Valley Forge, PA: Trinity Press International, 1995.

Greenberg, Joseph H. *The Languages of Africa.* 3rd ed. Bloomington: Indiana University Press, 1970.

Greenlee, J. Harold. *An Exegetical Summary of Hebrews.* Dallas, TX: Summer Institute of Linguistics, 1998.

Heim, S. Mark. *Saved from Sacrifice:, A Theology of the Cross.* Grand Rapids: Eerdmans, 2006.

Idowu, E. B. *African Traditional Religion: A Definition.* London: SCM, 1973.

Ilogu, Edmund. *Christianity and Igbo Culture: A Study of the Interaction of Christianity and Igbo Culture*. New York: Nok, 1974.

Jeremias, Joachim. *The Eucharistic Words of Jesus*. Translated by Norman Perrin. New York: Charles Scribner's Sons, 1966.

John Paul II, Pope. *Ecclesia de Eucharistia*: *On the Eucharist in Its Relationship to the Church*. Washington, DC: United States Conference of Catholic Bishops, 2003.

———. *Instrumentum Laboris: Encounter with the Living Christ: The Way to Conversion, Communion and Solidarity in America*. Washington, DC: United States Conference of Catholic Bishops, 2007.

———. *Pastores Dabo Vobis*. Washington, DC: United States Conference of Catholic Bishops, 1992.

———. *Redemptoris Missio: On the Permanent Validity of the Church's Missionary Mandate*. Washington, DC: United States Conference of Catholic Bishops, 1990.

Johnson, Luke Timothy. *Hebrews: A Commentary*. New Testament Library. Louisville: Westminster John Knox, 2006.

Jones, Cheslyn, et al., eds. *The Study of Liturgy*. Rev. ed. New York: Oxford University Press, 1992.

Jones, C. P. M. "The New Testament." Revised by C. J. A. Hickling. In *The Study of Liturgy,* edited by Cheslyn Jones et al. New York: Oxford University Press, 1992.

Jordan, John P. *Bishop Shanahan of Southern Nigeria*. Dublin: Clonmore & Reynolds, 1949.

Jurgens, William A. *The Faith of the Early Fathers: A Source-Book of Theological and Historical Passages from the Christian Writings of Pre-Nicene and Nicene Eras*. Collegeville, MN: Liturgical Press, 1970.

Kalu, Ogbu. *The Embattled Gods: The Christianization of Igboland, 1841– 1991*. Trenton, NJ: Africa World Press, 2003.

Küng, Hans. *Why Priests? A Proposal for a New Church Ministry*. Translated by Robert C. Collins. London: Collins, 1972.

Kunzler, Michael. *The Church's Liturgy*. Translated by Placed Murray et al. New York: Continuum, 2001.

Kurtz, J. H. *Offerings, Sacrifices and Worship in the Old Testament*. Translated by James Martin. Peabody, MA: Hendrickson, 2000. German original, 1863.

Levenson, Jon D. *The Death and Resurrection of the Beloved Son: The Transformation of Child Sacrifice in Judaism and Christianity*. New Haven: Yale University Press, 1993.

Maly, Eugene H., ed. *The Priest and Sacred Scripture*. Washington, DC: United States Conference of Catholic Bishops, 2007.

Maraldo, John Charles. "Syncretism." In *Sacramentum Mundi: An Encyclo-*

*pedia of Theology,* edited by Karl Rahner. New York: Herder & Herder, 1970. Vol. 6, pp. 201-3.

Marmion, Columba. *Christ, The Life of the Soul.* Translated by Alan Bancroft. Bethesda, MD: Zaccheus, 2005.

Marx, Alfred. "The Theology of Sacrifice according to Leviticus 1–7." In *The Book of Leviticus: Composition and Reception,* edited by Rolf Rendtorff and Robert A. Kugler. Supplements to Vetus Testamentum 93. Leiden: Brill, 2003.

Mbiti, John S. *Concepts of God in Africa.* London: Camelot, 1973.

———. *Introduction to African Religion.* London: Heinemann Educational Books, 1975. 2nd rev. ed., 1991.

McKenzie, John L. *A Theology of the Old Testament.* Garden City, NY: Image Books, 1974.

McLaren, Brian D. *A Generous Orthodoxy.* Grand Rapids: Zondervan, 2006.

Metuh, Ikenga. *African Religion in Western Conceptual Schemes: The Problem of Interpretation.* Jos, Nigeria: Imico, 1991.

———. *Comparative Studies of African Traditional Religion.* Jos, Nigeria: Imico, 1987.

Milgrom, Jacob. *Leviticus: A Book of Ritual and Ethics.* Continental Commentaries. Minneapolis: Fortress, 2005.

———. *Leviticus 1–16: A New Translation with Introduction and Commentary.* Anchor Bible 3. Garden City, NY: Doubleday, 1991.

Millgram, Abraham E. *Jewish Worship.* Philadelphia: Jewish Publication Society, 1971.

Mitchell, Alan C. *Hebrews.* Sacra Pagina. Collegeville, MN: Liturgical Press, 2007.

Muilenburg, James, and Henry Sloane Coffin. "Isaiah 40–66." In *The Interpreter's Bible,* edited by George Arthur Buttrick. Nashville: Abingdon, 1980.

Ngwoke, Emeka. *The Eucharist and Social Responsibility towards the Poor.* Enugu, Nigeria: SNAAP, 2005.

Nichols, Aidan. *Holy Order: The Apostolic Ministry from the New Testament to the Second Vatican Council.* Dublin: Veritas, 1990.

Niehaus, Jeffrey J. "'šn." In *New International Dictionary of Old Testament Theology and Exegesis,* edited by Willem A. VanGemeren. Grand Rapids: Zondervan, 1997.

Nwala, Uzodinma T. *Igbo Philosophy.* Lagos, Nigeria: Lantern Books, 1985.

Oakes, Edward T. *Pattern of Redemption: The Theology of Hans Urs von Balthasar.* New York: Continuum, 1994.

Obi, Celestine A., ed. *A Hundred Years of the Catholic Church in Eastern Nigeria, 1885 – 1985.* Onitsha, Nigeria: Africana-FEB Publishers, 1985.

O'Collins, Gerald O., and Edward G. Farrugia. *A Concise Dictionary of Theology.* New York: Paulist, 1991.

O'Connor, James T. *The Hidden Manna*. San Francisco: Ignatius Press, 1988.

Ogudo, Donatus E. O. *The Catholic Missionaries and the Liturgical Movement in Nigeria: An Historical Overview*. Vol. 1, *The Holy Ghost Fathers and Catholic Worship among the Igbo People of Eastern Nigeria*. Paderborn: Bonifatius, 1988.

Oko, Azu K. *Ancestor Worship: Roots/Biblicity*. Aba, Nigeria: Enuda Video House, 1992.

Okpalike, Chika. *Ichuaja in Igbo Traditional Religion*. Bloomington, IN: iUniverse, 2008.

Okwor, Joseph. *The Priesthood from an Igbo Perspective: A Theological Study Aimed at Improving the Formation of Catholic Priests in Igboland*. Enugu, Nigeria: Fulladu, 1998.

Okwu, Augustine. *Igbo Culture and the Christian Missions, 1857–1957*. Lanham, MD: University Press of America, 2010.

Opoku, K. A. *West African Traditional Religion*. Singapore: Fep International, 1978.

Onwubiko, Oliver A. *African Thought, Religion, and Culture*. Enugu, Nigeria: SNAAP, 1991.

Oranekwu, George N. *The Significant Role of Initiation in the Traditional Igbo Culture and Religion*. Frankfurt: IKO-Verlag, 2004.

Orr, William F., and James Arthur Walther. *1 Corinthians: A New Translation*. Anchor Bible 32. Garden City, NY: Doubleday, 1976.

Parrinder, E. G. *African Traditional Religion*. 3rd ed. London: Seldon, 1974.

Paul VI, Pope. "Mysterium Fidei: The Mystery of Faith." *Acta Apostolica Sedes* 57 (3 September 1965): 753–74.

Pelikan, Jaroslav. *The Christian Tradition: A History of the Development of Doctrine*. Vol. 1, *The Emergence of the Catholic Tradition (100–600)*; Vol. 3, *The Growth of Medieval Theology (600–1300)*. Chicago : University of Chicago Press, 1971, 1987.

Perry, John Michael. *Exploring the Evolution of the Lord's Supper in the New Testament*. Kansas City, MO: Sheed & Ward, 1994.

Pitre, Brant. *Jesus and the Jewish Roots of the Eucharist: Unlocking the Secrets of the Last Supper*. New York: Doubleday, 2011.

Prosic, Tamara. *The Development and Symbolism of Passover until 70 CE*. Journal for the Study of the Old Testament Supplement Series 414. London: T&T Clark, 2004.

Quinn, Frank C., O.P. "Ministry, Ordination Rites, and Language." In *The Theology of Priesthood,* edited by Donald J. Goergen and Ann Garrido. Collegeville, MN: Liturgical Press, 2000.

Rahner, Karl. *The Church and the Sacraments*. New York: Herder & Herder, 1964.

———, ed. *Sacramentum Mundi: An Encyclopedia of Theology*. New York: Herder & Herder, 1970. S.v. "Syncretism" by John Charles Maraldo.

Ratzinger, Joseph. *Behold the Pierced One*. San Francisco: Ignatius Press, 1986.
———. *God and the World: A Conversation with Peter Seewald*. San Francisco: Ignatius Press, 2002.
———. *Introduction to Christianity*. Translated by J. R. Foster. San Francisco: Ignatius Press, 2004. German original, 1968.
———. *Journey towards Easter*. New York: Saint Paul Publications, 1987.
———. *On the Way to Jesus Christ*. Translated by Michael J. Miller. San Francisco: Ignatius Press, 2005.
———. *The Spirit of the Liturgy*. San Francisco: Ignatius Press, 2000.
Richardson, Cyril, ed. and trans. *Early Christian Fathers*. Philadelphia: Westminster, 1953.
Rordorf, Willy, et al., eds. *The Eucharist of the Early Christians*. Translated by Matthew J. O'Connell. Collegeville, MN: Liturgical press, 1978.
Rowley. H. H. *Worship in Ancient Israel: Its Forms and Meaning*. London: SPCK, 1967.
Schleiermacher, Friedrich. *The Christian Faith*. Edited by H. R. Mackintosh and J. S. Stewart. New York: Harper & Row, 1963.
Schmemann, Alexander. *The Eucharist: Sacrament of the Kingdom*. Translated by Paul Kachur. Crestwood, NY: St. Vladimir's Seminary Press, 2003.
Schweitzer, Albert. *The Psychiatric Study of Jesus*. Translated by Charles R. Roy. Boston: Beacon Press, 1948. Reprint, 1968. German original, 1913.
———. *The Quest of the Historical Jesus*. Translated by W. Montgomery. New York: MacMillan Company, 1961. German original, 1913.
Segal, Judah B. *The Hebrew Passover, from the Earliest Times to A.D. 70*. New York: Oxford University Press, 1963.
Shaughnessy, James D., ed. *The Roots of Ritual*. Grand Rapids: Eerdmans, 1973.
Sheerin, Daniel J. *The Eucharist*. Wilmington, DE: Michael Glazier, 1986.
Tanner, Norman, ed. *Decrees of the Ecumenical Councils,* vol. 2. London: Sheed & Ward, 1990.
Tcherikover, Victor. *Hellenistic Civilization and the Jews*. New York: Athenum, 1970.
Thornton, John F., and Susan B. Varenne, eds. *The Essential Pope Benedict XVI: His Central Writings and Speeches*. San Francisco: HarperCollins, 2007.
Torrance, Thomas F. *Royal Priesthood: A Theology of Ordained Ministry*. 2nd ed. Edinburgh: T&T Clark, 2003.
Uchendu, Victor C. *The Igbo of Southeast Nigeria*. New York: Holt, Rinehart & Winston, 1965.
Udeani, Chibueze. *Inculturation as Dialogue: Igbo Culture and the Message of Christ*. Intercultural Theology and Study of Religions 2. Amsterdam: Rodopi, 2007.

Ukaegbu, J. O. *Igbo Identity and Personality vis-à-vis Igbo Cultural Symbols.* Salamanca: Universidad Pontificia de Salamanca, 1991.

Umeasiegbu, Rems N. *Words Are Sweet: Igbo Stories and Storytelling.* Leiden: Brill, 1982.

Uzor, Chika Justin. *Living between Two Worlds: Intrapersonal Conflicts among Igbo Seminarians – An Enquiry.* Bern: P. Lang, 2003.

Vaillancourt, Raymond. *Toward a Renewal of Sacramental Theology.* Translated by Matthew J. O'Connell. Collegeville, MN: Liturgical Press, 1979.

VanGemeren, Willem A., ed. *New International Dictionary of Old Testament Theology and Exegesis.* Grand Rapids: Zondervan, 1997.

Vanhoye, Albert. *The Old Testament Priests and the New Priest.* Translated by Bernard J. Orchard. Petersham, MA: St. Bede's, 1986.

Vaux, Roland de. *Ancient Israel: Its Life and Institutions.* Translated by John McHugh. New York: McGraw-Hill, 1961.

Vonier, Anscar. *A Key to the Doctrine of the Eucharist.* Introduction by Aidan Nichols. Bethesda, MD: Zaccheus, 2003–2004.

Weeks, Noel. *Admonition and Curse: The Ancient Near Eastern Treaty/Covenant Form as a Problem in Inter-Cultural Relationships.* London: T&T Clark, 2004.

Williamson, H. G. M. "The Origins of the Twenty-Four Priestly Courses: A Study of 1 Chronicles xxiii–xxvii." In *Studies in the Historical Books of the Old Testament,* edited by J. A. Emerton. Supplements to Vetus Testamentum 30. Leiden: Brill, 1979.

Winter, Michael. *The Atonement.* Collegeville, MN: Liturgical Press, 1995.

Wright, N. T. *The Challenge of Jesus: Rediscovering Who Jesus Was and Is.* Downers Grove, IL: InterVarsity, 1999.

———. *The Climax of the Covenant.* Minneapolis: Fortress, 1991.

———. *Jesus and the Victory of God.* Minneapolis: Fortress, 1992.

———. *The New Testament and the People of God.* Minneapolis: Fortress, 1992.

Young, Robert, ed. *Young's Analytical Concordance to the Bible; Also, Index Lexicons to the Old and New Testament.* Grand Rapids: Eerdmans, 1977. Originally published 1900.

Zimmerli, Walther. *The Church's Liturgy.* Translated by Placed Murray. New York: Continuum, 2001.

## Ecclesiastical Documents

Congregation for Divine Worship. *Lineamenta: The Eucharist: Source and Summit of the Life and Mission of the Church.* Washington, DC: United States Conference of Catholic Bishops, 2004.

———. *The New Roman Missal.* Totowa, NJ: Catholic Publishing, 2011.

Congregation for Divine Worship and the Discipline of the Sacraments. "Inculturation and the Roman Liturgy" (March 29, 1994). http://www. adoremus.org/VarietatesLegitimae.html.

Congregation for the Doctrine of the Faith. *The Catechism of the Catholic Church*, 2nd ed. Washington, DC: United States Conference of Catholic Bishops, 1997.

———. *Dominus Iesus, Declaration on the Unicity and Universality of Jesus Christ and the Church*. Washington, DC: United States Conference of Catholic Bishops, 2000.

Pius X, Pope. *Tra le sollecitudini, Instruction on Sacred Music* (November 22, 1903). http://www.adoremus.org/TraLeSollecitudini.html.

Pius XII, Pope. *Mediator Dei: On the Sacred Liturgy*. Vatican City, November 20, 1947.

Second Vatican Council. "Constitution on the Sacred Liturgy." In *Vatican II: The Conciliar and Post Conciliar Documents*. Edited by Austin Flannery. Northport, NY: Costello, 1996.

United States Conference of Catholic Bishops. "The Real Presence of Jesus Christ in the Sacrament of The Eucharist: Basic Questions and Answers." http://www.usccb.org/prayer-and-worship/the-mass/order-of-mass/liturgy-of-the-eucharist/the-real-presence-of-jesus-christ-in-the-sacrament-of-the-eucharist-basic-questions-and-answers.cfm.

### Articles

Angenendt, Arnold. "Holiness of the Person—Holiness of Space." *Studia Liturgica: An International Ecumenical Review for Liturgical Research and Renewal* 38 (2008): 53–63.

Horton, W. R. C. "God, Man and the Land in Northern Ibo Village-Group." *Africa* 26 (1956): 17–28.

Nkurunziza, Deusdedit R. K. "Towards a New African Paradigm of Evangelization." *African Ecclesial Review* 50 (March–June 2008): 58–70.

Ryder, A. F. C. "The Benin Missions." *Journal of the Historical Society of Nigeria* 2 (1961): 231–319.

———. "Portuguese Mission in Western Africa." *Tarikh* 3 (1969): 2–13.

Schofield, Alison, and James C. Vanderkam. "Were the Hasmoneans Zadokites." *Journal of Biblical Literature* 124 (2005): 73–87.

### Books Used but Not Cited.

Alison, James. *The Joy of Being Wrong: Original Sin through Easter Eyes*. Translated by Sebastian Moore. New York: Crossroad, 1998.

Balthasar, Hans Urs von. *Myth and Reality*. Translated by Willard R. Trask. New York: Harper & Row, 1963.

Barclay, William, ed. *The Gospel of Luke*. New Daily Study Bible. Louisville: Westminster John Knox, 2001.

———. *The Gospel of Matthew*. New Daily Study Bible. Louisville: Westminster John Knox, 2001.

Bernard of Clairvaux. *On the Song of Songs*. Translated by Kilian Walsh, OCSO. Spencer, MA: Cistercian Publications, 1971.

Burchfield, R. W., ed. *The Oxford English Dictionary*. 2nd ed. Oxford: Clarendon, 2000.

Chupungo, Anscar, ed. *Handbook for Liturgical Studies*. Collegeville, MN: Liturgical Press, 1997.

Davies, Brian, and G. R. Eited Evans, eds. *Anselm of Canterbury: The Major Works*. Oxford: Oxford University Press, 1998.

Day, John, ed. *Temple and Worship in Biblical Israel*. London: T&T Clark, 2005.

Delorme J. *The Eucharist in the New Testament: A Symposium*. Translated by E. M. Stewart. Baltimore: Helicon, 1964.

Dunhill, John. *Covenant and Sacrifice in the Letter to the Hebrews*. Cambridge: Cambridge University Press, 1992.

Fitzmyer, Joseph A. *The Gospel according to Luke, X–XXIV: A New Translation with Introduction and Commentary*. Anchor Bible 28A. Garden City, NY: Doubleday, 1985.

———. *Romans: A New Translation with Introduction and Commentary*. Anchor Bible 33. Garden City, NY: Doubleday, 1993.

Goppelt, Leonhard. *Typos: The Typological Interpretation of the Old Testament in the New*. Translated by Donald H. Madvig. Grand Rapids: Eerdmans, 1982.

Gottwald, Norman K. *The Tribes of Yahweh*. Maryknoll, NY: Orbis Books, 1979.

Gray, George Buchanan. *Sacrifice in the Old Testament*. Edited by Harry M. Orlinski. New York: Ktav, 1971.

Guillet, Jacques. *The Consciousness of Jesus*. Translated by Edmond Bonin. New York: Newman, 1972.

Haffner, Paul. *The Sacramental Mystery*. Leominster: Gracewing, 1999.

Haran, Menahem. "The Passover Sacrifice." In *Studies in the Religion of Ancient Israel,*. edited by G. W. Anderson and P. A. H. De Boer. Leiden: Brill, 1972.

Irwin, Kevin W. *Models of the Eucharist*. Mahwah, NJ: Paulist, 2005.

Jungmann, Josef A. *The Early Liturgy*. Translated by Francis A. Brunner. South Bend, IN: University of Notre Dame Press, 1959.

Kasper, Walter. *The God of Jesus Christ*. Translated by Matthew J. O'Connell. New York: Crossroad, 1984 .

Kilmartin, Edward. *The Eucharist in the Primitive Church*. Englewood Cliffs, NJ: Prentice Hall, 1965.

Kodell, Jerome. *The Eucharist in the New Testament*. Wilmington, DE: Michael Glazier, 1988.

LaVerdiere, Eugene. *The Breaking of the Bread*. Chicago: Liturgy Training Publications, 1998.

———. *Dining in the Kingdom of God*. Chicago: Liturgy Training Publications, 1994.

———. *The Eucharist in the New Testament and the Early Church*. Collegeville, MN: Liturgical Press, 1996.

Mazza, Enrico. *The Celebration of the Eucharist*. Translated by Matthew J. O'Connell. Collegeville, MN: Liturgical Press, 1999.

McCarthy, Dennis James. *Old Testament Covenant*. Oxford: Basil Blackwell, 1972.

Mendenhall, George E. "Law and Covenant in Israel and the Ancient Near East." *Biblical Archeologist* 27, no. 2 (1954): 26–44.

———. *The Tenth Generation*. Baltimore: Johns Hopkins University Press, 1973.

Metuh, Ikenga. *The Gods in Retreat: Continuity and Change in African Religions*. Enugu: Fourth Dimension, 1986.

Moloney, Raymond. *Problems in Theology: The Eucharist*. Collegeville, MN: Liturgical Press, 1995.

Vaux, Roland de. *Studies in Old Testament Sacrifice*. Cardiff: University of Wales Press, 1964.

# INDEX

# Other Titles of Interest

### Catholic Dogmatics for the Study and Practice of Theology
### by Gerhard Cardinal Müller

*Catholic Dogmatics for the Study and Practice of Theology* is the definitive text on the structure of Catholics Dogmatics, written by one of the most important authors in the Catholic Church today. Cardinal Müller oversaw the collected writings of Pope Benedict. The book will enhance both the scholar's and lay reader's knowledge of dogmatics.

978-0-8245-2232-2 cloth / 0-8245-2233-9 paperback
128 pages

### Handing on the Faith: The Church's Mission and Challenge
### by Robert P. Imbelli, Ed.

Renowned theologian and teacher Robert P. Imbelli introduces the work of leading Catholic theologians, writers, and scholars to discuss the challenges of handing on the faith and to rethink the essential core of Catholic identity.

978-0-8245-2409-8 paperback
264 pages

### Pope John Paul II
### The Saint for Shalom: How Pope John Paul II
### Transformed Catholic-Jewish Relations
### His Complete Texts on Jews, Judaism, and the State of Israel 1979–2005
### by Eugene J. Fisher, Ph.D., Rabbi Leon Klenicki, editors

Pope John Paul II's efforts can serve as a model for reconciliation, inspiring both believers and nonbelievers to pursue deeper understanding and work together in harmony to help improve the world and achieve Shalom, the Hebrew word for Peace, wholeness, and right-relationship, for all of humankind.

978-0-8245-2682-5 paperback
398 pages

### Encyclopedia of Theology and Church:
### Dictionary of Popes and the Papacy

"Gratitude to the editors of this impressive volume and to its many contributors. It contains a wealth of information about the papacy. No other work like it exists in English. Highly recommended."—Patrick Granfield, Catholic University of America

978-0-8245-1918-3 cloth
294 pages

*Support your local bookstore or order directly from the publisher at*
www.crossroadpublishing.com
*To request a catalog or inquire about quantity orders,*
*e-mail* sales@crossroadpublishing.com

## The Crossroad Publishing Company

www.ingramcontent.com/pod-product-compliance
Lightning Source LLC
Chambersburg PA
CBHW020704270326
41928CB00005B/262